CONCENTRATE Q&A
CRIMINAL LAW

FREE online study and revision support available at
www.oup.com/lawrevision

Take your learning further with:
- Multiple-choice questions with instant feedback
- Interactive glossaries and flashcards of key cases
- Tips, tricks, and audio advice
- Annotated outline answers
- Diagnostic tests to show you where to concentrate
- Extra questions, key facts checklists, and topic overviews

unique features

student-focused online support

CONCENTRATE Q&A CRIMINAL LAW

Mischa Allen
Associate Lecturer in Law
The Open University

THIRD EDITION

OXFORD
UNIVERSITY PRESS

OXFORD
UNIVERSITY PRESS

Great Clarendon Street, Oxford, OX2 6DP,
United Kingdom

Oxford University Press is a department of the University of Oxford.
It furthers the University's objective of excellence in research, scholarship,
and education by publishing worldwide. Oxford is a registered trade mark of
Oxford University Press in the UK and in certain other countries

Published in the United States of America by Oxford University Press
198 Madison Avenue, New York, NY 10016, United States of America

British Library Cataloguing in Publication Data
Data available

Library of Congress Control Number: 2020935467

ISBN 978–0–19–885348–0

Printed in Great Britain by
Bell & Bain Ltd., Glasgow

Contents

Guide to the book

Every book in the Concentrate Q&A series contains the following features:

Are you ready to face the exam? This box at the start of each chapter identifies the key topics and cases that you need to have learned, revised, and understood before tackling the questions in each chapter.

Not sure where to begin? Clear diagram answer plans at the start of each question help you see how to structure your answer at a glance, and take you through each point step-by-step.

Demonstrating your knowledge of the crucial debates is a sure-fire way to impress examiners. These at-a-glance boxes help remind you of the key debates relevant to each topic, which you should discuss in your answers to get the highest marks.

What makes a great answer great? Our authors show you the thought process behind their own answers, and how you can do the same in your exam. Key sentences are highlighted and advice is given on how to structure your answer well and develop your arguments.

Each question represents a typical essay or problem question so that you know exactly what to expect in your exam.

Don't settle for a good answer—make it great! This feature gives you extra points to include in the exam if you want to gain more marks and make your answer stand out.

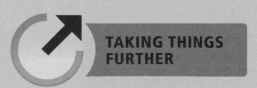

Don't fall into any traps! This feature points out common mistakes that students make, and which you need to avoid when answering each question.

Really push yourself and impress your examiner by going beyond what is expected. Focused further reading suggestions allow you to develop in-depth knowledge of the subject for when you are looking for the highest marks.

Guide to the online resources

Every book in the Concentrate Q&A series is supported by additional online materials to aid your study and revision: www.oup.com/uk/qanda/.

- Extra essay and problem questions with guidance on how to approach them.
- Video guidance on how to put an answer plan together.
- Audio advice on revision and exam technique from Nigel Foster.

Table of cases

Table of statutes

Table of international conventions

Exam Skills for Success in Criminal Law

1

The challenges of studying criminal law

Criminal law is usually attractive to students due to its media presence. However, this can give the impression that it is an easy subject. In fact, it is conceptually difficult, and technical, so great care must be taken over structure.

There is more topic overlap in criminal law than you will find in other subjects. Whilst there are distinct crimes to study, there are common features: *actus reus*, *mens rea*, and the defences.

Furthermore, the criminal law necessarily deals with issues of morality. It is political and policy-driven, which means that the cases sometimes contain contradictory decisions. One example of this is the way in which the courts apply subjective and objective tests for liability. Should a defendant accused of a crime be judged on the facts as he saw them, or according to the standards of a reasonable person? In *mens rea*, a subjective approach is usually used, but in the defences, an objective standard is becoming the norm. Finally, in order to understand current definitions, you will need to appreciate how the law has developed historically. You'll therefore need a keen understanding of statutory interpretation and the current common law rules. For example, in understanding the topic of recklessness, you will study how the House of Lords settled on an interpretation of this concept in the **Criminal Damage Act 1971 in 1957,** then changed its mind in 1982, before settling on a renewed definition in 2003. This has affected the concept of recklessness throughout the criminal law.

Your examiners want to see that you can deal with these challenges by demonstrating that you understand the law, can apply it with reason, and can also critically evaluate it.

This chapter explores some techniques to help you achieve this to a high standard.

Study skills for criminal law

The best route to good examination skills is to *develop good study and revision skills* from the outset. You should pay attention to the reading lists provided by your lecturers. You are likely to need a book of statutory material, especially if your module is assessed by exam. Attendance is key, especially at seminars, where you will be taught the fundamental skills for answering exam questions. These skills cannot be acquired by downloading notes, or even by attending lectures, but solely by practising exam-style questions. Examiners are interested in your ability to say *how* the law works in particular situations, not just in your ability to learn it by rote. In other words, you should avoid being too descriptive, and concentrate on *legal analysis*. When a question is set for discussion in seminars, you should treat it as a possible exam question. In this way you will acquire good habits, which may need only minor modification in the examination. Don't forget to take good notes, as these will be invaluable later on. One way of doing this is to make notes *before* the lecture on your set reading, or before the seminar on the questions set, then add to your notes during or after the session. In this way you are *making* notes from your reading, and *taking* notes from your lecturer or tutor. These are both crucial skills for success.

Closer to the time of the exam, *consolidate your material* as much as possible. You could prepare two separate lists for each topic. One list is a checklist of the main points to be considered when answering any question on that topic. The second is a list of the key cases and the key legal principle the case contains. Once you have mastered the 'bare bones' of each topic, you can concentrate on refining your answers, and working on critical analysis and evaluation.

Achieving success in exams

In the exam, *planning and time management* are essential. Make sure you answer all the questions set. Consider the instructions carefully. Stick strictly to your time plan, leaving one question and moving on to another when that time is up.

Relevance and structure are also vital. If you are answering a question in which a defendant in charge of a level crossing has left the gate open, leaving an express train free to pass, killing a man who crosses, you should get straight to the point, which is that in the case of *R v Pittwood* (1902) **19 TLR 37**, a breach of contract leading to death imposed a duty to act on the defendant. You should not simply write everything you know about liability for omissions. Irrelevant material, however well researched or presented, will gain no marks. If the man is a volunteer, however, you will gain extra marks for distinguishing your facts from the facts of *Pittwood* and you might base the duty on another head of liability, for example on the voluntary assumption of care found in the case of *R v Stone and Dobinson* [1977] 1 QB 354.

A good structure will help you cope with the challenge of overlap, and prevent your answer from becoming muddled. For example, if you are told that a defendant is under the influence of drugs or alcohol at the time of committing the offence, you need to consider the possibility that intoxication has negated *mens rea*, that a plea of automatism could be raised, or, in a murder case, that an abnormality of mental functioning arises for the purposes of diminished responsibility. The best thing to do is to consider the technical requirements of each 'defence' to enable you to make the correct decision.

You may be allowed to bring *statutory material* into the examination with you. Usually, the rules are that the statutes can be highlighted, but not annotated (marked, in any way). Make sure that you do not copy them out—there is no credit for this! A better technique is to write, say, in a theft question: 'in taking the book from Jo's bag, Millie has assumed one of Jo's rights and has therefore appropriated the book (**s 3** of the **Theft Act 1968**)'. In this way, you are demonstrating that you know the broad effect of the statute and can apply it.

Your lecturers will emphasize the importance of *critical analysis in answering questions in exams and other assessments*. In essay questions, this means that you need to be able to compare academic or judicial views on a topic, and formulate your own view. In problem questions, critical analysis comes from skilful application of the law to the facts. Students who write excellent answers will be able to use the judgments from the cases well in order to answer the question, and will be able to distinguish cases by using minority judgments of their own analysis.

Problem questions: planning and writing your answer

The best method to adopt, and the one adopted throughout this book, is IRAC—Identify the issues, explain the Rule, Apply the law to the facts, and reach a Conclusion. A long introduction to problem questions is not required. Instead, a sentence or two explaining what your answer will cover (eg the potential offences with which the defendant may be charged) should be sufficient.

Identifying the issues and relevant facts means that you will need to work out in general terms what area of criminal law the question is about. Most will concern some particular issue around the *actus reus/mens rea* of an offence or whether the defendant has the benefit of a defence. The facts of problem questions will not reflect decided cases exactly. They generally fall in between and include a range of issues, giving you an opportunity to demonstrate your skills and knowledge. You will need to highlight these issues for discussion.

The next step in the IRAC method is to explain the rules or principles of law involved. You should start by defining the relevant offences, using the correct common law or statutory definition. Deal with each defendant separately. What is the *actus reus* and *mens rea* of these offences? You should then consider defences. Some defences should be dealt with at the end of your discussion on *actus reus* and *mens rea*. Loss of control and diminished responsibility are examples of this type of defence. Other 'defences' such as intoxication are not, strictly speaking, defences, but a negation of one element of the offence.

Working through the structure of *actus reus*, *mens rea*, and defences for each defendant, you should explain the *rule of law* (the *ratio* of a case or a statutory provision) and explain it. For example, in discussing the **Adomako** test, discuss all four guidelines in the case to establish a finding of gross negligence manslaughter.

Your points must be backed up with authority (relevant cases and statutory provisions), and be *applied* to the facts. Your answer will also be improved by referring to opposing judgments and academic commentary. In an examination, you are generally not expected to include dates, courts, or citations (although they are included in this book for ease of reference). Do not 'invent' facts or describe the facts of cases. Sometimes the facts are deliberately ambiguous. Quite often you will need to argue in the alternative. For example, if the harm done to the victim amounts to a wound, then the answer is . . . ; on the other hand, if the harm is held not to amount to a wound the alternative lesser offences may be . . .

Now, consider your *conclusion*. Is the defendant guilty of murder or manslaughter? Do any defences work? What is the most likely outcome? There is no 'right' answer. Instead, credit will be given to those students who have presented a coherent argument, often for both the prosecution and the defence, which is logically argued.

Essay questions

Essay questions are quite different to problem questions. In problem questions, you are asked to give specific legal advice on a factual scenario. In essay questions, you are normally being asked to discuss or analyse a legal issue which is the subject of debate. You will very rarely simply be asked to explain or describe what you know about a certain area of the law. A good answer to an essay question will persuade the examiner of the argument. Ask yourself: 'Am I answering the question set?'

A common mistake in an essay question is the 'shotgun' approach—simply stating everything you know about a topic. This type of answer lacks focus, and will not gain high marks. Essay questions can be more difficult than problem questions, because you have to decide the parameters of your answer. You need to be familiar with the literature in the area, and have knowledge of areas due for or in need of reform. There is, however, no reason why you cannot do well in them as long as you have prepared the topics. Usually, you are provided with a quote from a case or an article which represents one view of the current state of the law. Your task is to say whether or not you agree with that interpretation. You may feel that you have nothing to contribute at this stage to an academic discussion on, say, the effect of the law following the **Coroners and Justice Act 2009** on victims of domestic abuse accused of murder. However, this is a topic which has been discussed at length by legal academics and judges—so do refer to and use these discussions in formulating your own conclusion in direct answer to the question.

Essentially, in a problem question you are being asked to use your legal knowledge to apply to a specific set of facts and to conclude, giving legal advice. In an essay question, you are being asked to analyse a legal problem (in the sense of a problematic area of law), and to to reach a conclusion. Therefore, you need to know what the law is, what it was previously, and how it might be changed.

Summary

The importance of exam technique cannot be overstated. Criminal law is a very technical subject, and answers can appear muddled if they are not properly planned and structured. The general structure of *actus reus*, *mens rea*, and defences should be adopted. For problem questions, focus on the issues straight away, and apply the law to the facts given throughout, using relevant authorities. Focus on the *ratio* of cases and the effect of statutory provisions. Don't forget to conclude. If you have several options, discuss these in turn. Finally, make sure you have answered the correct number of questions, and allocated the requisite amount of time to each one. In essay questions, ensure any points you have made are supported by evidence, that you have weighed up any proposals for reform, and that you have focused on the question set.

TAKING THINGS FURTHER

- Finch E and Fafinski S, *Legal Skills* (7th edn, OUP 2019).
- McVea H and Crumper P, *Exam Skills for Law Students* (2nd edn, OUP 2005).
- Strong S I, *How To Write Law Essays and Exams* (5th edn, OUP 2018).

Fundamental Principles of Criminal Liability— *Actus Reus* and *Mens Rea*

2

ARE YOU READY?

In order to answer questions on this topic, you will need to understand the following:

- the scope of criminal liability for acts and omissions;
- factual and legal causation and the rules on *novus actus interveniens* in causation;
- intention (direct and oblique);
- the development of recklessness in the criminal law;
- the coincidence of *actus reus* and *mens rea*.

KEY DEBATES

Debate: criminalizing omissions

Is there a 'Good Samaritan' duty to help those in danger? Ashworth (1989) has argued that a failure to intervene should be criminalized on the grounds of social responsibility. However, Smith (1993) argues that the focus ought to be on whether the defendant has *caused* the death of the victim, rather than any wider duty, as it is often too difficult to distinguish between an act and an omission.

Debate: the meaning of oblique intent

When the intention of the defendant is uncertain, judges must be sure to direct the jury appropriately. The current test, contained in the **Nedrick** direction, has not necessarily resolved the matter, despite the House of Lords' attempt to do so in **R v Woollin [1998] 4 All ER 103**. Ashworth (2016) welcomes the direction, stating that it affords the jury a certain amount of 'moral elbow room' to acquit those who may deserve it. Should the decision on intention be left to the jury? Lacey argues that it should, as jurors tend to have an innate sense of what the term means.

⊙

Debate: mercy killing

Whilst suicide is not unlawful, euthanasia is. Despite a number of high-profile cases, the courts have refused to rule on whether a relative helping a terminally ill victim to die should be immune from prosecution. A challenge to the **Suicide Act 1961** was brought to the High Court in 2017 in the case of **Conway v Secretary of State for Justice [2017] EWHC 2447 (Admin)**. Noel Conway argued that the Act is incompatible with **Article 8** of the **European Convention on Human Rights**, which guarantees the right to respect for private and family life. The High Court declined to offer a declaration of incompatibility, regarding it as a question for Parliament, not the courts. This decision maintains the approach in the earlier challenge in **Nicklinson**.

QUESTION | 1

David is thirty-five years old and lives with Mona, his mother, who is bedridden. David cares for Mona by providing her with food and changing her medical dressings. Mona gives David money to cover the costs of the food, and pays the mortgage on the house. David begins a relationship with Jane. After five weeks, Jane starts to stay at David's house at the weekends. One night, Jane surprises David by telling him that she has booked a holiday for them both—two weeks in Spain, departing the next day. David expresses his concern about who will look after his mother. Jane says that he has 'done his bit' and that David's sister Vera, who lives ten miles away, should help out for once. David telephones Vera and leaves a message on her answer phone telling her that she will have to look after Mona for the next two weeks. When Vera arrives home, she accidentally erases her telephone messages before she has the chance to replay them. Whilst David and Jane are on holiday, Mona's condition worsens considerably. When they arrive home, they find her unconscious, having become ill through lack of food and from infections caused by unchanged dressings. Shocked, David rushes her to hospital, where she is seen briefly by a harassed doctor, Simon, but is then left unattended in a hospital corridor. Mona dies shortly afterwards.

David and Jane have been convicted of manslaughter and wish to argue that there is no criminal liability for a failure to act, and that, furthermore, they did not cause Mona's death. Discuss.

CAUTION!

- Read questions carefully, noting who it is you are being asked to advise. With this type of question, you can waste valuable time discussing the liability of the doctor. The focus should be on whether David and Jane are guilty.

- Remember that *actus reus* consists of an act or an omission, plus evidence of causation. Even if medical treatment is negligent, it is unlikely to break the chain of causation, except in the most unusual cases.

■ Note that David is not liable simply because he is Mona's son—the courts still operate a fairly restrictive approach in familial relationships.

 DIAGRAM ANSWER PLAN

Identify the issues	■ *Actus reus* and *mens rea* in the context of homicide. ■ Is there a culpable omission giving rise to a duty of care in criminal law? If so, does that omission cause the death of the victim? ■ Consider gross negligence manslaughter—the *Adomako* test.
Relevant law	■ There is no general liability for omissions; however, a duty may arise either by contract (*R v Pittwood*) or via a voluntary assumption of care (*R v Stone and Dobinson*; *R v Instan*)? ■ Consider *Novus actus interveniens*: medical cases, *R v Smith*, *R v Cheshire*.
Apply the law	■ Duty of care and death are caused in fact and in law. Does the duty of care arise due to David's relationship, or is there a wider duty? ■ *Cheshire* is likely to apply here.
Conclude	■ Gross negligence manslaughter based on the principles in *R v Adomako*.

 SUGGESTED ANSWER

The first question to consider is whether David and Jane have committed a criminal act or omission which has caused Mona's death. As there is no positive act causing death here, liability can be based on the failure of either or both of them to prevent Mona's death.[1]

[1] Ensure that you emphasize the general rule: that there is no liability for omissions in English law.

Traditionally, the criminal law has drawn a clear distinction between acts and omissions. However, apart from the numerous statutes that impose a duty to act, for example **s 170** of the **Road Traffic Act 1988**, it appears that the common law will impose a duty to act in only very limited circumstances.

There can be no criminal liability imposed on David and Jane in respect of their failing to care for Mona unless the prosecution can establish that they were under a positive legal duty to care for her. Such a duty can be imposed by statute. That is not the case here.

As Mona gives David money to cover the cost of food, arguably a contract arises, as in *R v Pittwood* **(1902) 19 TLR 37**, where the defendant, a railway gate operator, was found guilty of manslaughter when a person was killed crossing a railway line. The defendant had left a gate open when a train was coming. On the other hand, in domestic relationships such as this one, there is a presumption that no legally enforceable relationship existed. There may be some liability for omissions on other grounds. In *R v Instan* **[1893] 1 QB 450**, liability for manslaughter was placed upon a niece who failed to care for her aunt with whom she was living, having been given money by the aunt to buy groceries. There might be a similar duty on David.[2]

[2] It is important to be very specific about the duty—which case does it emanate from?

With regard to David and Jane, a duty cannot be established on the basis of a family relationship. However, the prosecution might wish to argue that a positive legal duty arises at common law because Mona has grown to rely on their help. Whilst five weeks may not be a sufficient length of time to create a duty in Jane's case, the fact that David changes her dressings and buys her groceries, but then stops helping, may give rise to some liability. In *R v Stone and Dobinson* **[1977] QB 354**, the Court of Appeal upheld convictions for manslaughter by gross negligence on the basis that the defendants had allowed the victim to stay with them and had started to care for her. They then failed to discharge that duty and failed to summon any assistance. The court stressed that the duty to act arose not simply because of a blood relationship between one of the defendants (Mr Stone) and the deceased, but because of the reliance relationship—Mrs Dobinson had washed her and taken her food. It can be argued here that David did not discharge his duty in looking after Mona. He could have done more than simply making a telephone call.[3]

[3] Here, you are showing the examiner that you are not following the law blindly, but are able to distinguish your case on its own facts.

It could also be argued that a duty arises following the principle in *R v Miller* **[1983]**. In this case, the House of Lords upheld the defendant's conviction for criminal damage on the basis of the doctrine of 'supervening fault'. In other words, in creating a dangerous situation, and then failing to counteract it, the defendant had committed a culpable omission. In that case, the defendant had inadvertently fallen asleep smoking in bed, setting fire to the room. When he realized what had happened, he moved away rather than taking any action to stop the fire from spreading. It might be said that going on holiday and leaving Mona without checking that Vera could, in fact, take over responsibility for her care created a dangerous situation, which they failed to counteract.[4]

[4] Quoting directly from the case raises the bar of your answer.

The prosecution will now need to establish that David and Jane's omission caused Mona's death. Causation in criminal law is proven with the 'but for' test established in *R v White* **[1910] 2 KB 124**.[5] Would Mona have died but for David and Jane's departure? It seems

[5] In proving causation, look at factual causation first, then legal causation.

clear that she would not, as David would have been taking care of her. This stage is known as causation in fact. It is not necessary for the prosecution to prove that the omission was the sole or main cause of death, merely that this contributed significantly to the victim's death.

The defendants here will argue that a number of events occurred so as to make their omission insignificant in terms of liability. Vera did not get the message, and Simon, the harassed doctor, left Mona unattended in a hospital corridor. With regard to the first point, the defendants will argue that the defendant's conduct must be a substantial and an operating cause of death. Here, they might argue that the death of the victim was unforeseeable and they could not be expected to know that Vera would delete her phone messages.[6] To be legally significant, the defendant's conduct must be more than trivial, in accordance with the *de minimis* rule (the defendant's contribution must be more than minimal). The defendant's conduct does not need to be the sole cause of death. The question is whether the defendant made a *significant* contribution. The fact that there are two competing causes of death does not prevent the defendant from being responsible. It suffices that the defendant's contribution is more than merely trivial.

The defendants may try to argue that they are not to be held responsible on the grounds that Simon, the doctor, was negligent. This is also likely to fail. In *R v Smith* **[1959] 2 QB 35**, it was held that if, despite the medical treatment, the original injury was still an operating and substantial cause of death, the chain of causation would not be broken.[7] The chain would only be broken if the original wound was 'merely the setting in which another cause operates' or 'if the second cause is so overwhelming as to make the original wound merely part of the history'. In *R v Cheshire* **[1991] 3 All ER 670**, the court stated that negligent medical treatment would only break the chain of causation if it were 'so independent of the defendant's acts, and in itself so potent in causing death' that the contribution made by D's acts in causing death was rendered insignificant. Here, Mona is in hospital because she has become ill due to the lack of food normally provided by David, and, more recently, Jane. The fact that Simon has left her unattended, whilst clearly negligent, will not be sufficient to break the chain of causation.

David and Mona have a duty of care towards Mona and the prosecution are likely to succeed in arguing that they have caused Mona's death.[8]

A conviction for manslaughter by gross negligence may follow. In order to establish this, the prosecution will need to show, in addition to the requirements for a culpable omission and causation, that there was a risk of causing death and that the negligence was of a criminal nature (*R v Adomako* **[1995] 1 AC 171**). This is negligence which is so serious that a criminal conviction is justified.

[6] Don't forget to apply the law to the facts at each stage.

[7] Medical treatment, however negligent, does not generally break the chain of causation.

[8] Provide an overall conclusion summarizing the law and drawing a conclusion on the likely outcome.

LOOKING FOR EXTRA MARKS?

- In areas such as causation, structure is key. Ensure you deal with each defendant separately. You can build up a strong argument by quoting from cases and considering (or distinguishing) any potential argument on the part of the defence.

- Use the cases wisely, identifying the specific class of duty, and do not state the law blindly. Here, even if there is a voluntary assumption of care, it may not apply in these particular circumstances.

QUESTION | 2

To what extent is a defendant criminally liable for a failure to act?

CAUTION!

- You should avoid simply describing the law in a question like this. Try to ensure that some critical comment is made which adds value to the points being made. In particular, don't describe the facts of cases without explanation of how they apply.

- Some clear reference to the question set is crucial in a question like this. This is a straight-forward question on general principles, but an excellent structure will produce a clear, reasoned argument. This question is quite broad, so you can set your own parameters.

DIAGRAM ANSWER PLAN

Outline the law: the general rule is that there is no criminal liability for omissions. However, in certain closely defined circumstances the law will create a duty of care. These circumstances are quite limited.

▼

Provide case law examples: in *R v Pittwood*, it was held that a duty of care arose when a death occurred due to a breach of contract. The law was extended in *R v Stone and Dobinson*—where there has been a voluntary assumption of care which is subsequently abandoned, the law will create a duty. You can and should include recognized academic views on liability. Here, there are two clear opposing positions.

▼

Conclusion: although there are limits on the duty of care (eg in *R v Khan and Khan*), the courts may be widening the concept.

Every offence in criminal law requires proof of an *actus reus* on the part of the accused. In the majority of cases, statute or common law defines this *actus reus* in terms of a positive act. There are instances of statutory omissions.

The basic rule in English criminal law is that there is no general duty to act to prevent the commission of criminal offences or to limit the effect of harm caused by the actions of others. This position reflects an individualistic approach to liability. If D is at a swimming pool, and he sees P (a young child with whom he has no connection) drowning in the deep end, why should D be required to go to P's aid? D has no special responsibility for P, and did not cause the risk to arise. It is pure chance that D is in a position to help. Why should fate be the basis for imposing a liability for failing to prevent P's death? Ashworth (2011) argues for a 'social responsibility' approach to this issue. This view proposes that liability should arise for failing to attend to those in peril partly because of the moral obligation to do so, but also because it reflects a more complex social pact.[1] A positive duty to aid others would impose a responsibility but would also confer a corresponding benefit. D might one day find himself compelled to help P, but the next day he might be the beneficiary of the duty on P to aid D where D is in peril. Society benefits because less harm is suffered by individuals.

In practice, English criminal law does impose criminal liability for failing to act, but it does so on the basis of exceptions. Thus, D will not be liable for failing to act unless the prosecution can point to a positive legal duty.

The most common source of such legal duties is statute. Parliament creates liability for failing to act in two ways. At a very simple level it creates offences of omission. For example, the **Children and Young Persons Act 1933** places parents and guardians under a legal duty to care for children. Suppose that parents go out for the evening leaving a four-year-old child alone. Whilst they are out, he falls onto a fire and is killed. It is likely that the court would find that there was a culpable omission based on the breach of statutory duty, and liability could be imposed if causation and *mens rea* can also be established.

An alternative basis for establishing a legal duty to act is where D is subject to a contractual duty or holds an office that suggests the imposition of a duty. In the case of employees, the court will look at the express or implied terms of the contract to determine the extent and nature of the duties imposed on D. In *R v Pittwood* (1902) 19 TLR 37, a railway crossing gatekeeper opened the gate to let a cart pass, but then left his post, forgetting to close the gate. A hay cart

[1] In an essay question like this, try to go beyond the case law and include academic opinion to support your answer.

crossed the line and was hit by a train. The defendant was convicted of manslaughter. He argued that the only duty he owed was to his employers, with whom he had a contract. It was held, however, that his contract imposed a wider duty upon him to users of the crossing. Thus, the duty arising under a contract inures to the benefit of those who are not privy to the contract—ie the passengers on the train.[2] In *R v Instan* [1893] 1 QB 450, D was given money by her aunt to buy groceries. D failed to care for her aunt, who subsequently died. It is unlikely that any contractual duty existed in this case, as the agreement was a domestic one, hence there was no intention to create legal relations—a requirement for a legally enforceable contract.

There are situations where, despite the absence of any statutory or contractual duty to act, liability ought to be imposed. In such cases, it falls to the common law to perform its residual function of identifying the omission. Judges 'discover' new common law duties to act because it is felt they ought to exist. *R v Instan* is a case in point.[3] For the last twelve days of her life, the aunt was suffering from gangrene in her leg and was unable to look after herself. Only D knew this. D did not provide her aunt with food, nor did she obtain medical attention. This omission accelerated the aunt's death. D's conviction for manslaughter was upheld, the court proceeding on the basis that a common law duty was simply a moral duty so fundamental the courts had to enforce it. As Lord Coleridge CJ observed, a legal common law duty is nothing else than the enforcing by law of that which is a moral obligation without legal enforcement.

The court in *R v Gibbins and Proctor* (1918) 13 Cr App R 134 accepted that a duty could be imposed upon a common law wife to care for her partner's child because, although the child was not hers, she had assumed a duty towards the child by choosing to live with the child's father and to accept housekeeping money to buy food for them all.

Imposing liability for omissions where D undertakes to care for P and P becomes reliant on D may even be counterproductive. In *R v Stone and Dobinson* [1977] QB 354, the defendants were convicted of the manslaughter of Stone's sister Fanny because they took her in but failed to care for her adequately. With hindsight, they might have been advised not to help her in the first place. The law therefore sends mixed messages.[4] One ought to care for others, but one should not start to do so unless one is able to discharge that duty properly.

The common law duty to act was developed further by the important House of Lords decision in *R v Miller* [1983] 1 All ER 978. D, who was squatting in an empty house, fell asleep whilst smoking a cigarette. Whilst he was asleep the cigarette set fire to the mattress. D woke, realized the mattress was on fire, but took no steps to douse the fire. The house was damaged in the ensuing blaze. He was obviously not under a statutory duty to put the fire out, nor was he

[2] A more in-depth discussion of the reasons for establishing the duty will attract more marks.

[3] *R v Instan* was decided on a quasi-contractual basis. However, it was also held that there was a legal duty, rather than a moral one.

[4] The scope of the law was extended in this case, on the grounds of a voluntary assumption of care.

under a contractual duty to do so. At the time, the common law duties to act were based on duties owed to blood relatives, or arising from reliance. The House of Lords had little choice but to 'discover' a new legal duty at common law. Such a duty arises where D accidentally causes harm, realizes that he has done so, and it lies within his power to take steps, either himself or by calling for assistance, to prevent or minimize the harm.

[5] It is useful to explain how the law has been applied recently.

The doctrine has since been applied to killing by gross negligence in *R v Evans (Gemma)* [2009] EWCA 650,[5] where it was held that awareness of having caused a dangerous situation could of itself give rise to the duty of care (effectively the duty to act) that forms the basis of the offence. Whilst the ruling in *R v Miller* is socially desirable (there is great social utility in D being required to limit the effect of his careless actions), there are many uncertainties. What is it that D is required to do once he realizes he has caused harm? Must he act as the reasonable person would have done, or does he simply have to do his best?

Even where a positive legal duty to act can be identified, uncertainties may arise as to whether D has been or can be absolved from that duty. Some clarification is provided by the House of Lords' decision in *Airedale NHS Trust v Bland* [1993] AC 789, where it was held that doctors were under a duty to treat a patient where it was in the patient's best interests to do so. Where, however, all hope of the patient recovering had disappeared, the duty to nourish and maintain the patient would also cease.[6]

[6] The 'best interests' doctrine has been criticized on the grounds that it does not respect patient autonomy.

The courts are prepared to recognize the existence of a duty where it would be fair to do so. In 2017, in the unreported case of *R v Bowditch*, a duty of care was found to exist in a case where the defendant had no prior relationship with the victim and none of the classic duty situations were satisfied. This can be seen to demonstrate a less narrow approach to finding a specific legal duty to impose liability.

Williams (1991) and Hogan (1968) both argue that the duty should be limited, due to the fine line between acts and omissions and the fact that causation is a crucial element of criminal liability. As we have seen, Ashworth (1989) would extend the duty.

It can be argued that criminal liability should only arise where the defendant can be held to have caused the death of the victim. To do otherwise would render the law uncertain. Furthermore, it can be argued that to criminalize omissions blurs the lines between a positive act and a failure to act. With regard to the former argument, J C Smith (1996) argues that causation should be a sufficient foundation for liability:

it would be much more conducive to clarity of thought if we spoke of conduct and causation. If any proposition is self evident it is that a person cannot be held to have caused an event he did not cause … in my view … references to duty are unhelpful. The issue in *R v Pittwood* was simply whether the defendant had caused the death of the victim with the relevant mens rea.

Ashworth's position (1989) is that there are two opposing points of view on criminal omissions. The first, which he calls the 'conventional view', holds that there is a moral distinction between acts and omissions: liability should only be opposed in very clear circumstances. The other view, held by Ashworth, is the 'social responsibility' view.

It may be morally correct to say that we should assist those who are in danger, especially when the risk to ourselves is minimal. This is true, especially in circumstances when the victim is vulnerable in some way, or when the helper has a particular legal or moral duty to act. At present, a failure to do so in the absence of a duty is not a criminal offence. On the other hand, personal freedom may be compromised if one were obliged to intervene. The uncertainty in the law might give rise to an argument that the current position contravenes **Article 7** of the **European Convention on Human Rights**, which guarantees certainty and predictability in the law. It is submitted that the French model of a general statutory duty of easy rescue would be a good compromise. This would not lead to liability for manslaughter, but criminalizes the omission itself, on the basis of social responsibility.[7]

[7] It is useful if you can present alternatives or proposals for reform in your conclusion.

LOOKING FOR EXTRA MARKS?

- In an essay question, refer to academic argument such as the debate between Williams (1991) and Ashworth (1989). You should also ensure that you discuss what the limits of the law are. This may involve a reference to policy.

- There are relatively few proposals for reform in this area, so concentrate on the anomalies contained within the cases. Judges, however, have created new precedents in this area of law. Quotes from the judgments will show that you can appreciate the reasons for the development of the law and therefore raise the bar of your answer.

QUESTION | 3

Darren deals regularly in drugs. He meets Viv, his friend's daughter, at his flat one evening and gives her a quantity of heroin, which she injects into her own arm. He also injects himself. Viv, who is fifteen, has never tried heroin before. They carry on chatting that evening, and Viv falls asleep on the sofa. In the morning, she is unconscious. Darren sees this, but is late for work. He covers Viv up with a blanket, and leaves the flat, intending to call an ambulance on the way. As there is no one on the road, he decides to speed up and is soon travelling at sixty miles an hour through the centre of town. He is in a built-up area. Unfortunately, he runs out of petrol and the car stalls, running into Maisie, another driver. Maisie is also travelling to work, and sees Sam trying to cross at a pedestrian crossing. She tries to stop but ends up hitting him. Sam is seriously injured and an ambulance is called. By now the streets are very busy and the ambulance is delayed. Sam eventually arrives at hospital where he is given a transfusion of the wrong type of blood by Bo, a junior doctor, and injected with an antibiotic for which he has an allergy. Sam dies. In the commotion, Darren forgets to call an ambulance for Viv and runs off. The police follow him into a disused warehouse. Unknown to him or the police, the warehouse is being used by Annie, an artist. Annie is walking along the corridor to get some more supplies when she bumps into Darren and screams. When he sees Annie, he grabs her and shouts out that he has a knife. The policeman, John, sees a shape at the end of a corridor and shoots, killing Annie instantly. When the police go to Darren's flat, they find Viv dead.

How should the judge direct the jury on causation in this case?

CAUTION!

■ This question tests your ability to extract the rules on causation. Be systematic, working through the steps of factual and legal causation in order.

■ Be sure that you do not confuse causation with *mens rea*, and that you are able to distinguish all the elements of constructive and gross negligence manslaughter. Advise the defendant only, not the other characters!

DIAGRAM ANSWER PLAN

Identify the issues	■ Discuss liability for gross negligence manslaughter and manslaughter by an unlawful and dangerous act. ■ Discuss causation—*R v Pagett/R v Kennedy*.
Relevant law	■ The criteria in *R v Adomako* should be discussed and outlined. ■ Consider the decision in *R v Kennedy*. ■ Discuss causation and *novus actus interveniens*.
Apply the law	■ Consider whether there is a duty of care. ■ Consider whether Darren caused the deaths in fact and in law. ■ Discuss whether there is liability for gross negligence manslaughter.
Conclude	■ Conclude with liability for gross negligence manslaughter and/or manslaughter by an unlawful and dangerous act on the facts above.

In order to prove criminal liability for involuntary manslaughter (there does not appear to be sufficient evidence of *mens rea* here for murder), the prosecution will have to satisfy the court that the defendant, Darren, has committed an act or omission which caused a death. There are three recognized types of involuntary manslaughter: manslaughter by gross negligence, manslaughter by an unlawful and dangerous act, and subjectively reckless manslaughter (the last category is rarely used). Objectively reckless manslaughter no longer exists in the criminal law following the House of Lords' decision in *R v Adomako* [1995] 1 AC 171.

In relation to Viv, Darren may have committed manslaughter by gross negligence. The first thing to be satisfied of is whether he owes a duty of care to Viv. If he does, the court will need to be satisfied that this duty has been breached, that a risk of death was reasonably foreseeable, that death was caused by the defendant, and the negligence was 'gross'—ie capable of amounting to a criminal act or omission.[1]

[1] Set out the criteria for the relevant offence. This creates a structure for the rest of your answer.

Whether a defendant owes the victim a duty of care is determined by tortious principles.[2] In the specific situation of the supply of drugs, in *R v Khan and Khan* [1998] **Crim LR 380**, the defendants' appeals were allowed even though they had not summoned assistance. The court did not wish to extend the class of duties in criminal law, on the grounds that to do so would unnecessarily widen the law. In Darren's situation, however, the court may be inclined to draw parallels with *R v Evans (Gemma)* [2009] 1 WLR 1999. In this case, the defendant gave heroin to her sister. A duty was created when she realized that her sister had succumbed to an overdose. When Darren puts a blanket over Viv, a duty may arise. In the case, Lord Judge CJ held:

[2] Note that the criminal standard of duty of care mirrors the tortious standard. There is some lack of clarity in the law here, as the criminal law espoused a narrow approach until *R v Adomako* (see later).

when a person has created or contributed to the creation of a state of affairs which he knows, or ought reasonably to know, has become life threatening, a consequent duty on him to act by taking reasonable steps to save the other's life may reasonably arise.

A similar point arose in *R v Miller*, in which a defendant caused a fire by falling asleep in bed holding a cigarette. He did not do anything about it, even when he realized. The fact that he had created a dangerous situation which he then failed to counteract created a duty of care.

The next question is whether Darren has breached the duty. This is not difficult to establish in criminal law when there is a death. The prosecution must prove that Darren caused the death. The breach of duty must involve a risk of death which is obvious to the reasonable person, even if the defendant does not personally appreciate it.

[3] Note that this test is an objective one.

In *R v Misra and Srivastava* [2005] 1 Cr App R 21, it was held that the circumstances must be such that a reasonably prudent person would have foreseen a serious and obvious risk of death.[3] This seems clear here, and in any event, Darren intends to call an ambulance.

Finally, the jury must be convinced that the breach amounts to 'gross' negligence.

In *R v Adomako* [1995] 1 AC 171, the court held that the question to be asked is as follows: was the defendant's conduct so bad in all the circumstances as to amount to a criminal act or omission? The test can be viewed as 'circular' in this definition of 'gross' negligence (a defendant's conduct is criminal if it is 'gross' negligence, and is classified as 'gross' negligence if it is a crime). This circularity was acknowledged by Lord Mackay in the judgment in *Adomako*, who emphasized that the decision is one for the jury, and is a question of fact.[4] The key issue is whether the defendant's conduct goes beyond a mere matter of compensation between the parties.

[4] Some critique adds depth to your answer here.

Applying these concepts to Darren's case, it is clear that his breach of duty satisfies the above requirements. His negligence in failing to act beyond throwing a blanket over Viv, thereby causing her death, is criminally negligent given the existence of the duty of care.[5]

[5] Apply the law to the facts, making it clear how the circumstances amount to a duty of care.

The next question is whether Darren has caused Sam's death. If so, he may be liable for constructive manslaughter (manslaughter by an unlawful or dangerous act). Has Darren committed an act which causes death?[6] The first condition is that an unlawful act has been committed. Driving at speed in a built-up residential area is unlawful, and this is an act, not an omission. Causation is established by means of the two-stage tests of factual and legal causation.

[6] Note that an omission cannot form the basis of this offence.

The factual causation test is as follows. The prosecution must establish that the victim would not have died but for the defendant's actions (*R v White* [1910] 2 KB 124). Here, Sam would not have died if Darren's car had not stalled. A key factor in causation is whether an act is reasonably foreseeable. Is there an unbroken chain of causation between Darren's bad driving and Sam's death in the sense that death or serious bodily harm was reasonably foreseeable in the circumstances? Darren will want to argue that he could not help stalling, and that it was not reasonably foreseeable that he would then drive into Maisie, killing Sam. Only the free, deliberate, and informed act of a third party can break the chain of causation. In *R v Pagett* (1983) 76 Cr App R 279, a case in which the police shot at D, who was holding his girlfriend hostage, killing her instantly, the court said that although there were circumstances in which the act of a third party might break the chain of causation, a reasonable act performed in self-preservation does not. Here, Maisie was acting as a reasonable, legal driver might act. Darren will therefore not be able to argue that the chain of causation was broken. It is not an unforeseeable event for a car to stall. Maisie was not acting voluntarily in hitting Sam. She was acting in self-preservation, or to prevent a worse harm. To succeed here, Darren will have to show that Maisie was also driving dangerously. This does not appear to be the case here, but we cannot be sure.[7]

[7] You can offer alternative arguments.

Darren will try to argue, further, that Bo's possibly negligent medical treatment has caused Sam's death, rather than Darren. The first question will be whether the doctor was acting negligently in administering a transfusion of the wrong type of blood, and in giving Sam an antibiotic to which he is allergic. The rules on medical negligence as a potential *novus actus interveniens* were considered in the cases of *R v Smith* [1959] 2 QB 35, *R v Jordan* (1956) 40 Cr App R 152, and *R v Cheshire*. Medical negligence will not break the chain of causation provided the original injuries were a substantial and operating cause of death. Darren may try to rely on *R v Jordan* (1956) 40 Cr App R 152, in which the chain of causation was held by the Court of Appeal to have been broken by the 'palpably wrong' administration of large doses of an antibiotic to which D is allergic.[8] This was considered to be 'independent' of D's original wounds. It is unlikely that in this case much was known about Sam's blood group or drug tolerance in an emergency situation like this. In any event, it is unlikely that medical negligence will break the chain of causation. In *R v Cheshire* [1991] 1 WLR 844, the Court of Appeal held that even though medical negligence was the immediate cause of the victim's death, it did not exclude the defendant's responsibility. The negligence was not so independent of the defendant's acts, and in itself so potent in causing death, that the defendant's acts could be regarded as insignificant.[9]

[8] Set out the law, but here again, note that there are contrasting arguments.

[9] This case is useful if you cannot decide between the contrasting arguments above.

The subsequent events in the warehouse mirror the facts of *R v Pagett* (explained earlier). As stated earlier, any argument on Darren's part that he did not cause Annie's death, but that the police officer did, will fail.

In conclusion, Darren may be found guilty of manslaughter by gross negligence with regard to Viv, and manslaughter by an unlawful and dangerous act with regard to Sam and Annie.

➕ LOOKING FOR EXTRA MARKS?

■ This question deals with the essential principles of criminal liability. However, note that the area of causation has some conflicting case law decisions. You can use these to your advantage to build up a strong argument. If you can, include an awareness of weaknesses in the law, as this will show that you have really understood the topic. Here, it has been argued that gross negligence manslaughter is 'circular'.

■ The structure of this type of question is crucial. Deal with evidence of the act or omission before moving on to factual and legal causation in turn. In looking at the intervening act, choose your authorities carefully to ensure relevance.

QUESTION | 4

Whatever doubts there may have been in the past, the definition of intention in English Criminal Law is now settled.

Critically assess the validity of this statement with reference to relevant case law.

CAUTION!

- In oblique intention, the judicial guidelines are contained within the case of **R v Nedrick**, as confirmed in **R v Woollin**. You will need to consider previous case law in order to answer an essay question on this topic, but bear in mind the older cases are no longer current.

- Ensure that you refer to the question set, and provide some critical analysis, using the views of academic commentators.

DIAGRAM ANSWER PLAN

Outline the law: provide a brief definition of direct and indirect intention and its development, and in particular the decision of **R v Moloney** distinguishing between intention and foresight. How far have the courts settled on a meaning of intention?

▼

Provide case law examples: explain the decision in **R v Nedrick** and refer to the House of Lords' decision in **R v Woollin** and in **R v Matthews; R v Alleyne**—do these cases settle the debate?

▼

Conclude with an analysis and discussion of the role of foresight in intention. Include the changes made by **R v Woollin**, and the Law Commission's recommendations.

SUGGESTED ANSWER

[1] Identify the key arguments from the outset and avoid excessive description.

The concept of intention in English criminal law has been the subject of considerable debate and discussion. There is no statutory definition of intention, and the courts have not shown much consistency to date in attempting to define it.[1]

As intention is obviously a matter of the defendant's state of mind, it is difficult for the jury to assess it. Therefore, guidelines from the judge are needed. In the majority of cases, the word can be used in its ordinary meaning—that is, when it is the person's aim to bring about a particular consequence. This type of intention is clear and easy enough for a jury to follow on the facts of the case. As we shall see, its scope is wide enough to cover most cases. If a defendant stabs a victim several times anywhere on the body, it is clear enough from the circumstances that there was an intention to cause serious bodily harm or death.

However, a defendant may sometimes bring about a consequence that is different from that which he intended to achieve. This is known as *indirect* or *oblique* intention. The defendant could, for example, put a bomb under the pilot's seat on a plane owned by the defendant in order to destroy the plane and claim the insurance money. The deaths of the pilot and the crew are not an essential part of his purpose, but are almost certain to occur if the defendant succeeds in his plan to destroy the plane. It is theoretically possible for the crew and the pilot to escape, but the possibility is remote. The question then is whether intention should include a situation in which the defendant does not *directly* aim or desire to cause death or serious injury, but these results are an inevitable consequence of the course of action he chooses to take. In this type of case, a jury needs very clear guidance on the meaning of intention, and in what circumstances it may decide on a verdict of murder rather than manslaughter.[2]

[2] The concept of oblique intent is not a matter of law, but a matter of evidence. You should avoid referring to the 'definition' of oblique intent.

The question for the court is whether the defendant's intention (say, to frighten the victim) should be assessed subjectively or objectively. In case law spanning three decades, the law moved from an objective analysis of oblique intent to one which takes account of the defendant's knowledge at the time of the events leading to death. In this way, it can be argued that there is now a clear distinction between murder and manslaughter. In *R v Woollin* **[1998] 4 All ER 103**, judges in the House of Lords emphasized that the lines between intention and recklessness, and therefore murder and manslaughter, should be kept separate. This was not always the case, as will become clear.

In *DPP v Smith* **[1961] AC 290**, a case regarding the killing of a police officer, the trial judge directed the jury that if it was satisfied that the defendant 'as a reasonable man must have contemplated that GBH was a likely result and that such harm did happen and that the officer dies as a consequence, then the accused is guilty of capital murder'.

[3] Note that this case is no longer considered to be good law.

This case was heavily criticized on the grounds that such an objective test was not suitable for such a serious crime, and, furthermore, that it failed to take account of the defendant's state of mind, a crucial element in criminal liability.[3] This case led to the enactment of **s 8** of the **Criminal Justice Act 1967** which bound juries to look beyond the fact that the defendant had caused the result, and to draw inferences from all the evidence available to them.

Section 8 explains how intention should be inferred or found from the evidence. It does not define intention. If intention is disputed by D, **s 8** states that the jury will need to take into account all the *evidence* in the case in order to draw an inference of (or to find) intention. Suppose, for example, D denies an intention to kill but has no plausible alternative explanation of his state of mind at the time of committing the crime. The jury will be directed to weigh up the facts and all the evidence tendered on behalf of the parties in order to infer or find D's state of mind at the time of the act. What D thought would happen as a result of his actions and the degree of risk of harm foreseen will be significant. So too will be the testimony of police officers, other witnesses, and experts. The jury will look at forensic and circumstantial evidence such as DNA, motive, fingerprints, weapons, documentary evidence, and any earlier admissions, silence, or lies by D in the police station. If the evidence is strongly against D, then, despite a denial of intention, and in the absence of any reasonable explanation, the jury will be invited to draw the conclusion, or to find that the harm was intended. The judge will direct the Jury, who decides issues of fact, on the legal meaning of intention and on the weight of the evidence, leaving it to the jury to decide whether D's state of mind was intentional or not. Whether a result was actually intended is essentially a question of fact for the jury, not the judge.

The case law following *DPP v Smith* moved towards subjectivity, but seemed to confuse the concepts of foresight and intention. Thus, in *Hyam v DPP* [1974] 2 All ER 241 the House of Lords upheld a conviction for murder where the accused had set fire to a victim's house by putting burning newspaper through her letterbox. This caused the death of the victim's two children, who, unknown to D, were in the house at the time. D stated that her intention had only been to frighten the victim. The House of Lords held that D would have the *mens rea* for murder if she knew that it was *highly probable* that her act would cause death or serious injury. The result of this case was that foresight of a high probability of death or serious harm resulting from her conduct would be enough for the *mens rea* for murder. This applied whether or not such foresight amounted to intention. Under *R v Nedrick* [1986] 3 All ER 1, it is unlikely that she would be convicted.

The issue of intention was further debated by the House of Lords in *R v Moloney* [1985] 1 All ER 1025 and *R v Hancock and Shankland* [1986] 1 All ER 641. In the former case, Moloney shot his stepfather from point blank range and was convicted of murder after the trial judge directed the jury that in law a man intends the consequence of his voluntary act when he desires it to happen (whether or not he foresees that it probably will happen) or when he foresees that it will happen, whether he desires it or not. The House of Lords quashed the conviction on the basis that this was a misdirection, Lord Bridge stating that:

the judge should avoid any elaboration or paraphrase of what is meant by intent, and leave it to the jury's good sense to decide whether the accused acted with the necessary intent, unless the judge is convinced that, on the facts and having regard to the way the case has been presented to the jury in evidence and argument, some further explanation or elaboration is strictly necessary to avoid misunderstanding.

This decision was followed by the House of Lords' ruling in *R v Hancock and Shankland*, where Lord Scarman also made the point that if intention required a detailed direction, it was best to leave this to the discretion of the trial judge. He added that the trial judge could not do as Lord Bridge suggested and simply direct the jury to consider whether the defendant foresaw death or serious injury as a 'natural consequence' of his actions. Instead, Lord Scarman stated that the trial judge must refer to the concept of probability—the more probable the consequence, the more likely the accused foresaw it and intended it. However, these do not always amount to the same thing. The defendants in this case may well have foreseen that throwing the blocks would result in injury, but this did not mean they intended to kill.[4]

Despite clear House of Lords *dicta* to the contrary, the Court of Appeal in *R v Nedrick* [1986] 3 All ER 1 laid down some guidelines to the effect that the jury should not infer intention unless it considered that the accused foresaw the consequence as a virtual certainty. However, this decision has attracted criticism, and the Court of Appeal in *R v Walker and Hayles* [1989] 90 Cr App R 226 stated that 'we are not persuaded that it is only when death is a virtual certainty that the jury can infer intention to kill'. The most current interpretation of oblique intent, therefore, may still be open to criticism.[5]

Nevertheless, the status of *Nedrick* was confirmed by the House of Lords' discussion in *R v Woollin* [1998] 4 All ER 103. The House stated that where the simple direction was not enough, the jury should be further directed that it was not entitled to find the necessary intention unless it felt sure that death or serious bodily harm was a virtually certain result of D's action (barring some unforeseen intervention) and that D had appreciated that fact.

This decision also illustrates one of the difficulties of the present approach: when is the issue of intention so complicated as to warrant a detailed direction? In *R v Walker and Hayles*, the Court of Appeal decided that 'the mere fact that a jury calls for a further direction on intention does not of itself make it a rare and exceptional case requiring a foresight direction'. On the other hand, in *R v Hancock and Shankland*, the House of Lords confirmed that the trial judge was right to give a detailed direction, even though the content of the direction was wrong.

Does the *Nedrick* test provide a definition of intention? This depends on whether the necessary degree of foresight represents a definition of intention, or whether it is merely evidence of it. This is important because without a clear definition, a jury may to mistake recklessness for intention, and arrive at an unjust verdict.

[4] It is crucial to distinguish between foresight and intention clearly, as it is central to the debate. It is also the issue that has produced the most uncertainty.

[5] At this stage, refer back to the question. This case casts doubt on the assertion in the quote that the 'definition' is settled.

Unfortunately, juries may have different ideas as to what constitutes intention, some insisting on purpose being necessary, and others being prepared to accept that only foresight of a probable consequence is required. It might be argued that we should not leave such an important decision in the hands of the jury. Lacey holds that juries have an innate understanding of what intention is, and that no further judicial direction is required. Wilson (1996) agrees, arguing that in a case such as *Hyam*, the defendant may have both intended to kill and intended to frighten. Foresight of a low probability of a risk occurring need not necessarily lead to recklessness. In *R v MD* **[2004] EWCA Crim 1391**, it was emphasized that the direction is not to be used in every case where there is doubt about the defendant's intention. In fact, it need only be given to juries where the defendant does an act causing death without the purpose of killing or causing serious injury and where there is evidence that D would fulfil the criteria in the test. In other cases, there is room in the simple direction (ie giving intention its ordinary meaning) for the judge to direct the jury.

In *R v Matthews and Alleyne* **[2003] EWCA Crim 192**, the prosecution argued that the rule in *Nedrick* was a substantive rule of law, not just one of evidence.[6]

[6] This is important because if it is only a rule of evidence, then the jury still has some room to acquit if it feels it is deserved.

Ashworth ([2003] Crim LR 553) argues that this may lead to inconsistency:

The upshot is that a court that is satisfied that D foresaw the prohibited result as a virtual certainty may properly decide not to find that D intended that result. The court cannot find intention if D foresaw the result as less than virtually certain; but foresight of virtual certainty may not be sufficient in some cases.

It can be seen that there is still some ambiguity in the direction, although the *Nedrick* direction is remarkably similar to it. In **[1998] Crim LR 890**, J C Smith described the *Nedrick* formula as involving 'some ineffable, indefinable notion of intent locked in the breasts of jurors'. Given the criticisms of *R v Nedrick* in the cases which followed it, the guidance given in that case does not settle the definition. The problem may lie instead in the mandatory life sentence for murder, which, if modified, may resolve some of the remaining tensions.

 LOOKING FOR EXTRA MARKS?

■ The key issue in oblique intent (and the issue which has caused the courts the most difficulty) is in the distinction between foresight and intention. Make sure that you can explain this carefully, using the case law.

■ Think about providing some alternative to the current definition, for example by discussing proposals for reform. The Law Commission has considered homicide and intention a number of times but suggested a definition in its 2006 report (*Murder, Manslaughter and Infanticide* (LC 304, HC 30)). Note also the development of the concept in the leading judgments.

Explain why the House of Lords in *R v G and Another* [2003] **4 All ER 765** settled on a definition of subjective recklessness in the context of **s 1** of the **Criminal Damage Act 1971**.

CAUTION!

■ This is a classic case of the criminal law's struggle between an objective and a subjective approach to liability (see Chapter 1).

■ Ensure that you address the reasons for the definition and do not simply describe the decision in the case.

DIAGRAM ANSWER PLAN

Outline the development of recklessness in the courts and in particular the interpretation of recklessness in the **Criminal Damage Act 1971**.

▼

Outline the law: provide a brief definition of recklessness and the difference between objective and subjective liability.

▼

Discuss the problems caused by the subjective definition: *R v Cunningham* and *R v Stephenson*.

▼

Consider the decision in *R v Caldwell* and the objective test [1981].

▼

Discuss the decision in *R v G and Another* and the reasons for overruling *R v Caldwell*.

▼

Conclusion: discuss the return to a subjective analysis of recklessness.

SUGGESTED ANSWER

The concept of recklessness is to be distinguished from that of intention. A defendant may be considered to be reckless if it is not his aim to achieve a result or where he is not aware that it is virtually certain to occur. Instead, he may simply foresee that it may occur, without any degree of certainty.

The distinction between a subjective approach and an objective approach is crucial in understanding the development of the law of recklessness. The current definition is contained in the case of *R v G and Another* [2003] UKHL 50.

[1] Give a brief summary of the current state of the law.

Subjective recklessness requires the court to determine the defendant's state of mind and level of knowledge at the time of committing the offence.[1] In *R v Cunningham* [1957] 2 All ER 412, the Court of Appeal held that a defendant was reckless only if he took an unjustifiable risk and was aware of the possibility of that risk. The defendant took a gas meter from an empty house to steal money from it. He left behind a broken pipe from which gas escaped. He was convicted of maliciously administering a noxious substance so as to endanger life under s 23 of the **Offences Against the Person Act 1861** as he was aware of the risk in dislodging the pipe, but continued to take that risk.

[2] Identify problems with the existing law.

A problem could arise if the defendant failed to see that there was a risk.[2] If the defendant was not aware of the risk, he could not be convicted of an offence for which the *mens rea* is subjective recklessness. In *R v Stephenson* [1979] QB 695, a defendant was found not guilty of criminal damage when he set fire to a haystack to keep warm. The defendant was schizophrenic and did not recognize the risk of the fire spreading—he was not, therefore, reckless.

[3] Add some critical comment to your discussion, to add value and analysis to what you are saying.

This seems a fair decision. It does not take account, however, of a defendant who deliberately closes his mind to the risk, or one who cannot see the risk because he is intoxicated.[3] The judicial approach of subjective recklessness was changed in the case of *Metropolitan Police Commissioner v Caldwell* [1981]. The defendant's conviction for criminal damage (under s 1(2) of the **Criminal Damage Act 1971**) was upheld by the House of Lords. The offence is damaging property with intent to endanger life. The defendant had got drunk and set fire to a hotel as an act of revenge against the owner. The defendant alleged that he was drunk at the time of the event and that it had not crossed his mind that he may be endangering life. Intoxication cannot be a defence to a basic intent crime, such as criminal damage. The judges took the opportunity to redefine recklessness in objective terms. Lord Diplock stated that:

a person is reckless if (1) he does an act which in fact creates an obvious risk that property will be destroyed or damaged and (2) when he does that act he either has not given any thought to the possibility of a risk or has recognised that there is some risk involved and has nonetheless gone on to do it.

[4] This highlights the development of the law in this area.

This ruling changed the approach of the courts to recklessness in the context of criminal damage from a subjective one to an objective one.[4] This seemed to resolve the problem of the previous rule in that it took account of a defendant who refused to see the risk, but it risked being unfair to a defendant who was not able to see the risk.

In *Elliott v C (A Minor)* [1983] 2 All ER 961, the Divisional Court held that no account should be taken of the fact that the defendant was a fourteen-year-old girl of limited intelligence, who was tired and hungry. She had spilt some white spirit on the wooden floor of a garden shed, and then dropped a lighted match near it. A reasonable person would have recognized the risk, and it did not matter that even if D had thought about it, she might not have been able to recognize it.

The decision in *MPC v Caldwell* thus narrowed the scope of recklessness, but meant an unfair decision in circumstances such as that described above. Also, there was the argument that '*Caldwell* recklessness' was not acceptable as a form of *mens rea* because it was not based on the defendant's state of mind. Whilst Lord Diplock's efforts to penalize thoughtlessness in terms of a social policy initiative were applauded by some, the real question was whether he was right to pursue this via a radical judicial reinterpretation of the term 'recklessness'. As far as recklessness is concerned, the subjectivist argument has found favour again, as evidenced by the House of Lords' decision in *R v G* [2003] 4 All ER 765, where it was held that a defendant could not be properly convicted under s 1 of the **Criminal Damage Act 1971** on the basis that he was reckless as to whether property was destroyed or damaged when he gave no thought to the risk and, by reason of his age and/or personal characteristics, the risk would not have been obvious to him, even if he had thought about it.[5] Lord Bingham observed that recklessness should at least require a knowing disregard of an appreciated and unacceptable risk of, or a deliberate closing of the mind to, such risk. In his view, it was not clearly blameworthy to do something involving a risk of injury to another if one genuinely did not perceive the risk.

[5] Try to identify the overall impact of changes in the law.

Lord Bingham's reasons were as follows:[6]

[6] The *ratio decidendi*, or reasons for the decision, are important here, as the House of Lords overruled itself on this issue.

1. In serious crimes, the defendant's state of mind must be culpable. An objective test effectively makes the crime one of strict liability. Lord Bingham asserted that it is not clearly blameworthy to engage in conduct where there is a risk of injury if the defendant does not genuinely perceive that risk. Lord Bingham approved the dissenting judgment of Lord Edmund-Davies in *Caldwell*, where he had said that a man cannot close his mind to risk unless he first realizes that there is a risk, in which case he is subjectively reckless, as had already been decided in *Parker (Daryl)* [1977] 1 WLR 600. Furthermore, *Caldwell* was potentially unjust and contrary to the **UN Convention on the Rights of the Child** in force in the UK in September 1999.

2. The approach in *Caldwell* sometimes compelled juries to commit what they perceived as obvious unfairness towards defendants. The context of *Caldwell* did not require consideration of the young or mentally handicapped. No modification of *Caldwell*

could correct its inherent injustice. A lapse of care due to inca-
pacity, absent-mindedness, or foolishness would be negligent,
whereas if it was due to excitability or rage it might be reckless.
The defendant in *Elliott* had not chosen to commit harm in a
rational sense.

3. The decision in *Caldwell* itself was held to be a misinterpretation of the law contained in the **Criminal Damage Act 1971**.
He asked what Parliament had meant in using the word 'reckless'
in **s 1(1)** and **(2)** of the **1971 Act**. In treating *Cunningham* as
irrelevant, the majority in *Caldwell* fell into 'understandable but
demonstrable error'.

4. Lord Steyn thought the decision would lead to impractical
consequences:

the surest test of a new legal rule is not whether it satisfies a team of logicians
but how it performs in the real world. With the benefit of hindsight, the verdict
must be that the rule laid down in *Caldwell* failed this test … experience suggests that in *Caldwell* the law took a wrong turn.

In a commentary to the decision in *Caldwell*, J C Smith (1981) argued
that it would not only lead to unfairness, but that the intention of
Parliament, was largely ignored in the case. The defendant, such as
Caldwell, who acts recklessly through impulse or anger, could still be
caught within the former definition. The rule had been changed from
a subjective view to an objective view rather unnecessarily.

In conclusion, *R v G* reflects a general judicial trend in favour of
subjectivity in criminal law, as evidenced in other decisions such as
B v DPP **[2000] 1 All ER 833**.

As a result of the decision in *R v G and Another*, the test for recklessness in criminal damage has returned to a subjective test—the
court must take into account any relevant characteristics in assessing
the defendant's state of mind. The rule in *Caldwell* applied only to
criminal damage.

Was the court correct in its decision to reverse *R v Caldwell*? This
depends on whether a subjective or an objective view of the criminal law is used. On the one hand, it can be argued that *mens rea* is
crucial in a society in which individuals are autonomous and have
the capacity and freedom to decide how to behave. Therefore, a person's state of mind at the time of the offence is significant. *Mens
rea* reflects the principle that liability should be imposed on those
who intended or knew of the risks of their behaviour. On the other
hand, it can be argued that the courts have a duty to protect the
public from reckless defendants.[7] Most people would agree that punishment should extend to people who knowingly choose to take a
risk of serious harm with others' safety and property. They would also
probably agree that, although not necessarily fully aware of the risk

[7] Conclude by weighing up the
arguments in your conclusion.

of harm at the moment of acting, a person still knows they are creating a risk if they would have been able to realize it given a moment's reflection. *R v G* demonstrates that a subjective test of recklessness should be able to include both of these states of mind. It is important that the courts maintain consistency, particularly in matters of blameworthiness.

LOOKING FOR EXTRA MARKS?

■ A direct comparison of Lord Bingham's judgment in *R v G and Another* and Lord Diplock's judgment in *R v Caldwell* will help to add real weight to your answer and will satisfy the examiner that you have attempted to critically analyse the issues arising.

TAKING THINGS FURTHER

■ Amirthalingam K, 'Caldwell Recklessness is Dead, Long Live Mens Rea's Fecklessness' [2004] MLR 491.

Argues that whilst the return to subjective recklessness in R v G is desirable as it assesses the individual defendant's liability, an element of objectivity is needed to assess guilt.

■ Ashworth A, 'The Scope of Criminal Liability for Omissions' (1989) 105 LQR 424–9.

Proposes a duty of easy rescue based on social responsibility.

■ Ashworth A, *Principles of the Criminal Law* (8th edn, OUP 2016).

Seminal textbook on the criminal process.

■ Ashworth A, 'A New Generation of Omissions Offences' [2018] Crim LR 2018 354–64.

Considers the expansion of criminalization to include 'preventive' criminal responsibility in the context of a 'new generation' of omissions liability.

■ Crosby C, 'Gross Negligence Manslaughter by Omission' (2018) J Crim Law 82(2) 127–37.

Considers the basis for the duty of care and criminal liability established in the recent unreported case of R v Bowditch and argues that there is a lack of clarity in the law.

■ Hart H L A and Honoré T, *Causation in the Law* (2nd edn, OUP 1985).

An in-depth discussion of the meaning of causation in the criminal law.

■ Hogan B, 'Omissions and the Duty Myth' in P Smith (ed), *Criminal Law: Essays in Honour of J C Smith* (Butterworths 1968).

Argues that the act/omissions distinction is unhelpful and that liability for omissions should instead be based on causation.

■ Lacey N, 'A Clear Concept of Intention: Elusive or Illusory?' (1993) 56 MLR 621.

Argues that we haven't reached consensus on the definition of intention, and explores the legal use of 'common sense' or 'ordinary' meanings.

■ Papadopoulou P, 'From Pretty to Nicklinson: Changing Judicial Attitudes to Assisted Dying' [2017] 3 EHRLR 298–307.

Discusses whether judicial attitudes on this area of law are taking account of how, and whether, the law ought to change.

■ Smith J C, 'Liability for Omissions in the Criminal Law' (1993) 57 J Crim Law 88.

Argues that causation should determine liability for omissions, rather than the wider concept of duty.

■ Williams G, 'Recklessness Redefined' (1981) 40 CLJ 252.

*A critique of the decision in **Caldwell**—still useful to understand the impact of the revival of subjective recklessness.*

■ Williams G, 'Criminal Omissions—The Conventional View' [1991] 107 LQR 90.

Argues against the social responsibility view of omissions advanced by Ashworth on the grounds of clarity of the law and the blurred lines between positive acts and omissions.

■ Wilson W, 'Doctrinal Rationality after Woollin' (1999) 62 MLR 448.

*Argues that the definition of intention is still unstable, despite the clarifications offered by **Woollin**.*

Online Resources

www.oup.com/uk/qanda/

For extra essay and problem questions on this topic, as well as advice on revision and exam technique, please visit the online resources.

3

Murder and Manslaughter

ARE YOU READY?

In order to answer questions on this topic, you will need to understand the following:

- the key distinctions between murder, voluntary manslaughter, and involuntary manslaughter;
- the *actus reus* for murder (see causation in Chapter 2);
- the *mens rea* for murder—direct and oblique intent (refer to *mens rea* in Chapter 2);
- the statutory provisions in the **Homicide Act 1957** and **Coroners and Justice Act 2009** on the defences of diminished responsibility and loss of control;
- the differences between gross negligence manslaughter, subjectively reckless manslaughter, and manslaughter by an unlawful and dangerous act (constructive manslaughter);
- the effect of the decision in *R v Kennedy* [2007] UKHL 38 in relation to the chain of causation in drugs cases leading to death.

KEY DEBATES

Debate: abused partners who kill

In the previous law contained in the **Homicide Act 1957**, an abused partner who killed had to have reacted suddenly in order to benefit from the defence of provocation, with no time lapse between the last act of provocation and killing. That defence was criticized on the grounds that it was unfair to female defendants, who tend not to react immediately to provocation. The defence of loss of control, introduced by the **Coroners and Justice Act 2009**, abolishes this requirement. In two articles in the *Criminal Law Review*, Alan Norrie (2009) and Ronnie Mackay (2009) provide a thorough analysis of the effect of the legislative changes, as well as reviewing the problems of

$\circledcirc$

the previous law on provocation and diminished responsibility, in particular concerning abused women.

Debate: the definition of involuntary manslaughter

It has been argued that involuntary manslaughter is too wide and covers a number of different circumstances. In gross negligence, there may be an overlap between civil and criminal law in establishing a duty of care. It is possible to be convicted of an unlawful and dangerous act such as manslaughter on the basis of quite a minor initial offence. It may also be argued that it is wrong that a defendant should be convicted of a serious offence when s/he did not intend the outcome. The Law Commission, in its 1996 report 'Legislating the Criminal Code: Involuntary Manslaughter' (LC 237), held this view and suggested that a defendant ought only to be convicted for causing a harm which he *chose* to risk. Duff (1990) (quoted in Law Commission Report LC 237 above) argues, however, that this approach is not realistic and would require the defendant to constantly be aware of all actions in what he describes as a 'constant silent monologue'.

QUESTION | 1

Tim and Karen had been married for six years. Recently, Karen had made a new set of friends and had become withdrawn from Tim and their relationship. She regularly went out to nightclubs without him and was drinking heavily. As a result, Tim was receiving treatment from his doctor for clinical depression. One night, he decided to follow Karen to the nightclub and found her dancing and kissing another man. At home, Karen told Tim that she had found a much better lover and that Tim bored her. Tim, furious and humiliated, reached for the poker next to the fire and hit Karen several times on the head with it. She collapsed. When Tim realized what he had done, he called the police and Karen was taken to hospital. When she regained consciousness, she took an overdose of painkillers which had been accidentally left next to her bed by an absent-minded nurse, and she died. Tim says that he did not want to kill Karen but was confused and angry.

Discuss Tim's criminal liability for murder, including the effect of any defences he may have.

CAUTION!

- Adopt a logical structure throughout, working your way through causation and the *novus actus interveniens*, then direct and oblique intent, including causation, then the partial defences to murder contained in the **Coroners and Justice Act 2009**.
- Make sure you do not confuse the issue of intent with the issue of diminished responsibility. Murder must be established before discussing this defence.

DIAGRAM ANSWER PLAN

Identify the issues
- The question raises the issue of murder and the relevant partial defences of loss of control and diminished responsibility.
- There is also an issue of intoxication, relating to *mens rea*.

Relevant law
- Discuss the *actus reus* of murder and work through the principles of causation. Is there an argument relating to *novus actus interveniens*?
- Discuss the *mens rea* of murder, including oblique intent and intoxication. Identify basic and specific intent.
- Discuss the provisions of **ss 52–55 Coroners and Justice Act 2009**.

Apply the law
- Tim's intoxication may affect *mens rea* (***DPP v Majewski***).
- Apply the provisions of the **Coroners and Justice Act 2009**.

Conclude
- Conclude on murder or manslaughter by reason of loss of control or diminished responsibility.

SUGGESTED ANSWER

[1] It is a good idea to start your discussion with a definition.

[2] Always start with factual causation, as this establishes the logical link between the defendant's act and the victim's death.

[3] Even though the case of ***R v Jordan*** suggests that the chain could be broken, this is very rare. Even if the medical treatment is severely negligent, it is unlikely to break the chain of causation if the 'operating' cause—that is, the reason that the victim is in the hospital—is the defendant's original action.

This question raises issues of Tim's liability for murder and any defences which may be available to him. The *actus reus* of murder is the unlawful killing of a human being.[1] The concepts of 'unlawful' and 'human being' are satisfied here. The first issue is causation. Tim is clearly the factual cause of Karen's death. Karen would not have died if Tim had not hit her on the head with the poker: ***R v White* [1910] 2 KB 124**.[2] A question arises over whether Tim's contribution to her death is too remote. In other words, will Tim's defence team be able to argue that the forgetfulness of the nurse causes Karen's death, and makes Tim's contribution insignificant (***R v Smith* [1959] 2 QB 35**, and ***R v Cheshire* [1991] 3 All ER 670**)?

As a general rule, medical treatment does not break the chain of causation. This is true even if the treatment is severely negligent. The key point is whether Tim can be considered to be a substantial and operating cause of Karen's death.[3] The common law defines the *mens rea* of murder as 'malice aforethought'. This is now understood as meaning an intention to kill or to do grievous bodily harm. In order for Tim to be found guilty of murder, the prosecution must prove that Tim had either the intention to kill or to do grievous bodily harm. Intent can be based on 'purpose/desire' or on evidence of foresight. It would appear to have been Tim's purpose to do some grievous bodily harm—this would suffice for the *mens rea* of murder. If it cannot be shown that his purpose was to cause serious injury, then the judge will direct the jury that it is only entitled to infer intention where death or serious injury is a virtually certain consequence of Tim's actions, and that Tim appreciated this to be the case. If necessary, the trial judge could give a '*Nedrick*' direction—*R v Nedrick* **[1986] 3 All ER 1**. This would involve asking the jury to consider whether or not there was evidence that Tim foresaw death or grievous bodily harm as virtually certain to result from his action. It seems likely that at least one of these circumstances will be satisfied. Only if there was evidence that Tim foresaw death or grievous bodily harm as virtually certain to result from his actions would a jury be entitled to infer that he intended death or grievous bodily harm.[4]

The loss of control defence requires Tim to provide evidence that he acted as he did due to a qualifying trigger.

The first of these under the 2009 Act is that he acted as a result of his fear of serious violence by Karen. This is not the case here. The Act provides a second possibility—that Tim's loss of self-control was attributable to things said by Karen that constituted circumstances of an extremely grave character such that they caused Tim to have a justifiable sense of being seriously wronged. A number of matters need to be considered here. First, s55 is clear that Karen's words alone can be sufficient.[5] Second, it would be for the prosecution to prove beyond all reasonable doubt that the words spoken did not amount to circumstances of an extremely grave character.

The prosecution may still argue that the 'anger' trigger is not available because **s. 55(6)(c)** expressly precludes its operation in circumstances where the thing said or done that is claimed to have triggered D's action constitutes sexual infidelity. However, in *R v Clinton* **[2012] EWCA Crim 2**, the Court of Appeal ruled that whilst s 54(4) of the **2009 Act** excludes sexual infidelity as a trigger for the loss of control defence, it should not be read as necessarily excluding evidence of sexual infidelity (as part of the context in which the issue of whether or not there was a qualifying trigger could be considered).

If the jury is satisfied that there is a qualifying trigger for Tim's actions, it will then have to consider whether a person of Tim's sex and age, with a normal degree of tolerance and self-restraint, and in Tim's circumstances, might have reacted as Tim did, or in a similar way. The purpose of this formulation is to prevent a defendant citing any personal characteristics that might affect his self-control. In doing so, it

[4] Don't forget to deal with both elements of the *Nedrick* direction.

[5] Do not forget to apply the law to the facts throughout.

reflects the approach taken by the Privy Council in *Attorney-General for Jersey v Holley* [2005] **UKPC 23**, in relation to the common law defence of provocation (since abolished by the **Coroners and Justice Act 2009**), which endorsed the view that a defendant pleading the defence of provocation had to be judged by the standard of a person having ordinary powers of control. Hence Tim's depression would not be relevant for these purposes. What the jury would be entitled to take into account are Tim's personal circumstances in so far as they explain the gravity of the words or actions causing him to lose his self-control, for example his marital difficulties and the fact that Karen has become withdrawn from the relationship. In *R v Rejmanski* [2017] **EWCA Crim 2061**, it was held that a mental condition was not relevant in so far as it reduced D's capacity for tolerance and self-restraint, although it might be relevant as one of D's circumstances. In that case, neither of the conditions (post-traumatic stress disorder and emotionally unstable personality disorder) were relevant to the standard of tolerance and self-restraint expected from them under **s 54(1)(c)**. If a condition was severe enough to provide an explanation for the killing, then the appropriate defence was diminished responsibility. Tim may not be successful in using the defence for these reasons, despite the fact that he lost his self-control, that he was not acting out of revenge, and that his actions came within the 'anger' qualifying trigger.

Bearing in mind that characteristics such as mental illness that have a bearing on the temperament of a defendant are excluded from the statutory defence of loss of control, Tim would be better advised to plead the defence of diminished responsibility, established under **s 2** of the **Homicide Act 1957**, as subsequently amended by **s 52** of the **Coroners and Justice Act 2009**. Under the amended **s 2(1)**, Tim would have to prove that, at the time of the killing, he was suffering from an abnormality of mental functioning arising from a medical condition. The facts indicate that he had been diagnosed and is being treated by a doctor for his depression.

Tim would also have to establish that this abnormality of mental functioning caused a substantial impairment in: (i) his understanding of the nature of his conduct; (ii) his ability to form a rational judgement; or (iii) his ability to exercise self-control. The Court of Appeal has confirmed that, for the purposes of the **2009 Act**, the concept of substantial impairment should be approached in the same way as was the case under the **Homicide Act 1957**; see *R v Brown* [2011] **EWCA 2796**. Hence, there should be evidence of more than some trivial degree of impairment, but there does not have to be evidence of total impairment; see *R v Lloyd* [1967] **1 QB 175**. In *R v Golds*

[2014] 4 All ER 64 it was held that the term 'substantial' must be explained as not simply 'more than minimal' or 'trivial'. The interpretation of the term is a matter for the jury.

[6] The legislation has substantially improved the law in this area by providing three distinct scenarios. Make sure you specify which one is most appropriate.

Of these three options, the impairment of self-control option is likely to prove the most fruitful for Tim,[6] provided the jury is satisfied that the impairment is substantial and, further, that the abnormality of mental functioning provided an explanation for Tim's actions in the sense that it was the cause or a contributory factor in making Tim act as he did. As indicated earlier, there is every prospect of this defence succeeding, and in consequence reducing Tim's liability to manslaugh-

[7] Try to give practical legal advice based on your argument.

ter, provided the expert evidence is sufficiently compelling. Tim should be advised that he is likely to be convicted of manslaughter by reason of diminished responsibility.[7]

LOOKING FOR EXTRA MARKS?

- Better answers may identify that responses to sexual infidelity are excluded by the Act in s 54(4)—however, the case of *R v Clinton* casts some doubt on this, and it should not be read as excluding evidence of sexual infidelity as part of the context of whether or not there was a qualifying trigger.

- Can you say which the better defence is, and conclude on the issue of whether Tim will be guilty of murder or manslaughter?

QUESTION | 2

The **Coroners and Justice Act 2009** aimed to create a more 'effective, transparent and responsive' justice service for victims, providing greater clarity and fairness (Explanatory Notes to the **Coroners and Justice Act 2009**).

Discuss this statement in relation to the defences of loss of control and diminished responsibility by abused women who kill.

CAUTION!

- With essay questions such as this, make sure you do not simply describe what the law is. You need to say whether you agree or disagree with the statement, based on evidence.

- The previous law on the characteristics of the defendants should not now be needed. However, in discussing the effectiveness of the new law, previous cases can expose some of the mischief the Act was trying to address.

DIAGRAM ANSWER PLAN

Explain the effect of the **Coroners and Justice Act 2009** on the two partial defences to murder: loss of control and diminished responsibility. The Act amends **s 2** of the **Homicide Act 1957** and creates a new defence of loss of control.

▼

Explain diminished responsibility and the medical requirement.

▼

Consider loss of control and the subjective test. The Act removes the sudden requirement.

▼

Discuss exclusion of sexual infidelity—*R v Clinton*.

▼

Consider the objective test—development of the law. Discuss a return to an objective test.

▼

Conclude by explaining that the Act still has some problems.

 SUGGESTED ANSWER

The defences to murder under the **Coroners and Justice Act 2009** amended the law in relation to diminished responsibility, and changed the law in relation to the defence of provocation, replacing it with a new defence of loss of control. These changes were brought about as a result of inconsistencies in, and criticism of, existing case law, and were the culmination of three Law Commission reports: 'Partial Defences to Murder' (LC 290, 2004), 'A New Homicide Act for England and Wales' (LC 177, 2005), and 'Murder, Manslaughter and Infanticide' (LC 304, 2006).

Diminished responsibility is defined under **s 2** of the **Homicide Act 1957** as amended by **s 52** of the **Coroners and Justice Act 2009**. The **Coroners and Justice Act 2009** provides for a new defence of loss of control, replacing the previous law of provocation, which was contained in the common law and in the **Homicide Act 1957**.

[1] In the introduction, refer to the rubric and state what you intend to do.

The changes in the **Coroners and Justice Act 2009** are discussed, and the effectiveness of the changes analysed.[1]

In relation to diminished responsibility, **s 52(1)** states that a person will not be convicted of murder if he was suffering from such abnormality of mental functioning which arose: (i) from a recognized medical condition; (ii) which substantially impaired his responsibility to do one of three things mentioned in **s 52(1)(A)**; and (iii) which provides an explanation for his acts and omissions in doing the killing. There must be a causal link between the defendant's condition and the killing. The definition of the abnormality of mind requirement in the previous law was much wider. The new law requires a 'recognised medical condition'.

This amendment appears to be an improvement to the law. It was not always clear which conditions were included in the definition. With particular reference to victims of abuse, battered women syndrome will continue to be part of the definition.[2]

On the other hand, as a recognized medical condition must be proven, it might be argued that some defendants, such as 'mercy' killers, will be excluded from the defence on these grounds.

The defendant has to establish that this abnormality of mental functioning caused a substantial impairment in: (i) his understanding of the nature of his conduct; (ii) his ability to form a rational judgement; or (iii) his ability to exercise self-control. There does not have to be evidence of total impairment.

The meaning of this word has given rise to several appeals. Until recently, it was held to mean 'more than trivial' as under the previous law (*Lloyd* **[1967] 1 QB 175**; *Brown (Robert)* **[2011] EWCA Crim 2796**). However, in *Golds* **[2016] UKSC 61**, the Supreme Court held that 'substantial', required something more than this, though it fell short of defining what that was. In *Squelch* **[2017] EWCA Crim 204**, the Court of Appeal emphasized that it was best to direct the jury using the words of **s 2**, 'without undue elaboration'. This may lead to inconsistency, as Gibson (2017) points out in an article in the *Criminal Law Review*.

There are clearly some problems with the new defence, as there were with the old. In particular, it can be argued that this is especially so in assessing abnormality of mental functioning, now confined to a medical condition. Whilst they have the benefit of expert evidence, these often conflict.

In certain cases, although diminished responsibility could be seen as a useful tool, it is arguable that it could only be used because provocation was unavailable due to the suddenness requirement.

Loss of control has replaced the defence of provocation. To begin with, the judge will determine whether there is sufficient evidence of loss of control to put before a jury. In **ss 54 and 55** of the **Coroners and Justice Act 2009**, there must be a loss of control (**s 54(1)(a)**) due to a qualifying trigger (**s 54(1)(b)**), due to a fear of serious violence from the victim or a thing done or said which constituted circumstances of an extremely grave character and caused the defendant to have a justifiable sense of being seriously wronged (**s. 55(4)**). It excludes situations of revenge or violence by the defendant.

[2] Back up and analyse your opinion, giving reasons for your answer. Here, the law has improved due to a tightening of the definition.

[3] Referring to the rationale for a particular legislative provision can help you to see whether it has achieved its aims. *Hansard* can be a useful research tool here.

Parliament was keen to make a clear distinction between genuine cases of loss of control and so-called revenge killings.[3]

Furthermore, incidences of sexual infidelity triggers are excluded.

The subjective test had been criticized in the past due to its unfairness towards women. The requirement for a 'sudden' loss of control required a 'snap' reaction, which is typically the reaction of men rather than women. In cases such as *R v Thornton* and *R v Ahluwalia* [1993], any delay between the last abuse and the killing was interpreted by the courts as the conscious formulation of a plan for revenge. Although some attempt was made by the Court of Appeal to recognize 'cumulative provocation' in cases of domestic violence, the delay often meant that the defence was rejected. In cases such as these, the defendant was not successful in pleading provocation, but had to plead diminished responsibility instead, effectively labelling the defendant as mentally ill.[4]

[4] You can comment on the law in its social context. Here, this was a particular disadvantage of the unavailability of the defence to certain groups of people.

In this respect, the **Coroners and Justice Act 2009** and its subsequent interpretation has improved the law. A defendant who has been abused will no longer need to prove that the loss of control was sudden, and will not be forced to plead the defence of diminished responsibility instead of loss of control. However, the law excludes cases of sexual infidelity, **s 55(6)(c)**.

The exclusion of sexual infidelity as a qualifying trigger is difficult, particularly in relation to things 'said'. Confessions of betrayal may or may not be true and may or may not count as sexual infidelity. The relevant words may take the form of reports from third parties or things said. Nevertheless, sexual infidelity as a thing 'done or said' is to be disregarded as a qualifying trigger.

The cases of *R v Clinton, Parker and Evans* [2012] EWCA **Crim 2** and *Dawes, Hatter and Bowyer* [2013] EWCA Crim 322 cast some doubt on this section and that evidence of the infidelity might be allowed in certain circumstances. The second case confirms this doubt and also held that concepts of cumulative provocation, which were previously recognized under the old law, should continue to be recognized under the Act. It has been argued that decisions casting doubt on the sexual infidelity exclusion in fact undermine the intention of Parliament in withdrawing it from the jury. D J Baker and L X Zhao, 'Contributory Qualifying and Non-Qualifying Triggers in the Loss of Control Defence: A Wrong Turn on Sexual Infidelity' [2012] JCL 254, argue that allowing it to be considered, against the intention of Parliament, effectively creates a third qualifying trigger. Furthermore, they argue that the aim of excluding the section was to give women greater protection:

the aim was to deny angry and jealous men a concession for killing in revenge and out of jealousy.

Further, in relation to the qualifying trigger, the sense of being wronged must itself be objectively justifiable: thus, in *Meanza* **[2017] EWCA Crim 445** it was accepted that D felt seriously wronged by conditions imposed on him by hospital and restriction orders. However, '[t]he emphasis must be on the adjective "justifiable". The appellant could have no justifiable grievance in relation to hospital and restriction orders that were lawfully imposed.'

The second area to be considered is the objective test. The **Homicide Act 1957** had stipulated that the jury had to ask whether a reasonable man would have acted as the defendant did. This raised the question of whether any particular information about the defendant could be put to the jury in order to help them to establish this. If certain characteristics could be put to the jury, then the defendant could be judged by his own reduced powers of self-control and not those of the reasonable man.[5] The case law on this point was far from clear. If the offensive conduct from the victim signified increased gravity to the defendant because it was aimed at a particular characteristic, then this characteristic could be taken account of by the jury. If the taunt was not about the particular characteristic to which the defendant was sensitive, then it could not be put to the jury. Later cases, however, dispensed with this idea of the mode of provocation and allowed nearly all characteristics to be put to the jury. This was the case even if this knowledge was prejudicial, and even if it was likely to reduce self-control. As long as it increased the gravity of the provocation to the defendant, it was admissible. Thus, in *R v Smith (Morgan)*, the defendant's alcoholism and depression, which affected his powers of self-control, was admitted.[6] However, in the case of *Attorney-General v Holley* **[2005] UKPC 23**, the court stated that the test should be an objective one. The defendant's reaction will be compared to that of a normal person of the defendant's sex and age with normal tolerance and self-restraint. This endorses the view that a defendant pleading this defence is to be judged by the standard of someone having ordinary powers of self-control. In *R v Rejmanski* **[2017] EWCA Crim 2061**, the Court of Appeal considered two cases: one concerning a soldier who claimed that he had killed V after V's taunting triggered his post-traumatic stress disorder, and second, Gassman, whose emotionally unstable personality disorder made her unable to control her emotions at the time of killing. The Court held that a mental condition was not relevant in so far as it reduced D's capacity for tolerance and self-restraint, although it might be relevant as one of D's circumstances. Thus, neither Rejmanski's post-traumatic stress disorder nor Gassman's emotionally unstable personality disorder were relevant to the standard of tolerance and self-restraint expected from them under **s 54(1)(c)** of the **Coroners and Justice Act 2009**. If a condition

[5] The debate on which characteristics of the defendant could be taken into account for the purposes of the objective test was wide ranging. Comment on whether the Act has helped in this.

[6] Try to give case law examples wherever possible, even in an essay.

was severe enough to provide an explanation for the killing, then the appropriate defence was diminished responsibility.

Does the new law retain a purely objective test? At face value, it seems so. This is evident in the use of the words, 'a person with a normal degree of tolerance and self-restraint'. However, the provision includes the term, 'in the circumstances of the defendant'. The jury is therefore entitled to take into account the personal circumstances of the defendant to the degree that it affects the gravity of the provocation to him. If there is evidence that the defendant was not acting out of revenge, that his or her actions came within the qualifying trigger, and that they were those that might have been displayed by a reasonable person in his or her circumstances, then the defence of loss of control may be made out.

In conclusion, it can be said that although the **Coroners and Justice Act 2009** has attempted to help victims of domestic violence who kill, problems remain, particularly in cases of sexual infidelity and in the taking account of mental conditions. This is evident from the cases of *R v Clinton, R v Rejmanski*, and *R v Dawes*. In relation to the objective test, it is still difficult for juries to be able to establish exactly what they are allowed to take account of when asking whether a person with a normal degree of tolerance and self-restraint would have acted as the defendant did. The introduction of the **Coroners and Justice Act 2009** was meant to eradicate the obstacles faced by battered women who kill, but it appears they have only been reduced.[7] It is the education of the jury which appears to be an important factor in the success of the partial defence of loss of control, particularly due to the jury's understanding of what characteristics should be considered.

It remains however the woman's responsibility to prove that her actions were justifiable, which is difficult when comparing it to the reasonable man. Without personally experiencing domestic abuse, it remains difficult for a judge or jury to understand the actions of an abused woman, so using the partial defence of loss of control remains a risk. Due to the stringent objective test, many women have to resort to the partial defence of diminished responsibility, which is not a viable option as without a recognized medical condition this defence does not apply, leaving no further options. The **Coroners and Justice Act 2009** has not corrected this problem, leaving many victims of abuse without the necessary available defences.

It appears that the **Coroners and Justice Act 2009** has not addressed the problems regarding statutory interpretation.

Despite the continuing issues which have been raised regarding the 'loss of control' requirement, the introduction of the 'fear' qualifying trigger has been welcome. However, the interpretation of the Act still remains wide, and the requirement of loss of control still remains impossible for many to show. Without recognizing the full extent of the effect of the abuse, outside the requirement of a reasonable man,

[7] Refer back to the question.

the defence will remain unavailable to many. The Law Commission, whose recommendations led to the **Coroners and Justice Act 2009**, has proposed that the 'loss of self-control' requirement be abolished, but it still appears in the Act. This is confusing as 'loss of self-control' implies an impulsive reaction. Sexual infidelity is not defined, and nor is 'a considered desire for revenge'.

In conclusion, it can be said that although the law has attempted to iron out some inconsistencies, it may have created new ones. It may be no easier for juries to understand.

LOOKING FOR EXTRA MARKS?

- Try to use the law in its social and political context, but always back up with case law principles wherever possible. Here, the law has particular application to this set of victims, and the case law illustrates the difficulties.

- Refer to academic commentary in this area. For example, in relation to the objective test in loss of control, the debate on which characteristics should be put to the jury has attracted prolific commentary.

QUESTION | 3

Sid, who is seventy-five years old and quite frail, is queuing for his pension at the post office one morning. He is not feeling very well and has forgotten to take his medication for his heart condition. Jim enters the post office, furious that his unemployment benefit has not been paid on time. He is determined to speak to the cashier and so pushes to the front of the queue. In doing so he pushes Dee, an elderly lady also waiting to pick up her pension, out of the way. Dee falls on Sid, who falls over. Jim leaves the post office.

Meanwhile Sid has a heart attack. The cashier calls an ambulance and Sid is taken to hospital, where he is seen by Dr Peach, who advises that Sid should be kept under observation. Unfortunately, Sid develops a chest infection and he is connected to a ventilator. Dr Peach is too busy to check on Sid regularly, and so does not realize that the tube has become blocked. Sid dies of asphyxia.

Advise the Crown Prosecution Service on the liability of Jim and Dr Peach for Sid's death.

CAUTION!

- Structure is very important in this question, as there are two different types of manslaughter to be considered.

- The element of dangerousness in constructive manslaughter must be discussed very carefully. It cannot be confused with causation.

DIAGRAM ANSWER PLAN

Identify the issues	■ Identify unlawful and dangerous act manslaughter and manslaughter by gross negligence.
Relevant law	■ Is there an unlawful act? Does it have to be directed at the victim? Use unlawful and dangerous act manslaughter: give the definition of the *actus reus* and *mens rea* of a battery. Consider dangerousness using the **Church** test.
Apply the law	■ Apply battery. Has Jim caused the death of Sid? Is it dangerous? ■ Apply the test in *R v Adomako* and the test for gross negligence. ■ Discuss whether the doctor may be guilty of gross negligence manslaughter with the above criteria: *R v Adomako*.
Conclude	■ The chain of causation is unlikely to be broken. Gross negligence is unlikely.

SUGGESTED ANSWER

Jim's liability for the death of Sid will be involuntary manslaughter rather than murder, as there is no evidence that he has the *mens rea* for murder. The type of manslaughter will depend on the initial act or omission which led to Sid's death. Manslaughter by an unlawful or dangerous act (also known as constructive manslaughter) requires, first, an unlawful act. The unlawful act must be a crime and not a tort. In pushing Dee, Jim has committed a battery.[1] A battery is defined as the application of unlawful personal violence. This can be committed directly or indirectly. The result of this is that Sid was knocked over. In *R v Mitchell* [1983] 2 All ER 427, the accused was found guilty of this type of manslaughter when he hit a man who fell against an old woman, knocking her over, causing her death.

Furthermore, Jim may try to argue that it is not necessary that the unlawful act is directed at the victim. In *R v Dalby* [1982] 1 All ER 916, the Court of Appeal appeared to introduce a third condition into constructive manslaughter—that the act must be directed at the victim.[2] However, it now seems clear, following *R v Mitchell* and

[1] The *actus reus* and the *mens rea* of the unlawful act must be proven as the basis for this offence.

[2] It was thought that the unlawful act needed to be directed at the victim: it is now settled that it does not.

R v Goodfellow (1986) 83 Cr App R 23, that this is unnecessary. As Jim pushed Dee out of the way, the court will conclude that Jim's unlawful act did not have to be directed at the eventual victim.

[3] The concept of dangerousness has caused the courts some problems. Is it to be assessed subjectively or objectively? The case of *R v Dawson* appears to have been decided on its own facts. In any event, it must not be confused with causation.

The unlawful act must be dangerous. In *R v Church* [1965] 2 All ER 72, it was held that an act is dangerous if a sober and reasonable person would foresee the risk of some harm.[3] Following *R v Dawson* (1985) 81 Cr App R 150, the jury can conclude that the criminal act is 'dangerous' for these purposes if a sober and reasonable person at the scene of the crime, watching the unlawful act being performed and seeing what the defendant sees, would have foreseen the risk of some physical harm. As Sid is obviously frail and this would be obvious to the reasonable person, then Jim would have been aware of the risk. The reasonable person does not have the benefit of hindsight. Hence, in assessing the dangerousness of pushing Dee, the jury must ignore the fact that Sid had a weak heart, as this fact was not known to Jim.

Essentially there is no need to show that the defendant knew that his action was dangerous; instead, the question is whether a reasonable person, who knew what the defendant knew, would think it was dangerous. This approach is not without its problems. In *R v JM and SM* [2012] EWCA Crim 2293, the defendants got into a fight with some bouncers outside a club. One of the guards collapsed from a heart condition and died. It was held that this was dangerous as fighting carried a risk of some harm, even if the ultimate harm was not what was risked in the first place.

In terms of *mens rea*, Jim may argue that he did not know that his actions were dangerous, but this argument is unlikely to succeed, as the House of Lords in *DPP v Newbury and Jones* [1976] 2 All ER 365 confirmed that, as a question of fact for the jury, the prosecution does not have to prove that the accused recognized the risk of danger.

The next question to consider is whether Jim's actions have caused Sid's death. Sid would not have died if Jim had not barged into the post office—this satisfies the requirement of factual causation (*R v White* [1910] 2 KB 124). Jim is likely to want to argue that Dr Peach was negligent in looking after Sid once he was in the hospital, and that therefore the chain of causation is broken by the *novus actus interveniens* of negligent medical treatment.[4] The prosecution do not have to prove that Jim's actions were a sole—or even a main—cause of the victim's death, merely that they made a significant contribution. In *R v Smith* [1959] 2 All ER 193, the accused's conviction for murder was upheld, as the court held that as the original wound was still an operating cause of death, the chain of causation was not

[4] Raise the defendant's likely argument—then deal with how successful it is likely to be, given the decided case law.

broken. Similarly, in *R v Cheshire* [1991] 3 All ER 670, Beldam LJ stated: 'it will only be in the most extraordinary and unusual case that such treatment can be said to be so independent of the acts of the accused that it could be regarded in law as the cause of the victim's death to the exclusion of the accused's act.' The question will be whether the chest infection suffered by Sid is 'independent' of Jim's initial act. Furthermore, Jim might argue that Dr Peach's failure to check up on Sid breaks the chain of causation, especially as he was on a form of life support.[5] This argument was rejected by the House of Lords in *R v Malcherek; R v Steel* [1981] 2 All ER 422, where Lord Lane CJ stated 'the fact that the victim has died despite or because of medical treatment for the initial injury given by careful and skilled medical practitioners, will not exonerate the original assailant from responsibility for the death'. Given that the treatment is probably not the sole cause of Sid's death, it is submitted that Jim has 'caused' the death.

The *mens rea* for this offence is the *mens rea* for the unlawful act. If this is battery, then what is required is evidence that Jim either intended or was reckless as to the infliction of unlawful personal violence. In barging into the post office, he must have foreseen a risk of harm (*R v G* [2003] 4 All ER 765).[6]

The prosecution would appear to be able to satisfy the requirements of manslaughter by an unlawful and dangerous act. Alternatively, the prosecution may argue that Jim has committed manslaughter by gross negligence or by reckless manslaughter (the latter is more rare). It may be argued that Jim has created a dangerous situation by leaving the post office without summoning help. In *R v Miller* [1983] 1 All ER 978, the House of Lords upheld the accused's conviction for criminal damage where he had inadvertently caused a fire and then, when he realized what he had done, simply left without doing anything to summon help. As such, Jim may have a duty of care towards Sid. The question will be whether the other remaining criteria in *R v Adomako* [1994] 3 All ER 79 are also satisfied.[7] In particular, the jury will have to decide whether Jim's behaviour was grossly negligent.

The same criteria will be applied to Dr Peach. Doctors clearly owe their patients a duty of care, but it is likely that in this instance the doctor will not be found to be grossly negligent. According to *R v Adomako* [1994] 3 All ER 79, the requirements for the operation of this offence are as follows:

- the defendant owes the victim a duty of care;
- the defendant acted in breach of that duty;
- the defendant's conduct was grossly negligent;
- the conduct carried a risk of causing death.

[5] This is a different issue to Dr Peach's liability.

[6] Don't forget that recklessness is always assessed subjectively.

[7] Would a reasonable person have appreciated a risk of death?

[8] This seems unlikely. Apply the law to the facts.

In relation to Dr Peach, according to Lord Mackay, the jury will have to consider 'whether in all the circumstances the extent to which the accused's conduct departed from the proper standard of care incumbent upon him involving as it must have done a risk of death to the victim was such that it must be judged to be criminal'.[8] In the context of a busy casualty department, the doctor probably did not depart from those standards sufficiently to fall into this category.

LOOKING FOR EXTRA MARKS?

- A discussion of whether the unlawful act needs to be directed at the victim will add depth to your answer in this type of question.

- Try to show an ability to argue in the alternative. Note that this does not mean you should sit on the fence—you can explore two options and still come to a clear conclusion.

QUESTION | 4

Don is in a relationship with Sally. One day, Sally tells Don she is leaving him for Rob, who is the best lover she has ever had. Don is diagnosed with depression. That evening, Don angrily throws a burning paraffin-soaked rag through Rob's open window. He does not check whether anyone is inside. The fire spreads rapidly, trapping Millie, Rob's little sister, on the top floor. Bert, a neighbour, hears Millie's screams, but does nothing. Eventually, the fire brigade arrives. Fireman Fred discovers that he has forgotten to bring a tall enough ladder. Millie jumps from an upper window into the arms of the crowd gathering below. She suffers severe injuries. In hospital, Dr John gives Millie a blood transfusion of the wrong blood type. She dies a week later. In his statement to the police, Don said that he thought it possible that someone would be injured, but he had not wanted anyone to die. His aim was to frighten Rob into leaving Sally alone.

Discuss Don's criminal liability for murder or manslaughter.

CAUTION!

- This question is more difficult than it looks. You need to distinguish carefully between murder and manslaughter. This discussion hinges on *mens rea*. Structure is of the utmost importance as there are a number of issues to cover, with multiple defendants, offences, and potential defences.

- Make sure that you deal with the defences separately, but with all the technical requirements.

DIAGRAM ANSWER PLAN

Identify the issues	■ Identify and define the possible offences: murder or manslaughter. ■ Deal with the partial defences to murder—loss of control/ diminished responsibility.
Relevant law	■ Discuss murder as defined by Coke, and the *actus reus* of murder and causation. Discuss the duty of third parties, the *novus actus interveniens*, and *mens rea* of murder: **Nedrick**. ■ Consider the partial defences to murder under **ss 52–55 Coroners and Justice Act 2009.**
Apply the law	■ Does medical treatment count as a break in the chain of causation? Discuss **R v Cheshire**. Do both limbs of the **Nedrick** test apply? Discuss the objective test in loss of control: **Holley**.
Conclude	■ Discuss the result of a successful plea of loss of control and reach a conclusion.

SUGGESTED ANSWER

Where there is a death, the only possible offences are murder and manslaughter. Murder is defined by L C J Coke (in *Coke's Institutes*, 1628) as follows:

a man of sound memory, and of the age of discretion, unlawfully killeth within any county of the realm any reasonable creature in rerum natura under the King's Peace, with malice aforethought, either expressed by the party or implied by law, [so as the party wounded, or hurt, etc die of the wound or hurt, etc within a year and a day after the same].

The 'year-and-a-day' rule has now been abolished (**Law Reform (Year and A Day Rule) Act 1996**).

This definition has been interpreted as an act or omission which causes death intentionally.

Would Millie have died if Don had not thrown the rag through the open window? The answer is negative: R v White [1910] 2 QB. Don may wish to argue that other factors contributed to Millie's death.[1] In other words, rather than him being responsible, he might want to argue that Fireman Fred's negligence, Bert's failure to act, and Dr John's negligent medical treatment have been a greater

[1] *Novus actus interveniens* should be discussed at this point, even though the issues appear later in the question. Do not get sidetracked by the liability of the other defendants.

contributory factor to Millie's death than Don's action of throwing the paraffin-soaked rag through the open window. As Bert has no duty to act (given that he does not fall into any of the recognized categories), he is unlikely to break the chain of causation. Fireman Fred has a duty of care to the public as a contracted employee. However, the actions of a third party, especially when acting under a legal duty or a duty of self-preservation, will not break the chain of causation: *R v Pagett*. Finally, the court must consider whether the actions of Dr John have broken the chain of causation. The cases of *R v Smith* and *R v Cheshire* are clear on this issue. Even severe medical negligence usually does not break the chain of causation if the defendant is a substantial and operating cause of death. In this case, Millie would not have been receiving medical treatment if it had not been for Don's action. The fact that she receives a blood transfusion of the wrong type does not change this fact.

[2] Having established causation, you can now turn to intention.

Don states that he did not intend to kill anyone.[2] Therefore, it is appropriate to consider oblique intention. The *Nedrick* direction must be considered here. This states that the jury is not entitled to infer intention unless death or serious injury is virtually certain to occur, and that the defendant foresees this as a possibility. Applying this to the facts of the question, it can probably be said that although the first part of the test may be satisfied (it is likely that if a burning paraffin-soaked rag is thrown through an open window someone will be seriously injured), it may not be said to be virtually certain that

[3] Be prepared to consider defences in the alternative. If the facts of the question suggest the defences to murder, then discuss these accordingly.

Don knew this. If he is found to be reckless, then you may be able to consider reckless manslaughter or manslaughter by an unlawful or dangerous act. Recklessness is defined subjectively—that is, according to the knowledge of the defendant in question.[3]

Don's defences will depend on the level of *mens rea* decided. If he is found guilty of murder, then the partial defences to murder will need to be considered. The **Coroners and Justice Act 2009** covers the partial defences to murder. To begin with, it will need to be established whether there was a qualifying trigger which made Don act as he did. The qualifying trigger can be a fear of serious violence, or a

[4] Only choose to discuss that part of the test which applies in this scenario.

thing done or a thing said plus certain conditions. In the instant case, Sally's statement that Rob is the best lover that she has ever had may suffice.[4] However, the prosecution may still argue that the 'anger' trigger is not available because **s 55(6)(c)** expressly precludes its operation in circumstances where the thing said or done that is claimed to have triggered Don's action constitutes sexual infidelity. However, in *R v Clinton* [2012] EWCA Crim 2, the Court of Appeal ruled that whilst **s 54(4)** of the **2009 Act** excludes sexual infidelity as a trigger for the loss of control defence, it should not be read as excluding evidence of sexual infidelity as part of the context in which the issue of whether or not there was a qualifying trigger could be considered.

⁵ The objective test in loss of control precludes personal characteristics of the defendant.

If the jury is satisfied that there is a qualifying trigger for Don's actions, it will then have to consider whether a person of Don's sex and age, with a normal degree of tolerance and self-restraint, and in Don's circumstances, might have reacted in a similar way. The purpose of this formulation is to prevent a defendant citing any personal characteristics that might affect his self-control.⁵ In so doing, it reflects the approach taken by the Privy Council in *Attorney-General for Jersey v Holley* **[2005] UKPC 23**, in relation to the common law defence of provocation (since abolished by the **Coroners and Justice Act 2009**), which endorsed the view that a defendant pleading the defence of provocation had to be judged by the standard of a person having ordinary powers of control. In summary, therefore, if there is evidence that Don lost his self-control, that he was not acting out of revenge, that his actions came within the 'anger' qualifying trigger, and that they were those that might have been displayed by a reasonable person in his circumstances, his liability for the death of Millie could be reduced to manslaughter. The fact that Millie rather than Sally is the object of Don's anger should not matter: *R v Pearson*.⁶

⁶ Third-party provocation counts for the purposes of the Act: *R v Pearson*.

As an alternative, and bearing in mind that characteristics such as mental illness that have a bearing on the temperament of a defendant are excluded from the statutory defence of loss of control, Don would be advised to plead the defence of diminished responsibility, established under **s 2** of the **Homicide Act 1957**, as subsequently amended by **s 52** of the **Coroners and Justice Act 2009**. Under the amended **s 2(1)**, Don would have to prove that, at the time of the killing, he was suffering from an abnormality of mental functioning arising from a medical condition. The facts indicate that he had been diagnosed by a doctor as suffering from depression. This first requirement might be made out, provided the expert evidence satisfied the balance of probabilities test.

Don will also have to establish that this abnormality of mental functioning caused a substantial impairment in: (i) his understanding of the nature of his conduct; (ii) his ability to form a rational judgement; or (iii) his ability to exercise self-control. The Court of Appeal has confirmed that, for the purposes of the 2009 Act, the concept of substantial impairment should be approached in the same way as was the case under the **Homicide Act 1957**.

⁷ Here, you can conclude, and advise on the best course of action.

Of these three options, the substantial impairment of self-control option is likely to prove the most fruitful for Don, provided the jury is satisfied that the impairment is substantial and, further, that the abnormality of mental functioning provided an explanation for Don's actions in the sense that it was the cause or a contributory factor in making Don act as he did.⁷ As indicated earlier, there is every prospect of this defence succeeding, and in consequence reducing Don's liability to manslaughter, provided the expert evidence is sufficiently compelling.

LOOKING FOR EXTRA MARKS?

- Excellent answers will not only describe the different requirements for the different offences and defences and apply them, but will attempt to reach a conclusion on the best defence available.
- Don't forget to deal with all the requirements in a particular test and analyse on the facts.

QUESTION | 5

Although the abolition of objectively reckless manslaughter by the case of *R v Adomako* [1995] **1 AC 171** has simplified the law, there remain substantial problems in the law on involuntary manslaughter. Discuss.

CAUTION!

- This is not an easy question. You will need to demonstrate that you can identify the different types of manslaughter, but also how the law developed to its current position. You will then need to assess whether the law is satisfactory in its current form.
- In particular, you will need a good understanding of the dividing lines between the three remaining types of manslaughter.

DIAGRAM ANSWER PLAN

Clarify the scope of the question—the types of involuntary manslaughter.

Discuss constructive manslaughter—must the act be directed at the victim?

Look at the issues of constructive manslaughter—dangerousness.

Discuss reckless manslaughter and the redefinition in *R v Adomako*.

Discuss gross negligence manslaughter.

Consider the challenges to gross negligence manslaughter.

Draw a conclusion.

SUGGESTED ANSWER

This question covers the concept of involuntary manslaughter. This type of manslaughter can be charged where the prosecution cannot prove *mens rea* for the killing. It is now settled that there are three types of manslaughter: manslaughter by an unlawful and dangerous act (also known as constructive manslaughter); reckless manslaughter; and manslaughter by gross negligence.[1] These will be discussed below, and an assessment of the clarity of the law will be attempted.

Manslaughter by an unlawful and dangerous act is committed when the defendant commits an unlawful act. This act must be a crime. The crime must also involve an act; an omission will not suffice. The unlawful act must be dangerous; furthermore, it must cause the death in fact and in law. The *mens rea* for the crime is that of the unlawful act.

This seems clear enough; however, there are a number of controversies contained in the law. These are discussed below, and an assessment of the clarity of the law is attempted.[2]

Next, it is not always clear what constitutes a 'dangerous' act. The court in *R v Church* **[1965] 2 All ER 72** held that a dangerous act is one which is 'such as all sober and reasonable people would inevitably recognise must subject the other person to at least the risk of some harm'. This suggests an entirely objective test which would discount the views or knowledge of the defendant. However, in *R v Dawson* **(1985) 81 Cr App R 150** the defendant was not guilty of manslaughter where the victim died of a heart attack when the defendant and two others threatened him with weapons during an attempted armed robbery. The defendants did not know he had a weak heart.[3]

In *R v Watson* **[1989] 2 All ER 865**, the defendant could clearly see that the victim was a frail old man who was reacting badly to the experience. To the reasonable man armed with the knowledge acquired by the defendant during the burglary, there would have been no doubt that the burglary created a risk of personal injury to the victim. The test, therefore, can be described as an objective one, with the knowledge of the defendant to be incorporated. This is not entirely clear.

The unlawful act itself can be difficult to establish. A further issue which the courts have considered is whether the unlawful act must be directed at the victim. In *R v Dalby* **[1982] 1 All ER 916**, the Court of Appeal appeared to suggest that the act had to be directed at the victim. However, in *R v Goodfellow* **(1986) 83 Cr App R 23**, where the accused, intending to be rehoused by the council, set fire to his house, causing the death of some of his family, this doctrine was

---

1 Begin by setting out the current law on the topic under discussion.

2 Set out what you are trying to achieve in the essay—here, a discussion of the problems across the categories of manslaughter.

3 The key here is that the reasonable man is to be regarded as having the same knowledge as the defendant would have if he had been at the scene. This case is not easy to reconcile with the 'thin-skull' rule but it is about dangerousness, not causation.

rejected and the accused was convicted of unlawful and dangerous act manslaughter. Furthermore, in *Attorney-General's Reference (No 3 of 1994)*, Lord Hope confirmed that as long as there is an unlawful and dangerous act which causes the victim's death, it does not matter whether the act was directed to someone else.[4]

In addition to the unlawful act, the prosecution must establish that the defendant has caused the death in fact and in law. The House of Lords' decision in *R v Kennedy* **[2007] UKHL 38** now settles the debate over whether the victim's choice to self-inject with drugs supplied by the defendant breaks the chain of causation and thus exonerates the defendant. Thus, there is no liability in manslaughter in this situation. The court confirmed that provided the victim was a fully informed and responsible adult, it was never appropriate to find the supplier guilty of manslaughter.[5]

The debate over reckless manslaughter also now appears to be settled. This question has been problematic for the courts. The original position was that a defendant who was subjectively reckless, and caused death, was guilty of manslaughter. In *R v Pike* **[1961] Crim LR 114**, the defendant administered carbon tetrachloride to a woman in order to enhance sexual satisfaction, having done so to other women in the past without any ill effects. The woman in question died, and it was held that the trial judge had properly directed the jury that it should convict the defendant if they thought that he had been aware of the risk. Nonetheless, in *R v Lidar* **[2000] 4 Archbold News 3**, the Court of Appeal accepted that a category of subjective recklessness still exists.[6] They were inclined to accept that the risk which the defendant foresees must be one of serious injury rather than just some injury. The case is inconclusive, however, because the court was able to uphold the conviction, as it was satisfied that the defendant's conduct created a risk of some injury. Whether this should still be a separate category is a moot point, as the defendant could just as easily have been convicted of other types of manslaughter. Nonetheless, the category differs from unlawful and dangerous act manslaughter as it encompasses lawful as well as unlawful conduct, and omissions as well as acts.[7]

What is clear is that objectively reckless manslaughter has been abolished. In *R v Adomako* **[1994] 3 All ER 79**, the House of Lords overruled *R v Seymour*, which in turn had applied *R v Caldwell* to manslaughter. Since *R v G* has overruled *R v Caldwell* on the issue of recklessness, the only type of recklessness recognized in criminal law is subjective. If the defendant caused a death and there was a serious and an obvious risk of death, he was guilty of manslaughter even if he did not appreciate the risk. This is certainly an improvement in the law.

[4] This problem seems to be clarified now, and it is no longer necessary for the unlawful act to be directed at the victim.

[5] This House of Lords case settled this debate. There is a break in the chain of causation in cases like this.

[6] This case confirms the existence of a separate category of subjectively reckless manslaughter.

[7] It is important to highlight this issue, as otherwise there is no point having a separate category.

A defendant can be convicted of gross negligence manslaughter, according to *R v Adomako*, if the following criteria are satisfied. First, the prosecution must prove that the defendant had a duty of care towards the victim; second, that the defendant acted in breach of that duty; third, that the defendant's conduct was grossly negligent, and, finally, that the conduct caused the victim's death. The key issue is that it must be shown that the defendant's breach of duty was 'gross'. This means that his omission must be so bad that it justifies a criminal conviction. Several recent cases have confirmed the high standard to be met. In *Sellu* **[2016] EWCA Crim 1716**, D was a colorectal surgeon whose patient died after long delays in administering antibiotics and carrying out surgery. Quashing his conviction, Sir Brian Leveson P emphasized that 'even serious or very serious mistakes or lapses' are not grossly negligent unless they are 'truly exceptionally bad'.

There are a number of problems with this case. The majority of convictions for gross negligence manslaughter arise in a professional context, especially cases against health-care professionals. We might ask whether it is appropriate to convict an individual of homicide when they are part of a large organization such as a hospital, with organizational failings. In *Bawa-Garba* **[2016] EWCA Crim 1841**, the conviction was upheld in part because the jury had been directed that her conduct must be 'truly, exceptionally bad'. This seems like a straightforward test, but it may be difficult to distinguish between this and a serious lapse of judgement or in concentration.

Furthermore, it may not be clear which type of duty must be established—a duty in criminal law (which is very narrow) or a duty in tort. Herring and Palser (2007) argue that both must be established, but Elliott (2010) argues that the duty should be based on the ordinary principles of negligence as to conflate these concepts is confusing to juries.[8] This latter argument seems to follow Lord Mackay in *R v Adomako*. Furthermore, the jury is left with a wide discretion on whether to convict the accused. Finally, there may be a breach of the **European Convention on Human Rights (ECHR)**. In *R v Misra* **[2004] EWCA Crim 2375**, the ruling in *R v Adomako* was challenged first on the grounds that it was inconsistent with the ruling in *R v G* on recklessness and second that it may be inconsistent with the **ECHR**.

In relation to establishing the risk of death, it is not quite clear how great the risk must be. It might also be argued that the test for gross negligence is effectively circular, and given that the jury determines whether the negligence was sufficiently gross for liability, it is uncertain. A further issue to consider is the extent of the risk of death. *Adomako* makes clear that the risk of death must be obvious

[8] Include academic debate where you can in an essay like this.

to the reasonable person, but it has not always been clear whether there must be an obvious risk at the time the alleged offence is being committed. This has now been clarified in **R v Rose [2017] EWCA 1168**. In this case, an optometrist failed to notice a serious condition during a routine eye examination. She was convicted of gross negligence manslaughter when the victim, a young boy, died five years later of acute hydrocephalus, which it was claimed should have been noticed during her examination. The judge directed the jury to consider whether the risk would have been obvious to another professional optometrist if she had not been in breach of her duty to examine the boy properly (she admitted that she failed to examine the back of the retina properly). Her appeal was allowed on the basis that it was not appropriate to take into account what the defendant would have known had it not been for her breach of duty. If this were the case, according to Sir Brian Leveson, this would fundamentally undermine the established legal test in **R v Adomako** which requires proof of a 'serious and obvious' risk of death at the time of the breach. The implications for medical professionals would be very serious— they could be convicted of the offence by not carrying out routine tests which would reveal fatal conditions.

Finally, the requirement for 'gross' negligence can be problematic, as it leaves a very wide discretion to the jury so it can be difficult to predict decisions and therefore give legal advice. As noted earlier, the test is somewhat circular. The 'truly, exceptionally bad' standard in **Sellu** (earlier in this answer) may alleviate this to some degree, being a test which is easier to understand.

[9] Conclude by summarizing the issues, and referring back to the question.

In conclusion, it can be seen that the law on involuntary manslaughter has not been without controversy.[9] The courts have grappled with the meaning of recklessness, dangerousness, and causation. For the most part, however, the law now appears to be settled. *Mitchell* has argued that the development of the law may be based less on legal definitions than practical prosecuting decisions.[10]

[10] It is a good idea to highlight practical reasons for the anomalies you have highlighted.

LOOKING FOR EXTRA MARKS?

■ Try to make some critical comment as you proceed through the essay, referring to academic opinion. For example, there is some uncertainty surrounding the definition of the duty of care in criminal law and the law of torts. The article by Herring and Palser (2007) (see 'Taking Things Further') refers to this.

■ Refer back to the question at the end of each paragraph. This ensures that you do not lose focus.

TAKING THINGS FURTHER

- Baker D J and Zhao L X, 'Contributory Qualifying and Non-Qualifying Triggers in the Loss of Control Defence: A Wrong Turn on Sexual Infidelity' (2012) 76 J Crim Law 254.

  *Criticizes **Clinton** for failing to understand the workings of the loss-of-control defence and overlooking policy issues.*

- Dickson E, 'Mentally Relevant? When is a Loss of Control Attributable to a Mental Condition?' (2018) 82(2) J Crim Law 117–22.

  *Considers the conjoined appeals of **R v Rejmanski** and **R v Gassman** and the applicability of **s. 54(1)Coroners and Justice Act 2009** when the defendant has a mental condition affecting powers of self control.*

- Elliott C, 'Liability for Gross Negligence Manslaughter: Don't Let the Baby Drown' (2010) 74(2) J Crim Law 163–79.

  Argues that the concepts of duty to act and duty of care should not be conflated in this offence, as it is confusing to juries.

- Freer E, 'We Need to Talk about Charlie: Putting the Brakes on Unlawful Act Manslaughter' [2018] Crim LR 612.

  Considers the conviction of a cyclist for unlawful act manslaughter and argues that this offence is now too broadly interpreted.

- Gibson M, 'Diminished Responsibility in *Golds* and Beyond: Insights and Implications' [2017] Crim LR 543.

  Explores the impact of the Supreme Court's decision, drawing on three subsequent cases to argue that it narrows the scope of diminished responsibility and reflects a changing attitude to partial defences generally.

- Herring J and Palser E, 'The Duty of Care in Gross Negligence Manslaughter' [2007] Crim LR 24.

  Discusses public policy reasons in the formulation of a duty of care in gross negligence manslaughter.

- Laird K, 'The Evolution of Gross Negligence Manslaughter' (2018) Arch Rev 6.

  Considers the case law on this offence and argues that its recent development solely in relation to healthcare professionals is undesirable.

- Law Commission, Partial Defences to Murder (LC 290, Cm 6301, 2004).

  *Proposals for reform which led to the enactment of the **Coroners and Justice Act 2009**.*

- Leigh G, 'Deconstructing Unlawful Act Manslaughter' (2017) 81 J Crim Law 112.

  Suggests that unlawful act manslaughter could usefully be considered as having two forms: manslaughter by act of intended bodily harm, and manslaughter by unlawful and dangerous act.

- Mackay R D and Mitchell B, 'The New Diminished Responsibility Plea in Operation: Some Initial Findings' [2017] Crim LR 18.

  Reviews the impact of the updated definition of diminished responsibility upon homicide prosecutions.

■ Norrie A, 'The Coroners and Justice Act 2009—Partial Defences to Murder (1) Loss of Control' [2010] Crim LR 275, and Mackay R D 'The Coroners and Justice Act 2009—Partial Defences to Murder (2): The New Diminished Responsibility Plea' [2010] Crim LR 290.

Detailed comparisons of the new partial defences to murder under the **Coroners and Justice Act 2009** *and the* **Homicide Act 1957**.

Online Resources

www.oup.com/uk/qanda/

For extra essay and problem questions on this topic, as well as advice on revision and exam technique, please visit the online resources.

4 Non-Fatal Offences Against the Person

KEY DEBATES

Debate: consent as a defence

Should one be able to consent to physical or psychological harm imposed by another? It might be argued that the courts should not interfere when harm is inflicted with consent; on the other hand, one might argue that consent should not be freely given, especially when the harm is serious. In *R v Brown*, Lord Templeman decried the cult of violence which allowed such harm to take place, largely on moral grounds.

Debate: 'biological' grievous bodily harm

The deliberate transmission of sexually transmitted diseases has caused the courts some problems—is this form of harm to be treated in the same way as other forms of grievous bodily harm? Crucially, the *mens rea* can be difficult to establish in situations where a defendant is aware

○

of infection, but does not reveal this to a sexual partner. Conviction under **s 18** of the **Offences Against the Person Act 1861** for this offence is unusual, demonstrating at least that the law is developing in this area, if slowly (see *R v Daryll Rowe*, Lewes Crown Court, 15 November 2017). Matthew Weait (2005) and Loveless and Derry (2004) discuss the level of *mens rea* required and the difficulties in consenting to this type of act.

Debate: coercive control

This relatively new offence under the **Serious Crime Act 2015** recognizes that abuse which is not physical is just as serious for the victim. **Section 76** of the **Serious Crime Act 2015** defines the offence as 'controlling or coercive behaviour in an intimate or family relationship'. To an extent, this section means that prosecution is possible even where a non-fatal offence against the person would be quite minor. One potential problem with the legislation is that the victim must be personally connected to, or in an intimate relationship with, the defendant: this would not cover all situations, such as someone who is being cared for by the victim and is indirectly affected by the control.

QUESTION | 1

Mike and Karen are both lecturers at Crammershire University. Karen is a member of the university's karate club and she persuades Mike to join. The day of the next karate club meeting is Karen's birthday. Before the club meeting, she spends a few hours in the bar drinking with friends. By the time she leaves the bar to go to the training sessions, Karen has drunk six pints of lager and several vodka 'shots'. During the training session, Karen hits Mike in the face with her forearm. Mike falls awkwardly, hitting his head on a nearby bench. Mike's girlfriend Gaye, who had come along to watch the session, witnesses the attack on Mike and runs towards Karen screaming abuse. Karen, who is intensely jealous of Gaye's relationship with Mike, throws Gaye to the ground and kicks her in the head. Gaye suffers minor bruising and grazes. Karen, who is distressed, runs off to the changing rooms without bothering to attend to Mike. Other club members call for medical help. It later transpires that Mike has a broken leg and has lost the hearing in one ear.

The following week Mike sees Karen coming towards him in the corridor at the university. As she approaches, Karen raises her arm, intending to give Mike a hug and apologize for what she has done. Mike fears that she is about to hit him again. He pulls his mobile phone out of his pocket and thrusts it towards Karen's face, with the result that Karen suffers several broken teeth. In the weeks following these incidents, Gaye becomes increasingly depressed and neurotic and has to seek professional psychological help to cope with the trauma caused by Karen's attack.

Advise the Crown Prosecution Service as to the respective criminal liabilities of Karen, Gaye, and Mike.

CAUTION!

- Don't forget to identify and discuss any causation issues in a question like this—the provisions of the **Offences Against the Person Act 1861** referring to statutory assaults all require it to be proven, albeit with slightly different terminology.

- An omission, as well as an act, can trigger all of these offences.

DIAGRAM ANSWER PLAN

Identify the issues	■ The legal issues here are **ss 18, 20**, and **47** of the **Offences Against the Person Act 1861**. ■ The defences are consent and self defence. *Mens rea* may be affected by intoxication.
Relevant law	■ Discuss the *actus reus/mens rea* of the offences, starting with the most serious. ■ Discuss which defences apply, taking care to explain each requirement. ■ Explain the *R v Barnes* criteria. ■ Discuss the duty to act.
Apply the law	■ Karen may not have foreseen harm (intoxication). ■ Is Mike's consent valid? ■ Discuss the psychological harm to Gaye.
Conclude	■ Summarize the offences committed and advise. What is the effect of the defences? Discuss the *Majewski* test.

SUGGESTED ANSWER

This question relates to non-fatal offences against the person and the defences of self-defence, intoxication, and consent. Turning first to incidents arising out of the karate session, Mike suffers a broken leg and loss of hearing as a result of the fall. The broken leg and loss of hearing could each be classified as 'grievous bodily harm'

[1] Note that not all possible non-fatal offences have been included here. The best approach is to start with the level of harm, then go to the *actus reus* of the relevant offence.

(*R v Saunders* [1985] Crim LR 230). This opens up the possibility of charges under ss 18 and 20 of the **Offences Against the Person Act 1861**.[1] **Section 18** requires proof that Karen caused grievous bodily harm—but for her actions, Mike would not have suffered the harm. Causation in law requires proof that the harm was a reasonably foreseeable consequence of her actions. The fact that Mike falls and hits his head etc will not break the chain of causation. The *mens rea* for s 18 is intent. On the facts, it may be difficult to establish that Karen intended to do grievous bodily harm, given the additional factor of intoxication. A charge under s 20 of the **Offences Against the Person Act 1861** could be brought as an alternative. The harm required is either grievous bodily harm or wounding. The injuries suggest that he has suffered a wound. On the basis of *C v Eisenhower* [1984] QB 331, this requires proof of a break in the dermis and the epidermis. Under s 20, the grievous bodily harm must be inflicted, and there does not seem to be a problem here in that regard.

[2] The *mens rea* of these offences can be tricky—note that it is only an awareness of the possibility of *some* physical harm.

The *mens rea* under s 20 is satisfied by proof that Karen was reckless: see *R v Mowatt* [1968] 1 QB 421.[2] Karen must have been aware of the possibility of causing some physical harm. She does not need to have foreseen the harm actually caused.

Karen may seek to rely on Mike's consent to the harm inflicted. On the basis of *R v Donovan* [1934] 2 KB 498, a victim cannot validly consent to physical harm if it amounts to actual bodily harm or worse unless the activity comes within a range of policy-based exceptions. The issue would be whether karate classes come within this exception. Even if they do, a further issue would be the extent of the harm or risk of harm consented to by participants. What was accepted in one sport, such as the physical contact inevitable in martial arts, would not necessarily be covered by the defence of consent in another.

In *R v Barnes* [2004] EWCA Crim 3246, Lord Woolf CJ observed that if the defendant's actions are within the rules and practice of the game and do not go beyond it, that will be a firm indication that what

[3] This is a good example of applying the law and building up an argument on the facts.

has happened is not criminal. Karen is, on the facts, a more experienced martial arts professional and it could be argued that Mike consented to a restricted range of risks—ie that he did not expect to be hit by her.[3] The key point will be whether or not her actions can be regarded as having been so obviously late or violent as not to be seen as an instinctive reaction, error, or misjudgement in the heat of the contest. On the facts, it is submitted that Mike will be regarded as having validly consented to the risk of being hit.

If the defence succeeds, Karen will have a complete defence to charges under ss 18, 20, and 47 of the **Offences Against the Person Act 1861**.

[4] Note that intoxication is not, strictly speaking, a defence, but a denial of one element of the offence—namely, *mens rea*.

The alternative 'defence' would be self-induced intoxication.[4] If Karen was merely drunk, she has no defence as such—intoxication requires evidence that she was incapable of forming, and did not form, the necessary intent. On the basis of *DPP v Majewski* [1977] AC 142, her voluntary intoxication could be a defence to crimes of specific intent but not crimes of basic intent. Section 18 of the Offences Against the Person Act 1861 is a specific intent crime because only intention will suffice in order to use it.[5] If Karen was charged under s 18 and successfully pleads intoxication, her liability will be reduced to the 'lesser included' offence of s 20 of the Offences Against the Person Act 1861—a basic intent crime or one which includes recklessness in its definition. Hence, if she is charged under s 20 or s 47 of the Offences Against the Person Act 1861 or charged with common assault or battery, she will not escape liability on the grounds of self-induced intoxication, as these are all basic intent crimes. She cannot claim that her consumption of the alcohol was anything other than reckless: see *R v Hardie* [1984] 3 All ER 848. Therefore, her liability will be imposed on the basis that she was reckless in becoming intoxicated—and recklessness is sufficient *mens rea* in respect of any one of the basic intent offences.

[5] The terms 'specific intent' and 'basic intent' refer to the type of *mens rea* inherent in the definition of the crime. Crimes which require intention to prove liability are, generally speaking, crimes of specific intent. Crimes which have an element of recklessness in their definition are usually crimes of basic intent.

Karen may also have incurred liability in respect of the harm caused to Gaye. Psychological harm can amount to grievous bodily harm or actual bodily harm, depending on its seriousness: see *R v Burstow; R v Ireland*.[6] The prosecution will have to produce medical evidence to show that the harm is not transient and minor. On the facts, a charge under s 47 of the Offences Against the Person Act 1861 seems the most likely here.

[6] This was not always the case, but *Ireland* explored the issue in relation to silent telephone calls.

Minor bruising and grazes would most likely constitute actual bodily harm, contrary to s 47 of the Offences Against the Person Act 1861: see *R v Miller* [1954] 2 QB 282. Grazing would not amount to a wound unless the definition in *C v Eisenhower* was satisfied. As indicated earlier, the *mens rea* for s 47 would be intention or subjective recklessness. Provided Karen intended to assault Gaye, it does not matter that she might not have foreseen the actual bodily harm that actually transpired; see *R v Savage; R v Parmenter*.

Karen may raise the defence of self-defence in respect of Gaye. Karen is entitled to use reasonable force to protect herself. The question will be whether or not the force she used was reasonable in the circumstances; see s 76 of the Criminal Justice and Immigration Act 2008.[7] Karen will not be able to rely on the fact that she has misjudged the amount of force required, due to her being intoxicated. Section 76(5) of the Act makes it clear that a defendant is not entitled to rely on mistaken belief which is 'attributable to intoxication that was voluntarily induced'. This can be problematic, especially

[7] The Criminal Justice and Immigration Act 2008 largely reproduces the common law.

where the defendant has a long-term condition caused by prolonged intoxication, rather than a single incident (see *R v Taj* **[2018] EWCA Crim 1743**).

As to Gaye's possible liability, she makes no physical contact with Karen, hence the only possible charge could be in relation to a 'narrow' assault based on her threats. The problem for the prosecution would be in establishing that Karen apprehended any immediate physical harm. She may not have been perturbed by Gaye's threats. Gaye would need to have the *mens rea* for assault.

Gaye could rely on self-defence (ie reasonable force used in defence of another), on the basis that she was acting to protect Mike, but the court may be reluctant to permit this where the evidence is that she was the aggressor in the incident. Alternatively, she could invoke the statutory defence under **s 3** of the **Criminal Law Act 1967**—using reasonable force to prevent the commission of a criminal offence. **Section 76** of the **Criminal Justice and Immigration Act 2008** applies equally to the common law and the statutory defence under **s 3** of the **1967 Act** regarding how the court should approach the question of whether or not the force used was reasonable. Assuming Gaye did believe the facts were such as to warrant her acting in self-defence, **s 76(7)** provides that the court dealing with the issue should have regard to the fact that she may not have been able to 'weigh to a nicety' the exact measure of any necessary action; and that her evidence of having only done what she honestly and instinctively thought was necessary for a legitimate purpose may be enough to convince the jury.

In breaking Karen's teeth, Mike may have caused actual bodily harm contrary to **s 47** of the **Offences Against the Person Act 1861**. He appears to have caused the harm with the necessary *mens rea*—ie he was at least aware of the risk of harm: see *R v Savage*; *R v Parmenter*. The obvious defence would be self-defence at common law—considered previously. The issue to note here is that Mike is mistaken—there is in fact no need for him to defend himself. Following *Beckford v R* **[1987] 3 WLR 611**, and now **s 76(3)** of the **2008 Act**, Mike will be judged on the facts as he honestly believed them to be—hence, if he honestly believed he was about to be attacked again by Karen he could use force that would have been reasonable to defend himself in such circumstances. In conclusion, therefore, we may say that Karen can be convicted of **ss 20** and **47** of the **Offences Against the Person Act 1861** and a common assault, and that she may use the defences of self-defence and consent. She may argue that intoxication has affected the *mens rea* of these offences, but is unlikely to succeed, as these are offences of basic intent for the reasons explained above.

LOOKING FOR EXTRA MARKS?

- The way in which you deal with defences in a question like this will determine whether you gain a high mark—in issues such as intoxication and self-defence it is crucial to understand the rules, but then apply them properly to the facts. For example, in discussing intoxication, you will need to consider whether this is a crime of basic or specific intent.

- The rules on specific and basic intent usually apply, but better answers will refer to academic views on this issue, and the fact that the rules do not always hold true—see, for example, *Heard* [2008] QB 43, in which intentional touching on a sexual offence charge was held to be a crime of basic intent.

QUESTION | 2

Critically assess the position taken in English criminal law in respect of consent to the deliberate infliction of harm and participation in activities carrying a risk of serious harm.

CAUTION!

- As English criminal law is not codified, there is no statute that sets out the law's aims and functions, so it is necessary to consider case law, Law Commission reports, and the views of commentators. In this answer, attempt to cover all aspects of this issue, as the question is not simply an invitation to write all you know about *R v Brown* [1993] 2 All ER 75. Make sure you refer back to the question and offer some critical comment throughout.

DIAGRAM ANSWER PLAN

Start by discussing the general aims of the criminal law and the development of the defence of consent.

Discuss the decision in *R v Brown*.

Discuss Lord Templeman's rationale for his decision—especially the 'cult of violence' argument. Consider other cases which do not seem to be consistent with this argument.

Discuss law and morality and the role of judges, including the balance between autonomy and the public interest.

Consider **R v Dica** and informed consent. Discuss the Law Commission's proposals.

Draw a conclusion with reference to the question. Refer to the question set and summarize the problems which the case law illustrates.

 SUGGESTED ANSWER

There will never be complete agreement as to the correct aims and functions of the criminal law and, in the absence of a criminal code setting out a rationale containing fundamental principles, this issue will remain a topic of debate. This is especially true of acts inflicting violence. Questions can be raised on the role of the courts in matters of private morality. The defence of consent reveals several incongruities. The cases in favour of restricting the defence appear to do so on moral rather than legal grounds.

A successful plea of consent will provide a complete defence to a non-fatal offence. In addition to protecting the public from harmful activity, we also expect the criminal law to respect individual liberties and autonomy. It is this conflict between individual freedoms and collective interests which was one of the major issues in **R v Brown [1993] 2 All ER 75**.

[1] This case is key to an understanding of the public policy arguments surrounding the defence of consent.

In **Brown**, a group of men willingly participated in sadomasochistic activities that involved the deliberate infliction of wounds.[1] The men were charged with various offences, including assault occasioning actual bodily harm (**s 47** of the **Offences Against the Person Act 1861**) and malicious wounding (**s 20** of the **Offences Against the Person Act 1861**) and pleaded guilty when the trial judge ruled against their defence of consent. The Court of Appeal upheld their conviction, but certified the following point of law of general public importance: 'Where A wounds or assaults B occasioning him actual bodily harm in the course of a sado-masochistic encounter, does the prosecution have to prove lack of consent on the part of B before they can establish A's guilt under **s 20** or **s 47** of the **Offences Against the Person Act 1861**?' The House of Lords answered this question in the negative and dismissed the appeal. Lord Templeman, who gave the majority judgment, decided the issue using a mixture of precedent and public policy. He stated that consent is not a general defence where actual bodily harm or wounding has been caused. There are exceptions to this rule, and violence intentionally inflicted will not be a criminal offence if it occurs in the course of a lawful activity, such as contact sports, surgical operations, rough horseplay, or tattooing.

The question for the House therefore was whether or not sado-masochistic behaviour as occurred in *Brown* could be regarded as positively beneficial, or as falling within the domain of private activities that were of no concern to the state provided vulnerable persons were not being exploited.

Lord Templeman concluded that the criminal law had to provide sufficient safeguards against exploitation and corruption of others, particularly those who are young; weak in body or mind; inexperienced; or in a state of special physical, official, or economic dependence. He referred to three reasons leading to the conclusion that sadomasochistic behaviour was not in the public interest:

(a) it glorified the cult of violence ('pleasure derived from the infliction of pain is an evil thing');

(b) it increased the risk of AIDS and the spread of other sexually transmitted diseases;

(c) iIt could lead to the corruption of youth.

Lord Templeman concluded, 'I am not prepared to invent a defence of consent for sado-masochistic encounters which breed and glorify cruelty and result in offences under **s 47** and **s 20** of the **Act of 1861**.'

[2] Using minority and majority judgments in your essay, and commenting upon them, is a good way to evaluate an issue in a critical way.

The minority (Lords Mustill and Slynn) interpreted the relevant cases (*R v Coney* **(1882) 8 QBD 534**; *R v Donovan* **[1934] 2 KB 498**; and *Attorney-General's Reference (No 6 of 1980)* **[1981] QB 715**) and the public interest requirements differently.[2] Lord Mustill decided that the House could consider the question of whether the public interest required **s 47** to be interpreted as penalizing the conduct in question.

In relating the majority decision to aims and functions, many questions arise. First, in ascertaining public interest, how far should the Law Lords take into account society's morals? This involves reference to the Hart–Devlin debate (see Lord Devlin, *The Enforcement of Morals*, 1959) as to whether conduct should be criminalized simply because it is a moral wrong, and whether the criminal law should simply reflect society's moral standards or try to improve them. This is

[3] You can put forward personal opinions in an essay, but try to link them to a legal issue. If your opinion is logically developed from analysis, you may get some credit for originality of approach.

virtually impossible to answer briefly, but it is submitted that if it is not morally right to encourage deliberate injury through sadomasochistic activity, the majority decision does not conflict with this objective.[3] If the majority had not declared it unlawful, their decision could have been interpreted as condoning, or even encouraging, such activities.

Secondly, did the House of Lords' decision in *Brown* create new law, or did it give effect to the will of Parliament as expressed in the 1861 Act? Their application of the defence of consent was probably correct, even though there has traditionally been a reluctance on the part of the courts to extend its boundaries. This is partially due to the difficulties in deciding whether consent was freely given by a victim capable of understanding the nature of the act.

Thirdly, was this a situation where respect for individual freedom should have been outweighed by the need to protect society from such conduct? The participants were middle-aged men who were in control of the activities, but the Law Lords considered that because of the risk of future, younger, inexperienced participants, the accused's individual liberty had to be sacrificed. This confusion was compounded by the Court of Appeal in *R v Wilson* **[1996] 3 WLR 125**, where the defendant had his conviction for actual bodily harm contrary to **s 47** of the **1861 Act** quashed. He had agreed to his wife's request that he should brand his initials on her buttocks with a hot knife. The court took the view that the husband's activities could be regarded as coming within the tattooing exception, and that, in any event, as explained by Russell LJ:

it is not in the public interest that activities such as the appellant's in this appeal should amount to criminal behaviour. Consensual activity between husband and wife, in the privacy of the matrimonial home, is not, in our judgement, normally a proper matter for criminal investigation, let alone criminal prosecution.

In *Wilson*, therefore, individual autonomy overrode the public morality argument, whereas in *Brown*, the deciding factor was protection of the public. Both decisions were based to some extent on the concept of public policy.

The law distinguishes between situations where a victim consents to inevitable and deliberate harm, and those where the victim consents to the risk of harm. As outlined earlier, consent to inevitable harm can only operate as a defence within certain limits dictated by public policy. Hence deliberate harm of a minor nature can be incurred without criminal liability, as this falls within the permissible scope of individual autonomy. More serious deliberate harm may be permitted if it is in the course of justifiable surgical interference. Many other activities, however, carry only the risk of harm, for example engagement in sports, or dangerous exhibitions, such as where a member of the audience volunteers to stand in front of a knife-thrower's target as part of a show. The audience member is not consenting to being stabbed; indeed, it is doubtful that any such consent would be recognized as valid. What he or she is consenting to is the risk of harm, as the stunt cannot be conducted without some risk.

It follows that if consent to risk of harm is to be a more general defence than consent to inevitable harm, issues will arise as to the extent to which the victim's consent has to be fully informed. In *R v Konzani* **[2005] EWCA Crim 706**, the Court of Appeal held that the doctrine of informed consent should form part of the criminal law, hence the fact that a woman consented to sexual intercourse with a man, unaware that he was HIV+, did not mean that she consented to the risk that she might herself become HIV+.

[4] If you can give practical examples illustrating your point, you will clarify your arguments.

Applying this to the knife-thrower example earlier in this section, the volunteer from the audience assumes the knife-thrower is a professional who can perform the stunt without causing harm. If in fact the knife-thrower is an amateur who has never successfully performed the stunt, it would be difficult to argue that the volunteer had genuinely consented to the risk of harm, should the stunt go wrong.[4] Were the knife-thrower to reveal this fact before asking for a volunteer, then anyone volunteering would do so with the necessary knowledge, although this might still throw up the question of whether any adult should be permitted to run such risks just for the sake of public entertainment.

As Lord Woolf CJ explained in *R v Barnes* **[2004] EWCA Crim 3246**, participants in sports often consent to the risk of quite serious harm—the more competitive the sport and the more it involves physical contact, the higher the level of risk. Rugby union is probably a good example of this. Players can suffer horrific injuries resulting in permanent paralysis, but it does not mean a criminal prosecution must follow. Such injuries are a foreseeable risk arising from participation, even where they result from action that is in breach of the rules. What players do not consent to is the risk of deliberate harm being caused outside the normal run of play—such incidents can and have led to criminal prosecutions, as the defence of consent does not extend that far.

Recently, the Court of Appeal considered body modifications in the case of *R v BM* **[2018] EWCA Crim 560**—a case in which a professional and registered tattoo artist was convicted of **s 18** of the **Offences Against the Person Act 2018** in relation to three procedures—removal of an ear, removal of a nipple, and splitting of a tongue, all performed with the customers' consent. He had unsuccessfully appealed a decision that the consent of the customer had offered no defence. Lord Burnett stated that 'the criminal trial process is inapt to enable a wide-ranging inquiry into the underlying policy issues, which are much better explored in the political environment'. He held the view that this type of body modification was not the same as, for example, tattooing, given the risk to health, concerning as it does 'irreversible surgery with profound long term consequences'. Furthermore:

the personal autonomy of one individual does not extend to involving another in what would otherwise be a crime. In short, we can see no good reason why body modification should be placed in a special category of exemption from the general rule that the consent of an individual to injury provides no defence to the person who inflicts that injury if the violence causes actual bodily harm or more serious injury. The appellant's argument envisages consent to surgical treatment providing a defence to the person performing the surgery whether or not that person is a suitably qualified as a doctor, and whether or not there is a medical (including psychological) justification for the surgery. Even were we attracted by the argument, which we are not, such a bold step is one that could only be taken by Parliament.

This case follows the approach of *Brown*.

[5] Do try to sum up your arguments and make direct reference to the question set.

In conclusion, it can be said that the contours of the defence of consent, whether to the deliberate infliction of harm or the risk of harm being caused, are clear.[5] The law gets into difficulties where it attempts to moralize on what consenting adults should do in private. It then runs the risk of attracting criticism that it is out of date and paternalistic.

 LOOKING FOR EXTRA MARKS?

■ Where you are attempting an essay-type question that requires you to adopt a position, be prepared to put your own views forward, provided they are logically developed. You are more likely to get credit if your approach is original. For example, try to look at resources such as Law Commission reports to enhance the critical value of your answer.

 QUESTION | **3**

Femi is driving his car through central London. At a point where the road narrows from two lanes down to one, a car driven by Roy cuts in front of Femi's car. Femi is infuriated. As the traffic is at a standstill, Femi gets out of his car, pulls open Roy's car door, and shouts abuse at him. Roy is very frightened by this. Louise, a passenger in Roy's car, gets out to remonstrate with Femi, whereupon Femi headbutts her. Louise is wearing steel-rimmed glasses and, as a result of this attack, both she and Femi suffer deep cuts to their foreheads, the frame of the glasses having caused the lacerations. Chiquitta, an elderly woman, sees this disturbance and tries to intervene. Femi pushes her away, causing Chiquitta to lose her balance and fall heavily. Chiquitta suffers a fractured hip and receives hospital treatment for several months afterwards. Louise becomes increasingly ill in the weeks following the attack, and tests reveal that she has become HIV+. Subsequent tests prove that she contracted the condition from Femi who, it transpires, is a drug addict. As a result of sharing needles, he became HIV+ some months prior to his attack on Louise.

Advise the Crown Prosecution Service as to the criminal liability of Femi.

 CAUTION!

■ Although you are told that Femi is a drug addict, there is no evidence that he acts under the influence of drugs at the time of the assaults outlined in the question. In a question such as this, therefore, you should not consider the defence of intoxication in any depth.

■ Distinguish carefully between the *actus reus* and the *mens rea* of these different offences.

DIAGRAM ANSWER PLAN

Identify the issues	▪ Consider Offences Against the Person and common law assault. ▪ Look at the issue of psychological harm.

Relevant law	▪ Discuss **ss 18** and **20** of the **Offences Against the Person Act 1861**, paying particular attention to *mens rea*.

Apply the law	▪ Discuss Louise becoming HIV+, liability for grievous bodily harm, and Femi's attack on Roy.

Conclude	▪ Draw a conclusion on these facts, paying particular attention to distinguishing between the levels of MR when choosing which defence applies.

 SUGGESTED ANSWER

[1] It is immaterial that no physical contact has been made.

[2] Make sure you draw a mini conclusion after each point has been established.

The facts state that Femi shouted abuse at Roy, frightening him. Femi may have incurred liability for common assault. The *actus reus* requires proof that Roy apprehended immediate physical violence.[1] The events will be viewed from the perspective of the victim, not the reasonable person: see *Smith v Chief Supt Woking Police Station* **(1983) 76 Cr App R 234**. It is possible to commit a 'narrow' assault by words alone. The authority for this is the House of Lords' decision in *R v Burstow; R v Ireland* **[1998] AC 147**. Overturning earlier decisions such as *R v Meade & Belt* **(1823) 1 Lew CC 184**, Lord Steyn described the proposition that a gesture may amount to an assault but that words can never suffice as unrealistic and indefensible. The *mens rea* for assault is intention to cause the victim to apprehend immediate physical harm, or recklessness as to whether the victim apprehends such harm: see *R v Savage; R v Parmenter* **[1992] 1 AC 699**. The recklessness is subjective—Femi must at least be aware of the risk that Roy will fear immediate physical violence. It is submitted that Femi could be guilty of common assault on these facts and should be charged under **s 39** of the **Criminal Justice Act 1988**; see further *DPP v Little; DPP v Taylor* **[1992] 1 QB 645**.[2]

Roy is very frightened. This raises the possibility that Roy may have suffered some psychological harm as a result of the abuse from

Femi. Both *R v Chan-Fook* [1994] 2 All ER 552 and *R v Burstow; R v Ireland* make it clear that psychological disturbance can amount to actual bodily harm, or even grievous bodily harm, provided there is medical evidence to substantiate this. Merely being upset will not suffice. As Lord Steyn explained in *R v Burstow; R v Ireland*, '... neuroses must be distinguished from simple states of fear, or problems in coping with everyday life. Where the line is to be drawn must be a matter of psychiatric judgment.' If Roy's fright amounts to actual bodily harm, Femi could be charged under s 47 of the **Offences Against the Person Act 1861** with assault occasioning actual bodily harm. It would be for the prosecution to establish that this assault caused the actual bodily harm. The *mens rea* would be as for common assault, outlined earlier. It is not necessary to prove that Femi foresaw the risk of actual bodily harm: see further *R v Savage; R v Parmenter*.[3]

[3] This *mens rea* issue is quite subtle and must be explained carefully.

The harm done when Femi headbutts Louise, causing the deep cuts to her forehead, could amount to grievous bodily harm if the lacerations are categorized as 'serious harm': see *R v Saunders* [1985] **Crim LR 230**. Femi could therefore be charged with an offence under s 18 of the **Offences Against the Person Act 1861**. The difficulty with a s 18 charge would be proof of the necessary intent. Did Femi intend grievous bodily harm? The prosecution would have to prove that it was either his purpose to do some grievous bodily harm, or that in attacking Louise he foresaw such harm as at least virtually certain—thus permitting a jury to infer intent, as per *R v Woollin* [1998] 4 All ER 103.

The more likely charge is under s 20 of the **Offences Against the Person Act 1861.** The lacerations would clearly amount to 'wounding'—see *C v Eisenhower* [1983] 3 WLR 537. There has been a break in the surface of the skin.[4] The *mens rea* requires proof that Femi acted maliciously. On the basis of *R v Mowatt* [1967] 3 All ER 47, the prosecution must prove that Femi foresaw that some physical harm to some person, albeit of a minor character, might result from his actions. This direction was endorsed by the House of Lords in *R v Savage; R v Parmenter* [1992] 1 AC 699. On the facts there appears to be little doubt that the *mens rea* for s 20 will be established. There is evidence that Femi foresaw at least some physical harm being caused to Louise. The fact that he may not have foreseen lacerations being caused by contact with the frame of her glasses is not relevant.[5]

[4] Apply the law to the facts. Here, do not confuse 'wounding' with grievous bodily harm—only one of these is necessary.

[5] Again, give a proper explanation of the difficult *mens rea* issue.

It should be noted that if the lacerations are grievous bodily harm, as discussed earlier, Femi might also be guilty of maliciously inflicting grievous bodily harm contrary to s 20 of the **1861 Act**. Femi could also be charged with criminal damage in relation to the spectacles worn by Louise, provided he was aware of the risk that property might be damaged: see the decision of the House of Lords in *R v G* [2003] **4 All ER 765**, where a subjective approach to establishing reckless-ness was confirmed as being correct.

Can Femi incur further liability in respect of Louise becoming HIV+? The condition itself would undoubtedly amount to grievous bodily harm—see above. The most appropriate charge would be under **s 18** of the **1861 Act**. The prosecution would have to prove that Femi caused grievous bodily harm (evident) and intended to do so. The complication would be the *mens rea*. There is no evidence that Femi knew he was HIV+, although this could be inferred from his having shared needles.[6]

[6] This issue has been discussed in *R v Dica* and *R v Konzani*.

Alternatively, the prosecution can consider liability under **s 23** of the **Offences Against the Person Act 1861**. This requires proof that Femi unlawfully and maliciously administered to Louise any poison or other destructive or noxious thing, so as to thereby endanger her life, or to inflict grievous bodily harm on her. It is submitted that the term 'administration' is liberally interpreted. The virus could be the 'noxious substance'. Causing Louise to become HIV+ would amount to endangering her life. Again, the problem would be whether or not Femi was aware of his condition. If not, there could be difficulties in establishing that he foresaw the risk of the harm specified in **s 23**, assuming the courts apply *R v Mowatt*.

LOOKING FOR EXTRA MARKS?

- With regard to the contraction of HIV, a discussion of *R v Dica* [2004] and *R v Konzani* [2005] **EWCA Crim 706** on informed consent will add value to your discussion here.
- Note that you need some knowledge of the poisoning offences for this question as well as the grievous bodily harm/actual bodily harm offences.

QUESTION | 4

Ahmed, a builder, throws a small piece of concrete out of a third-floor window. It narrowly misses Janet, an elderly lady who is walking in the busy street below. She manages to dodge out of the way but it falls into a pushchair. The baby, Annabel, needs treatment for minor bruises. Dave, who works opposite, sees what has happened and goes into the building with Janet to complain. He sees Ahmed and says he will 'sort him out'. Ahmed is not threatened by this, and tells Dave to mind his own business. He throws a cardboard box over towards Dave. It misses Dave, but hits Janet on the shoulder. She is bruised and faints from the shock. Unknown to Ahmed, Janet has a heart condi-tion. Dave grabs Ahmed by the shoulders and flings him on the floor. He then spits at him. Ahmed slips and falls down a lift shaft and suffers a broken arm.

In his spare time, Dave plays amateur rugby. During a friendly match, he tackles Ollie, who badly bruises his face when he falls over due to the tackle. As the tackle was illegal, the referee gives the point to Ollie's team. At the end of the match, Dave whispers to Ollie that they will get him back. Ollie reaches into his pocket for his phone. Thinking he is reaching for a weapon, Dave lunges at him, catching his ring on Ollie's face. Ollie is badly cut. That evening, Ahmed receives a text message from Dave insulting Ahmed's religion. Ahmed starts feeling very emotional and is scared to go to work as a result of receiving this message.

When she returns home, Janet suffers heart palpitations and spends several weeks in hospital. She is traumatized by the events and is unable to sleep. She is receiving treatment from her doctor. There is medical evidence to show that Dave had been drinking heavily before he played the rugby match that day.

Discuss the criminal liability of Ahmed and Dave for the non-fatal offences contained in this question.

(!) CAUTION!

■ Make sure you deal with one defendant at a time, even if chronologically other defendants appear first.

■ Be careful with the *mens rea* of the statutory assaults—remember that with the *mens rea* of **ss 47** and **20**, the defendant does not have to intend or be reckless as to the full *actus reus*.

(O) DIAGRAM ANSWER PLAN

Identify the issues	■ Discuss indirect common law battery, ss **47** and **20**, self-defence, and consent.
Relevant law	■ Discuss the direct/indirect rule, an explanation of the *mens rea* in these offences, the parameters of self-defence and consent, psychiatric harm as part of the definition of actual bodily harm, and causation.
Apply the law	■ Discuss whether actual bodily harm is satisfied as medically treated, *mens rea*, whether consent applies as it is outside the rules of the game (*R v Barnes*, *R v Donovan*), and *mens rea* of ss **47** and **20** (*R v Mowatt*).
Conclude	■ Conclude on the **Offences Against the Person Act 1861** offences committed and their relevant defences.

A number of non-fatal offences have been committed in this scenario.

Ahmed may have committed a common law battery when he throws the concrete out of the window. It hits Annabel, the baby, who sustains minor bruises.[1] A battery is defined as an application of unlawful force to the victim (*Collins v Wilcock* **[1984] 3 All ER 374**). It is committed if the defendant intentionally or recklessly inflicts that harm. It can be committed directly or indirectly, so the fact that it was not directed at anyone in particular may not matter. It may be argued by the defence that Ahmed did not hit Annabel directly. This will not matter, as the battery can be carried out via an object. In *Fagan* **[1968] 3 All ER 442**, the defendant committed a battery by placing his car on the victim's foot and leaving it there. The question, regarding *mens rea*, will be whether Ahmed was reckless when he threw the concrete. Given that it is a busy street, we can say that Ahmed was at least aware of the possibility of harm.[2]

When he throws the cardboard box towards Dave, and it hits Janet instead, he has again committed an indirect battery. In *Haystead v CC of Derbyshire* **[2000] 3 All ER 890**, the accused hit a woman who was holding a baby, causing her to drop the baby. In this instance, the battery may be extended to a charge under **s 47** of the **Offences Against the Person Act 1861**. This provides:

whosoever shall be convicted upon an indictment of any assault occasioning actual bodily harm shall be guilty of an offence.

Actual bodily harm has been defined as 'any hurt or injury which is calculated to interfere with the health or comfort of the victim' (*R v Donovan* **[1934] 2 KB 498**). Fainting and bruising clearly falls into this category.[3] Janet also suffers heart palpitations and has to spend time in hospital, and is receiving treatment for sleeplessness. Furthermore, the sleeplessness, for which Janet is receiving treatment from her doctor, may fall into the category of psychiatric harm. In *R v Ireland* **[1998] AC 147**, the House of Lords held that psychological injuries could be included in the definition of actual bodily harm, but only if they were medically recognized conditions. Mere fear, panic, or distress would not be included (*R v Chan-Fook* **[1994] 1 WLR 689**). Janet's sleeplessness would appear to fall into this category.[4]

Section 47 of the Act requires that the defendant 'occasions' the actual bodily harm. This means causation. Ahmed may argue that he did not cause this result and did not know of her condition. These conditions all fall into this category. The 'thin skull' rule will apply here— Ahmed must take Janet as he finds her, meaning that any peculiarities, whether these be physical or social attributes, make no difference to his liability for her injuries—*R v Blaue* **[1975] 1 WLR 11**.[5] The prosecution will

---

[1] In questions on offences against the person, start with the harm caused. This will lead you to the correct offence.

[2] Recklessness, as always in the criminal law, must be assessed subjectively (*R v G* **[2004] 1 AC 1034**).

[3] Make sure you explain exactly which injury is actual bodily harm.

[4] This is quite a fine point so make sure you explain how this works in this scenario (it does so because Janet is being treated by her doctor).

[5] You should not quote verbatim from the case. Note how the *ratio* of the case has been applied to the facts here.

have to show that the result, ie the sleeplessness, was directly caused by the events in question.

Ahmed may try to argue that he did not intend to hurt anyone by throwing a cardboard box. However, the *mens rea* for this section is an intention or recklessness as to the initial assault or battery, not as to the resulting harm. As he probably intended at least a battery when he threw the box, he will be guilty of an offence under this section.

Dave's threat to Ahmed to 'sort him out' will probably not be a common assault, as Ahmed is not threatened by it. An assault is defined as an act which causes the victim to apprehend imminent unlawful force. When he spits at him, however, he has committed a battery. A battery requires proof of unlawful physical force, but not apprehension. As this action appears to be intentional, it satisfies the requirements of this common law offence. When Dave flings Ahmed on the floor, causing him to fall down the lift shaft, he has committed a **s 20** offence, at least. **Section 20** provides that where a defendant intentionally or recklessly wounds or unlawfully inflicts grievous bodily harm, he is guilty of this offence.

A broken arm can be interpreted as grievous bodily harm[6] which is 'really serious' harm—see *DPP v Smith* [1961] AC 290. Deliberately flinging him on the floor may be proof of an intent to cause this and therefore proof of a **s 18** offence, but this may be more difficult to prove. Dave may not have anticipated that flinging Ahmed on the floor would result in him sustaining a broken arm, but this will be irrelevant as long as he was aware of the possibility of his sustaining at least some physical harm (*R v Savage; R v Parmenter* [1992] 1 AC 699.[7] Dave need not have *mens rea* in respect of the actual injury caused.

When Dave tackles Ollie, he may have committed an offence under **s 47** of the **Offences Against the Person Act 1861**. The tackle is a common law battery, which is defined as the application of unlawful physical force. The bad bruising on Ollie's face was occasioned or caused by Dave's actions. Bruising interferes with Ollie's health or comfort and therefore may fall into the category of actual bodily harm—*R v Donovan* [1934] 2 KB 498. The *mens rea* is simply that Dave intended to cause the initial assault or battery—this is evident in this context.

Dave may want to argue that the common law defence of consent applies because Ollie has agreed to play rugby. In principle, a victim cannot consent, validly, to physical harm if it amounts to actual bodily harm or worse, unless the activity comes within a policy-based exception. Sports are such an exception. In *R v Barnes* [2004] EWCA Crim 3246, Lord Woolf CJ observed that if the defendant's actions are within the rules and practice of the game and do not go beyond it, that will be an indication that what has happened was not criminal. Here, the tackle was illegal, so the defence may not be valid.

[6] Note that in the *actus reus* of **s 20**, you need to choose between wounding and grievous bodily harm.

[7] *Mens rea* is a subtle point here, so make sure it is explained well.

The cut to Ollie's face is a wound. A wound consists of the breaking of both layers of the skin—see *C v Eisenhower* (1984) 78 Cr App R 48. This could be a **s 18** or a **s 20** offence—depending on the *mens rea*. Dave may not have anticipated that he would wound Ollie, perhaps intending only to cause a battery. However, he may be reckless as to the causing of at least some harm. The *mens rea* for **s 20** requires that the defendant foresees the possibility of some physical harm[8]— see *R v Mowatt* [1968], in which Lord Diplock said the following:

[8] Be careful with the *mens rea* requirement for this offence. It is not necessary that the defendant intended the full gravity of the statutory definition.

it is quite unnecessary that the accused should have foreseen that his unlawful act might cause physical harm of the gravity described in the section ie a wound or other physical injury. It is enough that he should have foreseen that some physical harm to some person, albeit of a minor character, might result.

It would appear that **s 20** is the more appropriate charge in this instance.

Dave may try to argue that he is acting in self-defence and that he made a genuine mistake when Ollie reached in his pocket for his mobile phone. **Section 76** of the **Criminal Justice and Immigration Act 2008** can apply here.[9] The force used by Dave must be reasonable. This is to be decided according to the facts as the defendant believed them to be. In *Williams (Gladstone)* [1987] 3 All ER 411, the defendant thought he had witnessed an assault by a police officer—D then assaulted the officer. An honest mistake will mean that the defendant is judged on the facts as he saw them. This is supported in **s 76(4)(b)**, which states that as long as the defendant genuinely held that belief, he is entitled to rely on it if it is mistaken, as long as the mistake was a reasonable one to have made.

[9] The common law is now entrenched in the Act.

However, For reasons of public policy, the availability of the defence may be restricted in circumstances where the defendant is intoxicated. **Section 76(5)** provides that the defendant is not entitled to rely on any mistaken belief attributable to intoxication. In these circumstances, it is unlikely that Dave will be able to benefit from this defence and will be charged as explained earlier.[10]

[10] It is useful to have a conclusion on the likely offence to be charged.

The text message containing a racial slur can be an assault occasioning actual bodily harm. The difficulty may be in establishing whether Ahmed's reluctance to go out is 'actual bodily harm' for the purposes of the legislation. In *R v Chan Fook* [1994] 2 All ER 552, mere emotional distress was not enough to constitute actual bodily harm. The prosecution will have to show that Ahmed apprehended an imminent use of force. Since we do not know what the message said, we cannot say for certain that it did; however, it stops Ahmed from going to work and we know that he is frightened. This may be sufficient. Whether this is an assault or an assault occasioning actual bodily harm, the racial element must be considered. Under the provisions of the **Crime and Disorder Act 1998**, a person who commits an assault or battery or an offence under **ss 47** or **20** of the **Offences**

Against the Person Act 1861, where that offence is racially or religiously motivated, may receive a more severe penalty for the commission of the offence.

LOOKING FOR EXTRA MARKS?

- Note that a battery can take many forms—direct and indirect.
- The religious and/or racial aggravation point can be easily missed. This is a procedural issue which impacts on sentencing, but an important one nonetheless, as it will have an impact on sentencing.

QUESTION | 5

The **Offences Against the Person Act 1861** is unfit for purpose and in desperate need of reform. **Discuss this statement in relation to the statutory assaults.**

CAUTION!

- The question directs you to a discussion of the statutory assaults, therefore you should not consider the common law.
- This is a typical essay question in which you are asked to evaluate the law. You should try to come to a conclusion on whether you agree or disagree with the statement. In other words, do not write everything you know about the area, but try to focus on the need for reform.

DIAGRAM ANSWER PLAN

Briefly explain the areas to be covered: the statutory assaults in the **Offences Against the Person Act 1861**.

▼

Discuss the problems of statutory interpretation.

▼

Consider the problems in outcome and sentencing.

▼

Discuss proposals for reform.

▼

Give a conclusion, referring back to the question set—is it in need of reform and why?.

The **Offences Against the Person Act 1861** covers, inter alia, the statutory assaults of actual bodily harm, grievous bodily harm, and grievous bodily harm with intent. It also covers the offence of administration of a noxious substance. **Section 47** builds on the definitions of assault and battery in the common law and creates an offence of an assault (or battery) occasioning actual bodily harm. **Section 20** is malicious wounding or inflicting grievous bodily harm, and **s 18** is intentional wounding or causing grievous bodily harm. This essay focuses on these areas and identifies areas which are in need of reform. It will evaluate the need for this reform, and consider specific proposals.[1]

¹ Start by setting out the parameters of the relevant law, and explaining the scope of the essay.

One of the problems with any legislation is that the courts do not always interpret the meaning of words as Parliament intended. This is especially true of the **1861 Act**, whose language can be described as archaic. Modern interpretations of the concepts are sometimes contradictory. Professor Ashworth (1991) has referred to the Act as being 'expressed in language which is difficult to convey to juries'.[2] Jonathan Herring (2016) holds that 'it is remarkable that the law on assaults is based on an Act which is 150 years old'. The courts have often had to stretch the meaning of the statutory language to fit the demands of modern society. It can be argued as a direct consequence of this interpretation, that the meaning of the statute is too widely interpreted. For example, it now includes the concept of 'biological grievous bodily harm'. Terms such as 'wounding' cover a broad range of circumstances, from a minor cut to a serious wound. This dates from a time when wounding was very serious, and could be life-threatening, so it was important to reflect this in the seriousness of offences. The terms 'inflict', 'cause', and 'occasion' in **ss 20, 18**, and **47** respectively seem to have the same meaning. After the decisions in *R v Burstow* [1998] AC 147 and *R v Dica* [2004] EWCA Crim 1103, it can be confirmed that these mean the same thing. The case of *Clarence* (1888) 22 QBD 23 had established that 'inflict' had a narrower meaning than 'cause' and a direct assault was required.[3] There is a need for statutory clarification on this point.

² In a problematic area of law, it is a good idea to include some academic commentary.

³ *R v Clarence* overruled *R v Dica* on this point.

The language is confusing, nonetheless. These different words to describe causation have caused problems for the courts and lead to confusion. On the other hand, it can be said that these terms are justifiable. The inclusion of the word 'wound' is important due to the number of injuries caused by knife wounds, for instance, and the means by which the wound is caused (in **s 20** with or without any weapon or instrument, and in **s 18** 'by any means whatsoever') seems indistinguishable in these two sections.

The meanings of actual bodily harm and of grievous bodily harm have been extended, through case law, to include the meaning of psychiatric harm. This was probably not envisaged by the legislators. On the one hand, this may be seen as a reason for reform of the original legislation and a justifiable need in modern society; on the other, as indication that judges have gone beyond the meaning of the language in the statute.[4] This is a constitutional argument of whether judges, in interpreting legislation, are acting outside their powers. Meanwhile, certain meanings such as 'assault', which have a very specific meaning at common law, are not defined in the Act at all.

Furthermore, it can be argued that the definition of **s 47** should not require proof of a battery or an assault, but proof of actual bodily harm.

Some of these interpretations are criticized on the grounds that they can be unfair to defendants.

The inclusion of 'biological grievous bodily harm' might mean that defendants can be convicted of a serious criminal offence for not being aware of their own sexual health, for example.[5] This is because the **s 20** offence can be proven on the basis of recklessness, not intention. In *R v Dica* **[2004] QB 1257**, the defendant, knowing he was HIV+, had consensual sex with two women who were subsequently found to have the disease. He was charged with offences under **s 20** on the basis that he had recklessly transmitted the disease to the women when they were unaware. Whilst this undoubtedly solved an issue of interpretation in the Act (consent to sex is not of itself to be regarded as consent to the risk of disease), it means that a defendant who does not intentionally transmit such a disease is guilty of an offence.

Stalking is now criminalized in **ss 2A** and **4A** of the **Protections from Harassment Act 2007** as amended by the **Protection of Freedoms Act 2012**.

The sentencing of the offences under **ss 20, 18,** and **47** of the Act is not logical. **Section 20** has a much more serious *actus reus* (that of wounding or causing grievous bodily harm), and requires that the defendant foresaw actual harm, rather than a mere assault or battery. They both have the same maximum sentences, however. This appears to be contrary to the central importance given to *mens rea* in the criminal justice system and to proportionality (the punishment should fit the crime).[6]

The disparity in *mens rea* in certain sections of the Act is a further problematic issue. It might be argued that in **ss 20** and **47** the defendant can be found guilty of an offence even where he did not have the *mens rea* for the full offence. It may be regarded as wrong to consider a defendant guilty of a criminal offence when he did not have the *mens rea* for committing that offence. In other words, if the defendant did not foresee the *actus reus* of the crime, he should not be found guilty of it.[7] *Mens rea* has central importance elsewhere in

[4] In a discursive essay like this, there will be more than one point of view. Acknowledge this by explaining the contrast.

[5] Arguably, this extends the scope of the Act and of this area of law.

[6] Often, public policy considerations play a role in the development of the law—you should acknowledge this in this type of essay.

[7] This is one of the most controversial aspects of the legislation (and the one which students find most difficult!). Make sure you express it clearly.

the criminal law. This is a point made by Ashworth (1991). John Gardner (1994) disagrees with this contention, on the grounds that this 'correspondence' principle has never been a central tenet of English law. It is important that every *actus reus* is accompanied by *mens rea*, but it does not have to be of equivalent gravity:

the guilty act must therefore be attended by a guilty mind in line with 'actus non facit reum nisi mens rea'. What need not be attended by any mens rea are the consequences and circumstances, the risk of which one bears because one committed the original crime.

Proposed reforms were laid out in the Criminal Law Revision Committee's *Legislating the Criminal Code: Offences Against the Person and General Principles* and followed by a draft bill by the government, modelled on the 1993 report.

This bill set out a much more coherent structure of offences. In particular, it deals with the correspondence principle set out earlier, and recognizes that a person ought only to be found guilty of an offence which he intended. The language has been substantially improved. Herring describes the language used in the bill as 'simple and readily comprehensible'. In November 2015, the Law Commission published a consultation paper recommending that these proposals be enacted. It also recommends the enactment of an offence of threats to kill and aggravated assaults. Although there are some differences in these two sets of recommendations, it is submitted that to enact these proposals would deal with many of the issues of clarity and unfairness which the current law can be criticized for.[8]

[8] A comment on your analysis of any proposals for reform is a good way to end the essay.

LOOKING FOR EXTRA MARKS?

- Try to give specific examples of unclear wording in the Act.
- Providing your own commentary on possible reform is likely to impress the examiner, as it will provide evidence that you have not only gone beyond the basic law, but have really thought about the issues raised.

TAKING THINGS FURTHER

- Ashworth A, *Principles of the Criminal Law* (OUP 1991).
  Wide-ranging text: in the context of non-fatal offences, the author criticizes the form and structure of the Act.
- Edwards S, 'No Defence for a Sado-Masochistic Libido' (1993) 19(143) NLJ 406.
  *Discusses the issues raised by **Brown** and argues that the sexual element should not obscure the violence involved.*

■ Gardiner J, 'Rationality and the Rule of Law in Offences Against the Person' (1994) 53(3) CLJ 502–23.

A critique of the structure and operation of the 1861 Act.

■ Gardiner S, 'The Law and the Sports Field' [1994] Crim LR 513 and M James and S Gardiner, 'Touchlines and Guidelines' [1997] Crim LR 41.

Articles consider consent to injury in sport and the dangers of increasing criminal regulation of organised sports; the second article focuses on the Scottish approach.

■ Gibson M, 'Getting Their "Act" Together? Implementing Statutory Reform of Offences against the Person' [2016] Crim LR 597.

A critique of the Law Commission's proposals.

■ Herring J, *Criminal Law: Texts, Cases, and Materials* (7th edn, OUP 2016).

Texts, cases, and materials in criminal law.

■ Law Commission, Scoping Consultation Paper No 217 (2014)

Identifies incomplete and unresolved areas of the law on non-fatal offences and invites submissions for final consultation. It proposes adoption of the Home Office proposals.

■ Loveless J, 'Criminalising Failure to Disclose HIV to Sexual Partners: A Short Note on Recent Lessons from the Canadian Supreme Court' [2013] Crim LR 215.

Contrasts Canadian and English approaches to criminalizing HIV transmission, with particular attention to issues of mens rea.

■ Loveless J and Derry C, 'R v Dica [2004]' 38(3) Int'l J Legal Ed 'The Law Teacher' 287.

Discusses the problems of consent and recklessness in the offence of 'biological' grievous bodily harm.

■ Murphy P, 'Flogging Live Complainants and Dead Horses: We May No Longer Need to Be in Bondage to Brown' [2011] Crim LR 758.

Suggests that opinion may be shifting away from the majority view in **R v Brown**.

■ Tolmie T, 'Coercive Control: To Criminalize or not to Criminalize?' (2018) 18 Criminol Crim Justice 50.

Explores the risks and disadvantages of the coercive control offence.

■ Weait M, 'Knowledge, Autonomy and Consent: R v Konzani' [2005] Crim LR 763.

Examines the case law and the role of the criminal law in regulating the transmission of sexually transmitted diseases.

Online Resources

www.oup.com/uk/qanda/

For extra essay and problem questions on this topic, as well as advice on revision and exam technique, please visit the online resources.

5 Sexual Offences

ARE YOU READY?

In order to answer questions on this topic, you will need to understand the following:

- the effect of ss 1–3 of the **Sexual Offences Act 2003**, including the effect of the presumptions as to consent under **ss 75 and 76**;
- the concept of reasonable belief under the **Sexual Offences Act 2003**;
- the distinction between consent and submission;
- the definition of consent under **s 74**;
- an outline knowledge of other sexual offences.

KEY DEBATES

Debate: reform of sexual offences

Convictions for sexual offences have historically been very low. The **Sexual Offences Act 2003** sought to remedy this situation. It created a new definition of rape, and shifted the responsibility for obtaining consent to the defendant in certain circumstances. It also created new offences, including sexual assault and assault by penetration, recognizing that these attacks can be just as traumatic for a victim as rape. Some problems remain, however, including the degree to which a victim may have consented when intoxicated. Furthermore, putting the onus of obtaining consent on the defendant raises wider issues of the presumption of innocence and the importance of the burden of proof in a criminal trial.

Debate: the meaning of consent

The term consent, as Professors Ashworth and Temkin have pointed out, is full of inconsistencies. In particular, it is especially difficult to identify it in cases where the victim may be intoxicated. The use of the terms 'freedom' and 'choice' may make matters worse and more vague. Herring argues that mistaken consent should have been specifically included in the Act. Gross, on the other hand, argues that this would enlarge the boundaries of rape, imposing public morality on private relationships.

QUESTION | 1

Discuss the extent to which the Sexual Offences Act 2003 is an improvement on previous law.

CAUTION!

■ As with all essays, ensure you add some value through critical comment and reference to the question.

■ Do not become drawn into discussion of social issues. The conviction rate was an important driver for the changes in the law, but you should concentrate on legal definitions and analysis within the **Sexual Offences Act 2003**.

DIAGRAM ANSWER PLAN

Outline the current law in the Sexual Offences Act 2003 and the legislation it was designed to replace. Consider the Law Commission's proposals for reform.

▼

Conisder the widening of the scope of the *actus reus* of rape.

▼

Discuss the meaning of consent and issues: **ss 75** and **76**, the previous common law, and consent and submission.

▼

Discuss intoxication and consent, and fraud as to the nature and purpose of the Act.

▼

Give a conclusion on the uncertainties described above.

SUGGESTED ANSWER

The **Sexual Offences Act 2003** was enacted in response to the problems of obtaining convictions for rape and sexual assault. Rape is now reported more frequently, but conviction rates are slow to improve. Following reporting, the police need to record the offence and investigate it before a decision is made to prosecute. Even then, despite attempts to improve this, the trial process remains a challenging one for victims who have to cope with cross-examination on previous sexual history in addition to the trauma already experienced.

[1] Reference to the background to the legislation demonstrates that you can put the law in context and have researched the problems.

The Act was the result of a review and subsequent consultation paper by the Home Office (*Setting the Boundaries: Reforming the Law on Sexual Offences*, vol 1, 2000; and *Protecting the Public*, Cm 5668, 2002).[1] In these reports, the previous law on rape was described as inconsistent and piecemeal. This essay attempts to evaluate to what extent the 2003 Act has been successful in replacing it.[2]

[2] Explain what you intend to achieve.

The Act swept away the former **Sexual Offences Act 1956** to create, inter alia, a revised offence of rape, and new offences of sexual assault and assault by penetration. A novel approach to consent in relation to sexual offences was also introduced.

In relation to rape, a new definition was created. The offence of rape is defined in **s 1** of the **Sexual Offences Act 2003**:

[3] Provide a brief definition of the law in question.

A person commits rape if (a) he intentionally penetrates the vagina, anus or mouth of another person (B) with his penis, (b) B does not consent to the penetration, and (c) B does not reasonably believe that B consents.[3]

Thus, the physical definition of rape has changed to include other parts of the body. **Section 1** of the **Sexual Offences Act 2003** has widened the scope of rape beyond sexual intercourse to include penile penetration of other body orifices on the grounds that such penetration is as degrading, demeaning, and damaging as sexual intercourse (Home Office *Setting the Boundaries*, 2000). Sexual intercourse was also a concept which implied completion of the act, whereas case law such as *R v Kaitamaki* **[1985] AC 147** had held that it was a continuing act and that consent could be withdrawn at any time before completion. This is, indeed, now specifically recognized by **s 79(2)** of the **Sexual Offences Act 2003**, which states that penetration is a continuing act from entry to withdrawal.

In relation to *mens rea*, the key issue is consent and the standard of reasonable belief in consent. Consent is further defined in **s 74** of the Act. This provides the following definition: 'a person consents if he agrees by choice, and has the freedom and capacity to make that choice.'

It is important to note that the offence requires that the complainant agrees and the onus is on the defendant to ascertain that agreement. Consent embraces consent to both the nature and purpose of the act. One of the reasons for defining consent in such terms was to draw a distinction between consent and submission (*R v Olugboja* **(1981) 73 Cr App R 344**).[4]

[4] This shows the relationship between the new legislation and the previous common law.

The concept of submission and consent has also been changed by the Act. The law was previously covered in the common law by the case of *R v Olugboja*, in which the judge had directed the jury that although the complainant had not struggled, and no threats had been made to her, it was open to the jury to consider that she had submitted rather than consented to the intercourse. Dunn LJ stated that full regard was to be had to the state of mind prior to the act. Furthermore, a full direction was required:

> they should be directed that consent or the absence of it is to be given its ordinary meaning, and if need be, by way of example that there is a difference between consent and submission: every consent involves a submission, but it by no means follows that a mere submission involves consent.

The last *mens rea* requirement is that the defendant must reasonably believe that A consents. This is an objective test. However, Temkin and Ashworth (2004) argue that the contextualization of requiring the defendant to ascertain consent has the effect of watering down the objective nature of the test.

Furthermore, in certain circumstances the court will presume that the defendant has not obtained consent. This presumption can be rebutted in certain circumstances, but not in others. Thus, **s 75** proscribes certain circumstances in which lack of consent will be presumed, provided the act of sexual intercourse has taken place.[5] These circumstances include putting the complainant in fear, where the complainant has a physical or mental disability, or where the victim has become stupefied due to the administration of a substance. The Act also provides an irrebuttable presumption whereby the court will conclusively find that there has been no consent (**s 76**). This provision applies in circumstances of fraud, such as intentional impersonation and inducement. In circumstances in which **s 76** does not apply, the courts may have recourse to **s 74** and the general definition of consent.

[5] Ensure that you understand how an evidential presumption works. In the case of **s 75**, it is rebuttable—meaning that the defendant can raise evidence against it. **Section 76** provides for an irrebuttable presumption, which is conclusive (no argument can be brought in rebuttal).

These provisions replace the common law rules with regard to fraudulent consent. One example of this is the decision in *R v Williams* **[1923] 1 KB 340**, in which a singing teacher told the victim that he needed to make an air passage to assist in her breathing and to help her to sing better.[6]

[6] Another example of the entrenchment of the common law.

A further change which the **Sexual Offences Act 2003** has made to the previous law is the impact on the decision in

DPP v Morgan **[1975] 2 All ER 347**. This controversial decision had required the defendant to be judged on the facts as he believed them to be. The requirement in the **2003 Act** for the defendant to ascertain whether the victim has consented effectively removes this decision. The concept of reasonable belief has not been extensively interpreted by the courts. However, the decision in *R v Whitta* **[2006] EWCA Crim 2626** seems to suggest that the provision may be interpreted quite widely.

[7] The key issue here is that of capacity.

One of the difficulties arising from the Act is that of the intoxicated victim.[7] In *R v Bree* **[2007] EWCA Crim 256**, the Court of Appeal observed that if, through drink, a complainant in a rape case temporarily loses her capacity to choose whether or not to have intercourse, she is not consenting. On the other hand, if she has voluntarily consumed substantial quantities of alcohol, but nevertheless remains capable of choosing whether or not to have intercourse, and agrees to do so, the defendant would not be guilty of rape. This will be a fine question of fact for the jury.

Another issue arises in relation to fraudulently obtained consent. This is ostensibly dealt with by the irrebuttable presumptions in **s 76**, but these do not cover all situations (see *McNally v R* **[2013] 2 Cr App R 28**).

There is inconsistency in the situations chosen for the two types of presumption. For example, there seems to be little logical distinction in keeping drug-assisted rape an evidential presumption, and fraudulently obtained consent a conclusive one.

It could be argued that placing the onus on the defendant to effectively prove that consent was obtained unfairly removes the presumption of innocence from the defendant in the criminal trial.

[8] Conclude by summarizing the arguments.

In conclusion, whilst the **Sexual Offences Act 2003** has sought to provide clarity in the law, it may have made the law more difficult for juries to understand, thereby increasing the risk of appeals. It might be argued that placing the onus of proof on the defendant in a criminal trial shifts the burden of proof from the prosecution to the defence, thereby undermining the presumption of innocence.[8]

Finally, whilst the law has entrenched some common law decisions into statute, and has reversed the effect of some problematic areas such as *DPP v Morgan*, the problem of the intoxicated victim is not directly dealt with in the Act.

 LOOKING FOR EXTRA MARKS?

■ A discussion of the issue of submission and consent and the issue of intoxication will demonstrate that you have thought critically about this legislation and its effectiveness.

Answer both parts (a) and (b).

(a) Steve is having a coffee with his friends Dave and Barry. They discuss women's attitudes to sex and Dave expresses the view that all women really mean 'yes' when they say 'no' to sexual intercourse. Steve invites Dave and Barry back to his house, where Linda, Steve's wife, is asleep. Steve tells Barry that Linda loves to have sex with men other than her husband, but also likes to pretend that she is being raped. Steve reassures Barry that any resistance on the part of Linda will be part of her 'play-acting'. Dave visits the bathroom and, in error, enters the bedroom where Linda is asleep in bed. He goes into her bedroom and starts to have sexual intercourse with Linda, who is still asleep. On waking, Linda tries to fight Dave off, but he continues to have sex with her.

Linda runs downstairs in distress. Barry takes this as his cue to have sexual intercourse with her on the sofa in the living room. Linda begs Barry to leave her alone, but he persists. Steve stands by watching the events unfold.

Discuss the criminal liability of Dave and Barry.

(b) One evening Rory walks past Lizzie's house and notices that the front door is not fully closed. He pushes the door open and has a look around inside the house. He discovers Lizzie asleep in her bed. Without waking Lizzie, he pulls her bedclothes aside and raises her nightclothes enabling him to see her naked body.

The next day Rory, seeking to impress, tells his friend Kasra how he went out on a blind date the previous evening with Lizzie. He tells Kasra that the evening culminated in them having sexual intercourse at her house. Rory concludes by telling Kasra that Lizzie is 'always dead keen for it'.

The following day, Kasra visits Lizzie's house posing as a double-glazing salesman. Lizzie agrees to let Kasra in so that he can give her an estimate. Whilst they are in her bedroom, Kasra suggests that she might like to have sex with him there and then. Lizzie is shocked and frightened but she remains calm, suggesting that Kasra gets himself ready whilst she visits the bathroom. Lizzie leaves the bedroom intending to call the police. Kasra, encouraged by her response, runs after Lizzie and, pushing her onto the hallway floor, proceeds to have sexual intercourse with her, despite her protestations that he should stop. Once Kasra leaves, Lizzie calls the police.

Advise the Crown Prosecution Service as to the criminal liability of Rory and Kasra. Do not consider Rory's liability as an accomplice to Kasra, or any potential liability Rory may have under Part 2 of the Serious Crime Act 2007.

CAUTION!

■ Do not be tempted to allow your own views of the defendant's behaviour to interfere with your legal advice.

■ Note the rubric to part (a) does not require consideration of Steve's liability, hence the answer does not cover issues relating to his accessorial liability. Similarly, you are told not to consider Roy's accessorial liability in part (b). Examiners will attach such limitation where necessary to keep the candidate's task within reasonable bounds, given the time constraints imposed by the examination format, or the word limits imposed on coursework.

DIAGRAM ANSWER PLAN

Identify the issues	■ The issues raised by this question are the offences in **ss 1, 3**, and **4** of the **Sexual Offences Act 2003**: the *actus reus* of rape. ■ Discuss the *mens rea* of rape—consent. ■ Consider **ss 3** and **4** of the **Sexual Offences Act 2003**. ■ Discuss evidential presumptions as to consent under **s 75(2)(a)** and **s 76**.
Relevant law	■ Outline the relevant law: statutory, general principles, and case law, in particular the evidential provisions as to consent and the concept of reasonable belief. ■ Consider trespass with intent to commit a sexual offence.
Apply the law	■ Consider the application of the law to the facts. Does **s 75** raise evidential presumptions? How will they apply?
Conclude	■ What offences are they guilty of? Ensure you provide advice to the defendants.

SUGGESTED ANSWER

Part (a)

On the given facts it is likely that Dave would be convicted of rape contrary to **s 1** of the **Sexual Offences Act 2003**. In terms of *actus reus*, the prosecution would first have to prove that Dave had penetrated the vagina, anus, or mouth of another person with his penis.[1] The fact that he started to have sexual intercourse with Linda would appear to satisfy this. The prosecution would have to establish that, at some time during the penetration, Dave had the necessary *mens rea*. The second element of *actus reus* to be established is that Linda did not consent to the penetration. The issue of consent is now governed by the rather complex provisions of **ss 74–76** of the **2003 Act**.

Under **s 76**, the jury will be entitled to conclusively presume[2] that Linda was not consenting if the prosecution can prove that, in order to have sexual intercourse with Linda, Dave intentionally deceived her as to the nature or purpose of what he was doing, or that he induced her

[1] Begin by identifying the issues and setting out the relevant law—here, in relation to *actus reus*.

[2] No argument can be brought in rebuttal.

to consent to sexual intercourse by impersonating a person known personally to her. There is no evidence to support either assertion.

The prosecution may be able to rely on **s 75**, which goes on to establish certain presumptions as to consent.[3] Where the defendant has:

(a) committed the *actus reus* of rape;

(b) the complainant was asleep at the time of the penetration; and

(c) the defendant knew that this was the case,

the complainant will be taken not to have consented to the sexual intercourse unless sufficient evidence is adduced to raise an issue as to whether the complainant consented.

This effectively places Dave under a burden to provide evidence that Linda was consenting, even though she was asleep—on the facts there would appear to be no such evidence.

In the event that the absence of consent cannot be resolved by reliance on **s 75**, **s 74** provides that a person consents if she agrees by choice, and has the freedom and capacity to make that choice.[4] A person who is asleep does not have the capacity to make decisions.

[4] In other words, the court would revert to the main part of **s 1**.

Turning to *mens rea*, Dave's penetration of Linda is clearly intentional, hence the only live issue will be as to whether or not he reasonably believed that Linda was consenting.

Under **s 75** of the **2003 Act**, the jury can *presume* that Dave did not reasonably believe that Linda consented to the relevant act, unless sufficient evidence is adduced by Dave to raise an issue as to whether he reasonably believed Linda was consenting. If **s 75** does not lead the jury to a conclusion that Dave had the necessary *mens rea*, it would be directed that, in any event, **s 1(2)** of the **2003 Act** provides that whether or not a belief is reasonable is to be determined having regard to all the circumstances, including any steps the defendant took to ascertain whether the complainant was consenting. There is no evidence of Dave having taken such steps, hence he will be guilty of raping Linda.

Barry's situation is very similar, except that Linda was clearly conscious at the time of the sexual intercourse. Again, the prosecution would have to prove that Barry penetrated the vagina, anus, or mouth of Linda with his penis, and that at the time she was not consenting. Given that the preconditions for the application of **s 76** of the **2003 Act** are not apparent on the facts, the starting point again is **s 75**. Under **s 75**, if it can be proved that:

(a) Barry had sexual intercourse with Linda;

(b) Barry was, immediately before the sexual intercourse, using violence against Linda, or causing her to fear that immediate violence would be used against her; and

(c) Barry knew that those circumstances existed,

Linda will be presumed not to have consented to the sexual intercourse unless sufficient evidence is adduced to raise an issue as to whether she consented.

[5] This is, of course, an objective test.

The problem here for the prosecution is the absence of any direct evidence that Barry used force on Linda, although if she did not want sexual intercourse with him, it may be implied that he would have had to physically overpower her for this to have happened.[5] If **s 75** cannot be relied upon to establish the absence of consent, the prosecution will turn to **s 74**, which provides that Linda consents if she agrees to the sexual intercourse by choice, and has the freedom and capacity to make that choice. The facts indicate that there was no free choice on her part.

The absence of any reasonable belief by Barry as to whether or not Linda was consenting can be resolved under **s 75** if it can be shown that, immediately before the sexual intercourse, Barry was using violence against Linda, or causing her to fear that immediate violence would be used against her; and that he knew that

[6] Ensure that you answer the question directly by analysing the facts of the problem set.

those circumstances existed. If **s 75** does not, of itself, dispose of the *mens rea* issue, the issue of whether Barry's belief in Linda's consent was reasonable is to be determined having regard to all the circumstances,[6] including any steps Barry took to ascertain whether

[7] This position is now reversed by the Act, and included in the concept of reasonable belief.

the complainant was consenting. Under the pre-**Sexual Offences Act 2003** law, *DPP v Morgan* [1975] 2 All ER 347 would have required Barry to be judged on the facts as he honestly believed them to be.[7] Hence, he could have relied on Steve's assurances as to Linda's consent. Under the **2003 Act**, the onus instead is on Barry to

[8] You can incorporate prosecution and defence arguments into your discussion in this way.

obtain Linda's consent. On the one hand, Barry will contend that he acted on Steve's reassurances. On the other hand, the prosecution will argue that the **2003 Act** requires the jury to have regard to the steps taken by Barry to ask Linda if she was consenting.[8] The test is now objective, but the reassurances by Steve may be seen as making Barry's assumptions as to consent reasonable.

Part (b)

When Rory enters Lizzie's house, he does so as a trespasser as he has no permission to be there. Where he subsequently pulls her bedclothes aside and raises her nightclothes to see her naked body, he probably does commit an offence contrary to **s 4** of the **Sexual Offences Act 2003**—causing a person to engage in sexual activity without consent. The prosecution would have to prove that the activity was

[9] Define each element of the definition.

'sexual' in nature. For these purposes, 'sexual activity' is defined by **s 78** as penetration, touching, or any other activity that, whatever its circumstances or any person's purpose in relation to it, a reasonable person would consider of a sexual nature.[9] Alternatively, it can be penetration, touching, or any other activity that, because of its nature, may be sexual and, because of its circumstances or the purpose of any person in relation to it (or both), is sexual. The test is clearly objective, although the court can take into account the defendant's purpose.

That Lizzie was not consenting to the activity is presumed from the fact that she was asleep, and the fact that Rory was aware of this. In terms of *mens rea*, Rory's actions are intentional in lifting the nightclothes. There is no need to prove that he was aware that the actions were sexual. Given the facts, there appears to be no basis on which he could argue that he reasonably believed Lizzie to be consenting.

The facts also raise the possibility of a charge of sexual assault contrary to **s 3** of the **2003 Act**. This provides that a person commits an offence if he intentionally touches another person, the touching is sexual, the complainant does not consent to the touching, and the defendant does not reasonably believe that the complainant consents. There is no evidence that Rory actually touches Lizzie, although he may have done so 'through' her nightclothes. Note that in *R v H* **[2005] All ER (D) 16 (Feb)**, it was held that where a person was wearing clothing, touching of that clothing constituted 'touching' for the purposes of the offence contrary to **s 3** of the **2003 Act**. If this technicality can be overcome, a **s 3** charge is possible.[10]

[10] Note that you need to deal with each issue specified in the Act. Here the term 'touching' is construed quite widely.

Assuming the *actus reus* is made out, the prosecution must prove the absence of any reasonable belief that the victim was consenting. Again, regard would be had to **s 75(2)(d)** of the 2003 Act—as Lizzie was asleep, the jury would be able to presume that there was no reasonable belief on Rory's part that she was consenting. Beyond **s 75**, whether Rory's belief in Lizzie's consent is reasonable is to be determined having regard to all the circumstances, including any steps he took to ascertain whether she was consenting. On the facts the *mens rea* seems evident.

Does Kasra commit rape when he has sexual intercourse with Lizzie? The facts make it quite clear that the *actus reus* of the offence under **s 1** of the **2003 Act** is made out. Kasra commits the act of penile penetration in respect of Lizzie and she was not consenting. If necessary, resort could be had to **s 75** of the **2003 Act**:

(a) Kasra had sexual intercourse with Lizzie;

(b) Kasra was, immediately before the sexual intercourse, using violence against Lizzie, or causing her to fear that immediate violence would be used against her; and

(c) Kasra knew that those circumstances existed.

On this basis, the jury could presume Lizzie was not consenting, unless Kasra can raise evidence to rebut the assumption.

[11] See the discussion earlier on ***DPP v Morgan***.

The problem area for the prosecution will be *mens rea*. Kasra will contend that he honestly believed Lizzie was consenting.[11] The absence of any reasonable belief on the part of Kasra as to whether or not Lizzie was consenting could be resolved under **s 75** if it can be shown that Kasra was using violence against Lizzie and he knew that those circumstances existed. Kasra will rely upon the fact that he did ask Lizzie if she would like to have sex. As a ploy to buy time to telephone the police, she gave him the impression that she would be willing. All of this is evidence that Kasra will rely on to contend that a reasonable person would have thought Lizzie was consenting, and that he checked to make sure that she was.

 LOOKING FOR EXTRA MARKS?

- Proper fact management and careful application of the statutory provisions will help you here. In particular, don't forget that the common law adds to concepts such as 'touching'.
- Don't forget to explain the effect of the presumptions.

 QUESTION | **3**

Jake, an artist, is a member of a cult which has persuaded him that women always want sex and that when they say 'no' they really mean 'yes'. The cult's mission is to encourage its members to 'give sexual pleasure to women'. Jake decides that to be faithful to the cult's mission he should have sex with Anna, his long-standing friend. Anna has always made it clear that they will never be more than good friends, but Jake now believes that she does not mean this. He goes to her bedroom, where she is asleep. He climbs into bed and has sexual intercourse with her. She only vaguely recalls this incident the next morning.

The following week Jake meets Fiona in a bar. While they are chatting, she tells him that she suffers from migraine headaches. Jake tells her that he is a faith healer with mystical powers and can cure such headaches through the medium of sexual contact. Fiona is doubtful, but thinks it is worth a try and they go to her house, where they have sexual intercourse.

Jake is then invited to the cult leader's house for dinner, where he meets Debbie, the leader's sixteen-year-old daughter. Jake and Debbie go out into the garden for a walk and, when out of view of the house, Jake asks Debbie to perform oral sex on him. Debbie does not want to, but has been taught by her father never to deny a man sexual pleasure, and so she agrees to Jake's request.

Assess the criminal liability, if any, of Jake.

CAUTION!

■ Do not allow your own personal view of the offences to lead you to a certain conclusion—stick to the law.

■ The structure of the sexual offences can be quite tricky. Deal with the questions in the usual way, explaining *actus reus*, then *mens rea*. *Mens rea* is based on reasonable belief, which is an objective test.

DIAGRAM ANSWER PLAN

Identify the issues	■ Discuss rape, reasonable belief, **s 75**, and consent by fraud, **s 76**.
Relevant law	■ Discuss the **Sexual Offences Act 2003, ss 1, 74, 75**, and **76**.
Apply the law	■ Consider Anna: in relation to submission and consent; consider **s 75**; what are the circumstances the court might take into account? ■ Consider Fiona: **s 76** and **R v Tabassum**. ■ Consider Debbie: **s 74** capacity and consent; submission and consent; and **R v Olugboja**.
Conclude	■ Discuss rape and submission/consent. ■ Discuss the open question of consent with regard to Debbie.

SUGGESTED ANSWER

[1] Set out all the requirements for the *actus reus*, but focus on the fact in issue.

[2] The **Sexual Offences Act 2003** encapsulates much of the previous common law, therefore it is a good idea to refer to it.

Jake has sexual intercourse with Anna. The central issue on the facts, however, is the question of consent.[1] In order to satisfy the *actus reus* of rape, the prosecution must prove beyond all reasonable doubt that the complainant did not consent to penile penetration. Some assistance is provided in the **Sexual Offences Act 2003** as to the legal definition of consent. **Section 74** states that 'a person consents if he agrees by choice, and has the freedom and capacity to make that choice'. The purpose of defining consent in such terms was to draw a distinction between consent and submission (**R v Olugboja [1982] QB 320**).[2] Therefore, a person will not consent to penetration unless there was agreement to the act, with the freedom to consent or refuse and the capacity to make such a choice. Previous common law cases stated that it was not necessary for the complainant to dissent. Therefore, sexual intercourse with a sleeping woman could never be construed as consensual on the basis that she had not dissented. The prosecution must prove lack of consent. In order to provide some clarification for juries, **s 75(2)(a)–(f)** set out six circumstances in which an evidential presumption regarding consent will arise. If the facts of a case fall within any of these circumstances, it will be presumed that the complainant did not consent to penetration and that D did not reasonably believe in consent unless he can adduce sufficient evidence to raise an issue as to both consent and reasonable belief. **Section 75** therefore casts an evidential burden upon D. **Section 75 (2)(d)** is of specific relevance to this question because it concerns a complainant who is 'asleep or otherwise unconscious'. Therefore, if the prosecution proves beyond all reasonable doubt that Jake intentionally penetrated Anna whilst she was sleeping and that he knew she was asleep, it will be evidentially presumed that she did not consent and that he did not reasonably believe she consented.

[3] **Section 75** is an evidential presumption. This means that the defendant can bring evidence to the contrary. This is not the case for the conclusive presumption in **s 76**.

However, he will be able to rebut these presumptions by adducing or establishing sufficient evidence so as to raise an issue as to consent.[3] It seems as though he will have little evidence to offer with regard to lack of consent. Indeed, the facts disclose that she only had a vague recollection of the incident the next morning. This would appear to indicate that she was asleep and did not consent. If these two aspects of the *actus reus* can be proved by the prosecution, the case will then proceed to *mens rea*.

Mens rea: here the prosecution must prove beyond all reasonable doubt that the penetration was intentional and that Jake did not reasonably believe in consent. Proof of the former is rarely a problem and would seem to be irrefutable here. The latter is by far the more difficult aspect of *mens rea*. Whereas the former law on rape required intention or recklessness as to lack of consent on D's part, the new law requires a straightforward lack of reasonable belief. This is an objective test, but **s 1(2)** provides that 'whether a belief is reasonable is to be determined having regard to all the circumstances, including any steps A (D) has taken to ascertain whether B consents'. The test is objective (see the reference to reasonableness) but also takes into account 'all the circumstances' and efforts D has made to obtain the complainant's consent.

[4] Be sure that you consider the circumstances in the problem.

The circumstances are that Jake and Anna have been long-standing good friends and that Anna has not previously indicated that she would consent to sexual relations with Jake.[4] If one accepts the question at face value, and Anna is asleep when Jake penetrates her, having taken no steps to ascertain her consent, the jury should decide in the light of all the facts and circumstances that Jake could not reasonably believe that Anna was consenting. However, the jury will also need to take into account Jake's committed belief that all women who say 'no' to sex really mean 'yes' and that this was the result of cult membership, the mission of which is to 'give sexual pleasure to women'. There can be no doubt that this is an unreasonable belief on his part and is unlikely to alter the jury's view that he lacked a reasonable belief in consent. If he should choose to defend himself on the basis of a mistaken belief in consent, his mistake needs to be both honest and reasonable. This is a reversal of the *Morgan* test of honest mistaken belief previously applying to sexual offences.[5] Clearly, he has not made a reasonable mistake in relation to Anna's consent.

[5] Prior to this, the defendant could make an honest mistake, even if it was unreasonable.

Jake's offence against Fiona: again, the relevant offence is rape as defined in **s 1(1)** of the **Sexual Offences Act 2003** set out earlier. Given that sexual intercourse has again taken place, it is clear that the prosecution will be able to prove beyond all reasonable doubt the *actus reus* element of penetration and the *mens rea* element that penetration was intentional. The *actus reus* issue which arises here is that of consent and whether Fiona's consent has been induced by fraud.

It might appear that Fiona has consented to sexual intercourse with Jake and that no offence has been committed. However, looking at the consent provisions in **ss 74–76** of the **Sexual Offences Act 2003**, it can be seen that the prosecution may be able to prove a lack of consent on her part by reference to **s 76**, which concerns consent induced by fraud. **Section 76** states that if it is proved that D did the relevant act (ie performed intentional penetration) and that any of the circumstances specified in **subsection (2)** existed, it is to be conclusively presumed that: (a) the complainant did not consent to the relevant act; and (b) that D did not believe that the complainant consented to the relevant act. If successful, the prosecution will prove that any consent given by Fiona to the physical act of intercourse was undermined by Jake's fraud and was therefore ineffective. It will be conclusively presumed that the complainant did not consent and that he knew this to be so.[6] He will therefore be guilty of rape. The **subsection (2)** circumstances are that: (a) D intentionally deceived the complainant as to the nature or purpose of the relevant act; and (b) D intentionally induced the complainant to consent to the relevant act by impersonating a person known personally to the complainant. It does not appear from the facts as though (b) applies because, although Jake has assumed what must be presumed to be false attributes or qualifications, he has not impersonated anyone that Fiona knows. This part of **s 76** is aimed at impersonation of a husband or boyfriend (*R v Elbekkay* [1995] **Crim LR 163**).[7] However, by professing mystical healing powers and the ability to cure headaches by sexual

[6] The defendant has no opportunity to bring extra evidence in these circumstances.

[7] Again, this is an example of the common law being entrenched in statute.

contact, Jake may fall foul of **s 76(2)(a)**: fraud as to nature or purpose. Previous common law cases indicate that by 'nature', **s 76** is aimed at fraud as to the 'sexual' nature of the act. Fraud as to the nature of the act means deceiving the victim as to the sexual nature of the act; see *R v Clarence* **(1888) 22 QBD 23** and *R v Flattery* **(1877) 2 QBD 410**, where sexual intercourse was falsely represented as a surgical operation, and *R v Williams* **[1923] 1 KB 340**, where it was falsely represented by a singing teacher as a breathing technique. **Section 76** now entrenches these common law rules into statutory form. Jake is falsely and intentionally claiming that sexual contact may mystically offer a medical remedy for the very headaches from which Fiona suffers. It would also be possible to view this as a fraud as to his purpose. *R v Tabassum* **[2000] 2 Cr App R 328** held that fraud as to a 'quality' of the act would negate consent. The victims consented to being touched for medical and no other purposes. **Section 76(2)(a)** reflects *Tabassum* through the use of 'purpose' in place of 'quality'. If it was Jake's purpose to have sexual intercourse with Fiona for his own purposes of sexual gratification as opposed to her purpose of medical cure for headaches, then he has intentionally deceived her as to his purpose. Consequently, it will be conclusively presumed that she did not consent to sexual intercourse, and that he did not reasonably believe that she did. No further enquiry into Jake's *mens rea* is necessary, and he will therefore be guilty of rape.

Jake's offence against Debbie: the relevant offence here is rape contrary to **s 1(1)** of the **Sexual Offences Act 2003**. Jake will have committed rape if he intentionally penetrated Debbie's mouth without consent and he had no reasonable belief in consent. The issue for the prosecution in relation to the *actus reus* will be whether she consented or not. **Section 74** provides that 'a person consents if he agrees by choice, and has the freedom and capacity to make that choice'. Although Debbie is sixteen, she is legally above the age of consent and there is therefore no issue regarding her capacity on age grounds.[8] However, does she lack freedom or choice to consent? Debbie appears to have been inculcated by her father not to deny men sexual pleasure, in other words, to agree to sexual activity even when she may not want to. This is a denial of her personal autonomy (ie choice or freedom), not to mention a highly dangerous state of mind to induce in one so young. Her father's coercion may therefore induce her to submit to sexual activity without real consent. There is a difference between submission and consent, as explained in *Olugboja* earlier. It is clear from her point of view that she does not wish to have oral sex with Jake. However, she agrees to his request so as not to disobey her father. Whereas in reality she has probably submitted, it is likely

[8] Capacity is a crucial part of **s 74**.

that her agreement, albeit reluctant, will be seen legally as consent. It is not possible to say with certainty, therefore, that the *actus reus* of rape has been satisfied.

Regarding *mens rea*, Jake's penetration was intentional and he is likely to have a belief in consent in view of Debbie's agreement. Whether his belief could be said to be both honest and reasonable as required by **s 1(c)** in view of the circumstances and his own misguided beliefs is an open question.[9]

[9] Note that sometimes you will not come to a definite conclusion. This does not matter as long as you have argued well.

LOOKING FOR EXTRA MARKS?

- In this type of question, it is tempting to say that the presumptions apply without looking at them in detail. Think about these carefully—a good answer will apply **s 75** to the facts and consider what evidence could be brought in rebuttal.

- The circumstances in which consent will be negated are rare in fraud cases. It is important, however, to distinguish between consent as to purpose and consent as to the nature of the act.

TAKING THINGS FURTHER

- Gross H, 'Rape, Moralism and Human Rights' [2007] Crim LR 220.
  Argues that a wider definition of rape is undesirable as the criminal law must be carefully defined.

- Herring J, 'Mistaken Sex' [2005] Crim LR 511–18.
  Examines the idea that traditionally the onus for establishing lack of consent was placed on the victim and that sexual autonomy and mistaken consent are inextricably linked. A better, more precise definition is required.

- Herring J, 'Human Rights and Rape: A Reply to Hyman Gross' [2007] Crim LR 228.
  Herring's response to the comments made by Gross.

- Home Office, *Setting the Boundaries: Reforming the Law on Sexual Offences* (2000).
  *Proposals for reform leading to the enactment of the **Sexual Offences Act 2003**.*

- Lacey N, 'Beset by Boundaries: The Home Office Review of Sex Offences' [2001] Crim LR 3.
  A critical analysis of the Home Office report.

- Laird K, 'Rapist or Rogue? Deception, Consent and the Sexual Offences Act 2003' [2014] Crim LR 491.
  *Considers the relationship between **s 74** and **s 76**, and the principles and policy issues underlying the law on consent gained by deception.*

- Selfe D, 'The Meaning of Consent under the Sexual Offences Act 2003' (2008) 178 Crim Lawyer 3–5.

  *Discusses the conclusive evidential presumptions under **s 76** and whether it replaces the common law.*

- Temkin J and Ashworth A, 'Rape, Sexual Assaults and the Problem of Consent' [2004] Crim LR 328.

  *Assesses the effectiveness of the **Sexual Offences Act 2003**, particularly with regard to consent.*

Online Resources

www.oup.com/uk/qanda/

For extra essay and problem questions on this topic, as well as advice on revision and exam technique, please visit the online resources.

Property Offences

6

In order to answer questions on this topic, you will need to understand the following:

- s 1 of the **Theft Act 1968**, including the concept of appropriation, *inter vivos* gifts, and consent;
- dishonesty using **s 2** of the **Theft Act 1968** and the common law test in *Ivey v Genting Casinos t/a Crockfords* **[2017] UKSC 67** (now confirmed as superseding the common law test in *R v Ghosh* **[1982] EWCA Crim 2**);
- the various fraud offences under the **Fraud Act 2006**;
- robbery under **s 8** of the **Theft Act 2006**;
- burglary and aggravated burglary under **ss 9** and **10** of the **Theft Act 1968**;
- making off without payment under **s 3** of the **Theft Act 1978**;
- criminal damage under the **Criminal Damage Act 1971**;
- blackmail under **s 21** of the **Theft Act 1968** and handling stolen goods under **ss 21** and **22** of the **Theft Act 1968**.

KEY DEBATES

Debate: appropriation

The law on property offences is contained in a number of different pieces of legislation. In theft, the courts have struggled with the concept of appropriation, holding, controversially, in *Hinks* **[2001] 2 AC 241**, following *R v Gomez* **[1993] AC 442**, that a defendant has appropriated property even where the victim has consented to him taking it. Shute (2002) is in favour of this decision, but Simester and Sullivan (2005) criticize the law's emphasis on the protection of proprietary interests at

(>)

the expense of individuals, especially when there is no harm to society. J C Smith (2001) argues in a similar vein, that the decision in *R v Gomez*, preceding *Hinks*, was incorrect as it contradicted Parliament's intention in enacting the **Theft Act 1968** by enlarging the definition of appropriation. This was contrary to the intention of Parliament. However, Gardner agreed with the decision in *Gomez* on the grounds that dishonesty is really the key issue in theft, and that the victim's consent does not usually alter this fact.

Debate: dishonesty

Dishonesty is a key concept in both theft and fraud. Griew (1985) argues that it is impossible to reach a common standard of dishonesty and that the *Ghosh* test may lead to longer and more complex trials. This common law test is now not likely to be followed in criminal cases, following the decision in *Ivey v Genting Casinos t/a Crockfords* [2017] UKSC 67, which sets an objective standard.

Debate: fraud

The **Fraud Act 2006** aimed to simplify the law by introducing a single and comprehensive offence definition of criminal fraud. For example, under the old law, a machine could not be deceived, as the deception had to operate on the mind of the victim. The definition in the **Fraud Act 2006** attempts to iron out these earlier problems, concentrating instead on dishonesty, and the intention of the defendant. Ormerod (2007) argues, however, that despite its practical advantages, the new offence is still drafted too widely—this may lead to unfairness.

QUESTION | 1

Frank is staying with Hattie for the weekend. Hattie, who works on Saturdays, called Frank from work on Saturday morning and told him to take £10 from her purse to pay the window cleaner. Frank had seen a suit in the window of his favourite clothes shop which he really liked. However, he had already spent all of his salary that month. In addition to the £10 for the window cleaner, he took two £50 notes out of her purse, intending to tell Hattie later that he would pay her back from next month's salary. He also took Hattie's Oyster travel card which had been prepaid to the value of £10.

He returned to the shop and bought the suit, which cost £49. Frank handed over the two £50 notes and received three £20 notes in exchange. When Frank realized that he had received too much change, he was delighted and treated himself to lunch in a restaurant, being careful that no one saw him leave the shop. He left the £10 as a tip for the waitress, who was very pretty. After his lunch he did not feel like walking home, so he took the bus, using £2.00 from the Oyster travel card. Just before he got home, he saw some flowers growing on the side of the road outside his neighbour's garden and picked five to give to Hattie. At home he did not say anything to Hattie, but replaced the Oyster travel card.

Frank said later that he didn't think that she would mind if he took the money and the travel card as they were sharing a flat.

Discuss Frank's liability under the Theft Act 1968.

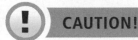

CAUTION!

- You need to make sure you have dealt with each element of theft, in order to secure a conviction. It is best not to dwell too long on one issue only as there are several incidents to cover.

- Take care not to spend too long debating on issues of fact, which are really in the province of the jury. You should still explain the guidance which the judge would need to supply to the jury clearly.

- **Sections 5(3) and 5(4)** can raise tricky issues about when property passes to the owner. In some circumstances, the court will assume that the property 'belongs' to another even where it is technically in his possession.

DIAGRAM ANSWER PLAN

Identify the issues	■ Consider the elements of theft contrary to **s 1** of the **Theft Act 1968**.
Relevant law	■ Consider appropriation in relation to property or belonging to another. ■ Discuss dishonesty and the intention to permanently deprive under **s 6**.
Apply the law	■ Consider Frank's arguments under **s 5(3)** and **(4)**. ■ Consider dishonesty under **s 2(1)(b)** and the ***Ghosh*** test (note the changes in ***Ivey v Genting Casinos***). ■ Look at **s 6**: intention to permanently deprive.
Conclude	■ Is Frank guilty of these counts of theft?

SUGGESTED ANSWER

¹ Start with a definition of the relevant statutory provision.

In taking Hattie's wallet from the table, Frank may have committed theft contrary to **s 1 of the Theft Act 1968.** Theft is defined as the dishonest appropriation of property belonging to another with an intention to permanently deprive that other of it.¹ Appropriation is defined under **s 3** as an assumption of any one of the rights of ownership (***R v Morris* [1984] AC 320**). Simply by taking the money, Frank has assumed one of Hattie's rights in the property. The money is property (**s 4(1)** of the **Theft Act 1968**), and it belongs to another (**s 5(1)** of the **Theft Act 1968**).

Frank may try to argue that he is not dishonest because if Hattie had been there, she might have lent or given him the money to buy the suit as they shared a flat. **Section 2(1)** states that a defendant is not to be regarded as being dishonest if the act was committed with any one of three beliefs: (i) a belief in a legal right to the property; (ii) a belief that the owner would consent; and (iii) a belief that the owner could not be found by taking reasonable steps.[2] Frank will not be regarded as being dishonest if he honestly believes that Hattie would have consented. This seems to be a large amount of money for such a belief. He could try to argue, following *R v Ghosh* **[1982]**, that even though his conduct appeared to be dishonest according to the standards of most people, he did not think that most people would find him to be dishonest. His assertion that he did not think that Hattie would mind is further evidence for this belief. The decision in *Ghosh* now no longer applies following the Supreme Court decision in *Ivey v Genting Casinos* **[2017] UKSC 67**. This decision will have far-reaching consequences for the law of property offences, including fraud, as it suggests that the test for dishonesty will be an objective one. It means that the prosecution will no longer need to prove that the defendant is aware that his actions are dishonest according to the standards of reasonable and honest people. Indeed, in *DPP v Patterson* **[2017] EWHC 2820 (Admin)**, Sir Brian Leveson commented that it would be difficult to imagine a court preferring *Ghosh* to *Ivey* in the future. Ivey has now been confirmed by the Court of Appeal in **Booth and Anor v R [2020] EWCA 575**. A court can therefore conclude that a defendant is dishonest on the basis of his actions and thoughts at the time of committing an offence. It will be up to the jury to decide whether these thoughts and actions are dishonest according to the standards of ordinary people.

The prosecution must also prove that Frank intended to permanently deprive Hattie of the property. Given that he states that he intends to return the money, the court will not treat this as a straightforward deprivation, but instead will invoke **s 6** of the **Theft Act 1968**.[3] Frank can be regarded as having the intention of permanently depriving Hattie of the money if it was his intention to treat the thing as his own, regardless of another's rights. This is the case here. Keeping the money until his next pay date indicates an intention to treat the money as his own, regardless of Hattie's rights. The money is clearly 'property' under **s 4(1)** and it belongs to another. With regard to the travel card, he might argue that he simply borrowed it. **Section 6** provides that if the borrowing is for a period and in circumstances making it equivalent to an outright taking or disposal, then this will also be an intention to permanently deprive the owner of the property. In *R v Lloyd* **[1985] QB 829**, the Court of Appeal held that there

[2] These are technically 'defences' rather than a definition of dishonesty. If none of these apply, or if they do not work, consult the common law test in *Ghosh*.

[3] Be careful with this: you should only use **s 6(1)** and **(2)** in cases of difficulty where the defendant needs to be deemed to have an intention to permanently deprive. Avoid a common mistake that candidates make—there is usually no need to prove that the owner was permanently deprived.

would be a sufficient intent to deprive if the accused in the course of borrowing changed the property so that all its 'goodness and virtue' was diminished. The Oyster card can be used again, but the money on it has been used, and Hattie is prevented from using the credit on it.[4]

[4] Remember to apply this complicated section to the facts.

When Frank receives too much change, he may argue that the property does not belong to the shop, but to him, given that he now has possession of it. **Section 5(4)** of the **Theft Act 1968** provides that where the defendant obtains property by mistake and is under an obligation to return it, he has an obligation to make restoration. The obligation to restore the property must be a legal one. This requirement was inserted into the **Theft Act 1968** to deal with the problem raised in the old law of larceny that a defendant could not be convicted for keeping excess wages paid to him by mistake.[5] The other requirements of theft will also need to be satisfied. As Frank spent the money, he appears to be dishonest. According to *R v Ghosh*, a defendant is dishonest if he would be dishonest according to the standards of reasonable and honest people. As explained above, following recent developments, the court will now be unconcerned with any contention by Frank that he did not realize he was being dishonest by ordinary standards. It is likely that the objective condition would be satisfied, as he checks to see that no one is watching him.

[5] An obligation must be shown for this section to operate.

The £10 destined for the window cleaner is also property (**s 4(1)**). Frank may try to argue that it is not property belonging to another because it is in his possession. Under **s 5(3)** of the **Theft Act 1968**, where the property is received by the defendant on account of another, and the defendant is under an obligation to the defendant to deal with the property in a particular way, then the property is to be regarded as belonging to another. Whether there is an obligation is a matter of law. For example, in *R v Hall* **[1973] QB 126**, the Court of Appeal quashed the conviction of a travel agent who had failed to use his client's deposit to book his holiday. A legal obligation could not be found. However, in *Davidge v Bunnett* **[1984] Crim LR 296**, the defendant was held to be under an obligation to her fellow occupants of the property from whom she had collected money to pay an electricity bill—she stole the money when she used it to buy presents. In the context of the other events here, Frank may well be regarded as being sufficiently dishonest to secure a conviction. Finally, the intention to permanently deprive the owner of the property is clear here, so recourse to **s 6(1)** is unnecessary.

[6] Where you cannot prove one of the elements of theft, you do not need to discuss the other elements.

Taking the flowers will not be regarded as theft, as the flowers are not property under **s 4(1)**.[6] It is not possible to 'steal' fruit, flowers, or foliage growing wild on any land unless this is done for reward or sale or other commercial purposes. As he picks a few flowers to give to Hattie, he does not do so for reward or for sale. These are not 'property' for the purposes of the Act. Once this is established, the other elements of theft need not be proven.

LOOKING FOR EXTRA MARKS?

- Careful management of the facts and application of the law to them is crucial in a question like this. You can deal with obvious issues fairly quickly, enabling you to concentrate on the more difficult problem areas such as **s 5**.

- Even though the reference to dishonesty in *Ivey v Genting Casinos* is, strictly speaking, *obiter*, show the examiner that you are aware of the impact of this important recent decision and its likely impact. The confirmation of Ivey in Booth can be explored further in the online resources.

QUESTION | 2

Saul and Tim go out one night looking for houses to break into. They see a ground-floor window open where Jen is working. Jen waves to Tim and beckons him in, thinking that it is her brother, Jason. Tim climbs in and Saul follows. When Jen realizes her mistake, she screams and tries to run away. Tim punches her and ties her to a chair, while Saul goes upstairs and helps himself to Jen's jewellery. On the way out, Tim grabs a knife which is on the kitchen table.

Saul and Tim visit an off-licence. While Andy, the assistant, is not looking, Tim takes some cans of beer from a shelf and puts them in his bag. Andy notices, and Tim points the knife at him. Andy is frightened and retreats. They leave the shop with the beer.

They then visit Saul's grandfather, Cyril. At Cyril's house, they both help themselves to some choco-lates on the sideboard and Saul takes a £20 note from Cyril's wallet.

Jen, a hospital administrator, is traumatized by her attack. The following week, she uses her broth-er's credit card to buy £1,000 worth of consumer goods without his knowledge and agrees to put a patient at the top of the operation waiting list in return for £500.

Saul says that he didn't think his grandfather would mind if he took the money and the chocolates.

Advise the Crown Prosecution Service on liability for property offences arising from these facts.

CAUTION!

- There is a lot of overlap between the different property offences of theft, robbery, burglary, and fraud. It is best to deal with them separately, as the questions can be very technical on the statute.

- Don't forget about the issue of continuing appropriation in robbery. This is more likely to appear than in theft.

DIAGRAM ANSWER PLAN

Identify the issues	▪ Look at robbery and burglary under **ss 8** and **9** of the **Theft Act 1968**. ▪ Discuss fraud under the **Fraud Act 2006**.
Relevant law	▪ Discuss continuing appropriation and the other elements of theft. ▪ Consider the timing of theft under burglary. ▪ Discuss fraud by false representation (**s 2** of the **Fraud Act 2006**).
Apply the law	▪ In relation to Tim and Saul, discuss burglary, and robbery and appropriation, and when the theft takes place. ▪ In relation to Jen, discuss fraud by representation—what is the representation? ▪ Again in relation to Jen, discuss fraud by abuse of position— is it financial?
Conclude	▪ Based on the above, advise whether the defendants are guilty of the three offences.

SUGGESTED ANSWER

This question raises issues of robbery, burglary, and theft offences. When Saul and Tim enter Jen's property, they may have committed burglary. This is defined under s 9 of the **Theft Act 1968**, and the relevant part in this case is s 9(1)(a), whereby a person is guilty of burglary if he enters any building or part of a building as a trespasser with intent to commit an offence as defined in s 9(2).[1] This includes stealing or attempting to steal anything from the property. They intend to look for houses to break into, so this is the appropriate section to use. It is not necessary to prove that they steal. They may argue that they were not trespassing, as Jen invited them in. In **R v Collins** [1972] 2 All ER 1105, the defendant, wearing only his socks, climbed a ladder and was perched on a bedroom windowsill. The eighteen-year-old girl inside assumed that her boyfriend had returned for a nocturnal visit, invited him in, and they had sexual intercourse. The defendant was convicted of burglary under s 9 (1)

[1] The difference between the two types of burglary is dependent on the moment the intent is formed.

(a)—note that at the time, burglary of this type included the intent to rape. Although the Court of Appeal quashed this because the trial judge had not properly directed the jury on the need for *mens rea* as to presence as a trespasser, later cases show that the defendant's entry must be effective, not just substantial. Jen's mistake would seem to negate any argument that the men are not trespassing.[2] Furthermore, it has been held that the defendant will be trespassing if he enters in excess of any permission he might otherwise have. In ***Jones and Smith* [1976] 3 All ER 54**, the two defendants entered the house belonging to Smith's father with the intention of stealing, and their convictions for burglary were upheld. This seems to imply that any person entering a building with an intention to exceed the terms of any express or implied permission to do so must be trespassing.[3] The *actus reus* of burglary along with the *mens rea* seems to be made out.

The defendants may also be guilty of robbery. **Section 8(1)** of the **Theft Act 1968** states that:

A person is guilty of robbery if he steals, and immediately before or at the time of doing so, and in order to do so, he uses force on any person or puts or seeks to put any person in fear of being then and there subjected to force.

Robbery is essentially aggravated theft. This means that the prosecution must first prove all the elements of theft, including that there has been an appropriation of property.[4] In ***R v Hale* [1978] 68 Cr App R 415**, two defendants went to their victim's house and while one was upstairs stealing a jewellery box, the other was downstairs restraining the victim. The Court of Appeal upheld the conviction for robbery, even though the box had been appropriated before any force was used against the victim. The theft was regarded as a continuing event, and the jury could conclude that it was in progress as the victim was being tied up. The facts of this question are almost identical.

A further count of robbery may be charged in relation to the events in the shop. The key difference between theft and robbery is that force or fear of force is used in robbery. This must be used in order to steal and before or at the time of stealing.[5] As the threat with the knife seems to take place after the theft of the beer, the elements of robbery will not be made out. The elements of theft will need to be satisfied. Theft is a dishonest appropriation of property with an intention to permanently deprive the other of it (**s 1 Theft Act 1968**).

Are the men guilty of burglary at Cyril's house? As discussed earlier, they may be regarded as having trespassed under the principle in ***Jones and Smith*** (discussed earlier). They have clearly appropriated

---

[2] It is now settled that entry must be effective.

[3] The key here is not the permission to enter, but is based on the defendant's behaviour once on the property.

[4] This does not have quite the same meaning as in theft; in robbery there may be a question of whether the appropriation is continuing or not at the time the other elements are complete.

[5] The timing is all-important here.

[6] This type of burglary requires an actual theft to have taken place.

the money and the chocolates. Therefore, they have committed burglary under s 9(1)(b).[6]

Jen may have committed fraud by representation and fraud by an abuse of position under **ss 2** and **4** of the **Fraud Act 2006**. On the assumption that her brother does not consent to the use of the credit card, using the card to buy £1,000 of goods constitutes an offence under **s 2** of the **Fraud Act 2006**. The *actus reus* of this offence consists of a representation (**s 2(1)**) which is untrue or misleading, and can be express or implied. Representation means any representation as to fact or to law, and can be express or implied (**s 2(4)**). Jen made an implied false representation to the cashier when she paid for the goods that she had the credit card company's authority to pay for the goods. The *mens rea* of fraud is the dishonest making of a false representation (**s 2(1)(a)**), knowledge that the representation is untrue or misleading, and an intention by that misrepresentation to make a gain or cause a loss to another or to expose another to a risk of loss. The 'gain' must be financial. Dishonesty is a key issue in fraud, and is likely to be defined according to the principles in the *Ghosh* test, subject to the case of *Ivey v Genting Casinos*. There is some debate about this applicability in a statute—in a commentary to the case, Karl Laird (2018) points out that in enacting the **Fraud Act 2006**, the *Ghosh* test, being included in the Explanatory Notes to the Act, was implicitly approved. Treating the *obiter* statement in *Ivey* as binding on all property offences may therefore be problematic. If *Ivey* is followed here, then the test will be whether ordinary people would be likely to regard his actions as dishonest—a question for the jury. The recent case of *Booth* in the Court of Appeal considered, and rejected, those concerns.

Alternatively, Jen may have committed fraud by abuse of position under **s 4** of the **Fraud Act 2006**. A person will commit this offence if he occupies a position in which he is expected to safeguard or not to act against the financial interests of another person (**s 4(1)**). The defendant must dishonestly abuse that position and intend to make a gain or cause a loss to another. An employment situation has been held to fall into this section. In *R v Gale* **[2008] 1 All ER 230**, a defendant was found guilty under this section when he falsified customs documents to show that he had inspected goods, when he had not. The court said that it was essential that employees trusted to do things of this nature showed a high level of trust and probity. Whether Jen would fall into this category is debatable, but when demand for operation waiting lists is high, it might be argued that a high level of trust and probity is required to ensure that the correct procedures are followed.

LOOKING FOR EXTRA MARKS?

- Proper fact management is required in these questions, when a number of different offences may have been committed.

- Make sure that you do not forget the dishonesty issue in fraud. An operative deception on the victim is no longer necessary (ie no causal link need be proven between the false statement and the loss suffered by the victim).

QUESTION | 3

Critically evaluate the current test for dishonesty for property offences. Is it fit for purpose?

CAUTION!

- This question requires an understanding of key developments in this area—in particular you will need to have read the judgment in *Ivey v Genting Casinos*. Note that this decision has now been confirmed by the Court of Appeal.

- You need to add critical value by explaining the impact of the decision on theft, fraud, and other offences. A discussion of fairness to the defendant will also help you to assess its effectiveness and purpose.

DIAGRAM ANSWER PLAN

> Outline the law—how is the concept defined under the **Theft Act 1968** and at common law?

⬇

> Discuss **s 2** and dishonesty providing only a defence and *R v Ghosh*.

⬇

> Consider *Ivey v Genting Casinos*.

⬇

> Consider the problems in *R v Ghosh*, which was superseded by *Ivey*—has *Ivey* solved the problems?

⬇

> Draw a conclusion—is the law fit for purpose?

Dishonesty is a key concept in a number of property offences, including theft and fraud. There is no legislative definition of dishonesty. The **Theft Act 1968** provides a partial definition in **s 2** which provides circumstances in which a defendant is not to be regarded as dishonest. Otherwise, the common law has developed to provide guidance from a judge to juries who have to determine the state of mind of the defendant in a criminal case. Achieving unanimity in such circumstances is no easy task. The following essay considers the development of the law on dishonesty and argues that recent developments have not necessarily resolved all the issues in the previous common law tests.[1]

The first port of call in deciding dishonesty is to consult the partial definition of dishonesty in **s 2** of the **Theft Act 1968**. The Act does not define theft, but rather provides three scenarios in which the defendant will not be regarded as dishonest.[2] **Section 2(1)(a)** provides, first, that where the defendant appropriates the property in the belief that he has in law the right to deprive the other of it, he is not to be regarded as dishonest. This claim of right defence might apply, for example, where the defendant thought that the victim owed him money. Second, where the defendant appropriates the property in the belief that he would have the other's consent if the other knew of the appropriation and the circumstances of it, he will not be regarded as dishonest. Third, the defendant will not be regarded as dishonest if he appropriates the property in the belief that the person to whom the property belongs cannot be discovered by taking reasonable steps.[3]

Where the **s 2** situations do not apply, the courts traditionally fell back on the common law direction from judges to juries relating to dishonesty, which was contained in **R v Ghosh [1982] QB 1053** and was a question of fact for the jury:

(a) whether according to the standards of ordinary, reasonable, and honest people what was done was dishonest. If it was not dishonest by those standards, that is the end of the matter and the prosecution fails. If it was dishonest by those standards, then the jury must consider

(b) whether the defendant himself must have realized that what he was doing was by those standards dishonest.

This test aimed to carve a path between a purely subjective approach, where the belief of the defendant would be all important, and a purely objective approach, where the latter is ignored and the standard of the reasonable man is invoked, no matter what the defendant believed. However, this approach meant that a number of problems arose.

[1] It is useful to provide some context and background in your introduction, as well as an indication of the structure of the essay.

[2] It is crucial to remember that this is a *mens rea* issue. It does not matter, for example in **s 2(1)(c)**, whether reasonable steps to find the owner are actually taken.

[3] Note that these are beliefs on the part of the defendant—there is no need, for example, to show that reasonable steps were actually taken.

The problem with leaving this decision in the hands of the jury is that it is very difficult for a jury of twelve to reach a decision on what is honest when individual opinions may be very diverse. This is especially true in situations in which a defendant thinks that he is 'doing the right thing'. A defendant who takes £50 from his employer's cash register intending to replace it may be regarded as dishonest by one jury, but gain sympathy (and acquittal) from another.[4]

[4] Try to give practical examples where you can—this adds critical value to your answer.

In his seminal article, Edward Griew (1985) argues that the **Ghosh** test would lead to longer trials, as the decision is so difficult for the jury to achieve. The test assumes that reasonable people, sitting on a jury, will all think in the same way, but in fact the behaviour that people find to be dishonest varies hugely. Griew refers to this difficulty as the fiction of community norms.[5] Furthermore, juries may find it difficult to apply the tests in situations they have no experience of themselves, such as fraud trials.

[5] Reference to academic criticism, such as Griew's here, will help you to strengthen your argument that the law was not satisfactory. See also Laird (2018) and Spencer (2018) below.

The second limb of the **Ghosh** test required the jury to 'look into the mind' of the defendant and ask whether s/he would realize that the actions taken were dishonest according to the standards of reasonable and honest people.

In the recent case of **Ivey v Genting Casinos**, the Supreme Court considered the future validity of this test.

Mr Ivey was a professional gambler who sought to recover his winnings (£7.7 million) from the casino after playing a game called Punto Banco Baccarat. He used a technique called edge sorting, which involved looking at the edges of cards and spotting very small differences and design irregularities, which he did by persuading the croupier to rotate the cards so that he could see them clearly. The technique improved his chances of winning. He told her that he always did this, as he was superstitious. The casino refused to pay out his winnings, alleging that he had cheated and therefore had breached an implied term of his gaming contract with them (not to cheat). He argued that he could not have cheated, as he was not dishonest—what he had done was simply an example of good gamesmanship. The definition of dishonesty under the **Ghosh** test required that that defendant knew that what he was doing was dishonest according to the standards of reasonable people. It was this limb, he argued, which was not satisfied: he did not consider himself to be dishonest according to the standards of reasonable people.

The Supreme Court held that where a definition of dishonesty is necessary, it should not contain an element which assesses the defendant's view of whether his actions are dishonest according to the standards of ordinary people. Instead, the court must ascertain the defendant's view of the facts. This should be followed by an assessment of whether these acts are dishonest according to the standards of reasonable people. What is not required is the defendant's appreciation that others would regard his behaviour as dishonest.

Note that the discussion of dishonesty is, strictly, *obiter*, since the Supreme Court held that dishonesty did not have to be proved in this case. However, given the terms in which it was set out and the fact that it was agreed unanimously by five Supreme Court judges, it is likely that future courts will follow it. In the same year, the case of **DPP v Patterson [2017] EWHC 2820 (Admin)**, an appeal by way of case stated, appeared to confirm the decision in **Ivey**. Sir Brian Leveson stated, 'it is difficult to imagine the Court of Appeal preferring **Ghosh** to **Ivey** in the future'. Commenting on this decision in a note to the case (Crim LR [2018] 5, 395–9), Karl Laird states that 'the tone of the Supreme Court's judgment strongly suggests that it intends for its *obiter* analysis of **Ghosh** to be treated as binding by the lower courts'. He further suggests that it would be possible for the Court of Appeal to depart from **Ghosh** without the matter returning to the Supreme Court.

In **Hayes [2018] EWCA Crim 1944 Cr App R 10**, the Court of Appeal indicated again that the **Ghosh** test would need to be reconsidered.

[6] This is a good opportunity to link the discussion above to the question set in the essay and to introduce more academic commentary. This can be summarized and repeated in the conclusion.

This decision will have far-reaching consequences for the law of property offences, including fraud, as it seems to suggest that the test for dishonesty will be an objective one.[6] It means that the prosecution will no longer need to prove that the defendant is aware that his actions are dishonest according to the standards of reasonable and honest people. A court can therefore conclude that a defendant is dishonest on the basis of his actions and thoughts at the time of committing an offence. It will then be up to the jury to decide whether these thoughts and actions are dishonest according to the standards of ordinary people.

[7] It is a good idea to contrast views you find in the literature in order to present a balanced view in your evaluation.

Some academic commentators are in favour of the decision.[7] Galli (2018), for example, states:

Ivey and **Genting Casinos** was the opportunity that the Supreme Court needed to clarify the test for determining dishonesty both in civil and criminal cases … the Supreme Court 'grasped it with both hands'. This raises an important point— that the tests for dishonesty in civil and criminal law were quite different.

Other commentators foresee problems, however. Dyson and Jarvis (2018) argue that what the Supreme Court failed to consider was the *effect* on other offences such as fraud. In enacting the **Fraud Act 2006**, Parliament implicitly approved **Ghosh**. They further argue:

The Supreme Court did not directly consider whether the approach in *Ivey* was compatible with the fundamental right of the individual to be able to foresee the consequence which a given course of conduct may entail.

Laird (2018) has concerns about precedent and *stare decisis*:

(the decision) raises questions about the propriety of the Supreme Court making obiter comments with the intention of them being treated as ratio and therefore binding. Should they be followed or should we wait for **Ghosh** to be specifically overturned? [...]The Supreme Court has distorted principles that are fundamental. The Court failed to appreciate the legal system's structure and operation … the decision has the potential to wreak havoc.

Continuing on this theme, J R Spencer ([2018] **8 Arch Rev 4–6**) emphasizes the value of the second limb of the *Ghosh* test:

> rejecting the belief of anyone who genuinely believes his conduct to be proper by the ordinary standards of honest and reasonable people can be seen as an important limit … rejecting it extends the offence of theft even further. The abolition of the second limb needs deeper thought than the Supreme Court gave to it in *Ivey* and the Court of Appeal should think not twice but many times before it decides to accept the *obiter dicta* in this case.

This extensive commentary suggests that opinion is divided. On the one hand, it can be said that bringing the criminal law definition of dishonesty in line with the civil law definition improves consistency and reduces absurd decisions as juries grapple with the test. On the other hand, there are concerns about the status of an *obiter* statement, and the loss of the subjective element of the previous test, including the effect on the fundamental rights of the defendant. e d

In conclusion, the pivotal concept of dishonesty is controversial and may lead to inconsistent decision making. It is submitted that a better statutory definition may avoid these problems.[8]

[8] Try to refer back to the question set in your conclusion. This will remind the reader that you are thinking about the question, and are staying relevant.

LOOKING FOR EXTRA MARKS?

■ Refer to academic opinion in essay questions. Griew (1985), for example, argues that the *Ghosh* test in dishonesty creates too many problems for juries and leads to inconsistent verdicts.

■ Show your knowledge of recent legal developments—for example *Ivey v Genting Casinos*. Note that the decision in Ivey has now been confirmed in the case of Booth - the above answer should be read in the light of that case. Further details on this, along with commentary, can be found in the online resources for this title.

QUESTION | 4

Martina contacts Andrew for a quotation to renovate a bathroom at her house, having searched on the internet and seen a page stating, 'Andrew Holter Bathrooms—use the best. Experience, reasonable prices and quality workmanship guaranteed.' Andrew has just set up his own business after leaving college with a diploma in marketing. He tells her the materials will cost £15,000, which he requires in advance as this is a trade requirement. This is untrue.

Martina agrees to hire him to renovate her bathroom. Andrew goes to the local DIY store to buy the materials, which cost him £5,000. Knowing he has insufficient credit on his credit card, he uses his father's credit card, for which he knows the PIN number. Before entering the store, he is approached and asked if he would like his van cleaned, for which he must pay £5 when he leaves the store. He agrees. When he leaves the store, he sees that his van had been washed but he drives off without paying.

When he returns to Martina's house to start work, she is just leaving. She tells him that she has left some money on the kitchen table to pay the window cleaner. When the window cleaner calls later that morning, Andrew tells him Martina did not leave any money for him. Andrew then uses the money to buy his lunch. Three weeks after completing the building job, the shower stops working and the plasterwork starts to crumble. Martina has to have it rebuilt.

Andrew's neighbour, Vince, has been observing and following Andrew and threatens to post details all over his website and call the police if he does not pay him £10,000. As he is secretly in love with Martina, he plans to give this to her as compensation for the money she has lost and therefore be in her favour.

Discuss the liability, if any, of Andrew and Vince.

CAUTION!

- This question covers a number of property offences, so deal with them all in turn. There will be overlap between the offences, so be careful and don't worry about repetition. This might particularly apply to theft and making off without payment.

- When discussing fraud, avoid a common error and ensure you give due weight to the *mens rea*.

DIAGRAM ANSWER PLAN

Identify the issues	■ Look at fraud under the **Fraud Act 2006**. ■ Consider theft under the **Theft Act 1968**. ■ Discuss making off without payment under **s 3** of the **Theft Act 1978**.
Relevant law	■ Discuss **s 2** of the **Fraud Act 2006**—the concept of representation. ■ Discuss **s 11** of the **Fraud Act 2006**—obtaining services dishonestly. ■ Consider making off without payment—**s 3**—payment on the spot?
Apply the law	■ Has he committed a **s 4** fraud offence? ■ Discuss 'position'. ■ Consider *mens rea*—is he dishonest under the test in ***Ivey***?
Conclude	■ Advise on the basis of the above discussion.

SUGGESTED ANSWER

Andrew may be found guilty of fraud under the **Fraud Act 2006**. He may also be guilty of theft under the **Theft Act 1968** and of making off without payment under the **Theft Act 1978**.

The advertisement placed on the internet seems to imply that he has experience in building work, whereas he has in fact just left college with a diploma in marketing. This statement is untrue. **Section 2** of the **Fraud Act 2006** states that a fraud by false representation has occurred where the defendant makes a false representation. A representation means any representation as to fact or law, including a representation as to the state of mind of the person making it or any other person (**s 2(3)**). The advertisement falls into this category, as the subsequent work was shown to be unsatisfactory (the shower has stopped working and the plasterwork has started to crumble).[1] Furthermore, his assertion that the materials would cost £15,000 when they cost one-third of this amounts to a false representation, especially when viewed in the context of the poor workmanship.

The *mens rea* of this offence of fraud is defined as the dishonest making of a false representation. Dishonesty here is now defined following ***Ivey v Genting Casinos* [2017] UKSC 67**. This will be a question of fact for the jury. The court will need to determine the defendant's state of mind, and then ask whether by the standards of ordinary people, he is dishonest. There is no longer a requirement that the defendant was aware that the defendant was dishonest according to the standards of ordinary people (the previous second limb of the ***Ghosh*** test). This has now been confirmed by the Court of Appeal in R v Barton and Booth [2020] EWCA 575.

In these circumstances, it seems unlikely that the jury would regard Andrew as an honest bathroom renovator. This aspect of the *mens rea* would appear to be satisfied.[2]

The work is clearly carried out with a view to gain (**ss 2(b)** and **5** of the **Fraud Act 2006**).

A further offence under **s 2** of the **Fraud Act 2006** may have arisen when he uses his father's credit card. Under **s 2(4)**, a representation can be express or implied. Here, Andrew makes an implied false representation to the cashier that he has the credit card company's authority to use the card and is within the credit limit (***Lambie* [1981] 1 All ER 332**).[3] The *mens rea* requirements of dishonesty and intention to make a gain appear to be met here: Andrew knows what he is doing when he uses the credit card. Furthermore, **s 2(5)** states that a representation is regarded as having been made if it is submitted to any system or device designed to receive, convey, or respond to

---

[1] Apply the law to the facts from the outset.

[2] Do not dwell too long on matters that are for the jury to decide, such as dishonesty—just explain the new test.

[3] This aspect of the common law has now been entrenched into the new Act.

communications (with or without human intervention). The fact that a human being is not deceived is irrelevant.

Andrew then drives off without paying.[4] He may be guilty of an offence under **s 2** of the **Fraud Act 2006**. By agreeing to pay, he has made a representation which he knows to be false. **Section 11** states that a person is guilty of an offence if he obtains services dishonestly, knowing that the service is made available on the basis that payment is required, and with an intention either not to pay or to pay in full. He may also be guilty of **s 3** of the **Theft Act 1978**, which refers to making off without payment. This section applies where a person, knowing that payment on the spot (for goods supplied or services done) is required or expected, dishonestly makes off without paying. The fact that he knows he has insufficient credit probably indicates that he does not intend to pay and has no intention of paying.[5]

Andrew may also have committed theft under **s 1** of the **Theft Act 1968**. He may argue that he has not appropriated property 'belonging to another', but the principle in *Turner (No 2)* **[1971] 55 Cr App R 336** will mean that he may be regarded as having done so. **Section 5** states:

property shall be regarded as belonging to any person having possession or control of it, or having any proprietary interest.

In that case, the defendant was convicted of the theft of his car because at the time he drove it away, the garage had lawful control of it and had a proprietary interest in it (the debt owed by the owner to the garage). When Andrew drives his van away, he is doing something similar.

The *mens rea* of the fraud offences and of the theft offence must now be dealt with. Is Andrew dishonest? The *Ivey* test will apply and ordinary and reasonable people are likely to believe Andrew to be dishonest.[6]

With regard to theft, the prosecution must further prove that Andrew intended to permanently deprive.

With regard to the money left for the window cleaner, Andrew may be found guilty of theft contrary to **s 1** of the **Theft Act 1968**. There is a dishonest appropriation of property belonging to another with an intent to permanently deprive. Andrew may try to argue that the property does not belong to another as he has the money in his possession within the meaning of **s 5(1)**. According to **s 5(3)** of the **Theft Act 1968**, he will be regarded as having taken property belonging to another if he has a legal obligation to retain this money and deal with it in a particular way.[7]

There may also be a fraud by abuse of position contrary to **s 4 of the Fraud Act 2006** or fraud by misrepresentation contrary to **s 2 of**

---

[4] In this situation, there are several offences you could choose from. The best thing to do is to work through the technical requirements of each.

[5] Don't forget to apply the law to the facts.

[6] As the second part of the *Ghosh* test is obsolete, you no longer have to ask whether Andrew thought that he was being dishonest according to the standards of reasonable people. His state of mind, though, is not completely irrelevant—it should be taken into account by the jury in deciding, objectively, whether he is dishonest according to the standards of ordinary people.

[7] This must be a legal obligation.

the **Fraud Act 2006**—when he uses the money to pay for his lunch, he represents that the money belongs to him.

Vince may be guilty of blackmail contrary to **s 21** of the **Theft Act 1968**. There needs to be a 'demand', which there clearly is here. A reasonable person would realize that a demand is being made (*R v Collister and Warhurst* (1955) 39 Cr App R 100). There is also clearly a 'menace' here. On the basis of *R v Clear* [1968] QB 670, the threat is such as would influence the mind of an ordinary person of normal stability and courage so as to make them accede unwillingly to the demand. Vince's threat is made with a view to gain. Although Vince's motives are to impress Martina, he intends to gain £10,000 to give to her. Under **s 34(2)(a)(i)**, gain and loss are to be construed as extending only to a gain or loss in money.

The prosecution would also have to prove that the demand was unwarranted. A demand with menaces is made in the belief that there are reasonable grounds for making the demand and that the use of the menaces is a proper means of reinforcing the demand. These con-ditions would seem to be satisfied here, as Vince believes that Martina is at an unfair advantage.

LOOKING FOR EXTRA MARKS?

- You may find that in questions on property offences, issues such as dishonesty are repeated several times. There is nothing wrong with 'referring above', *within the context of the same question*. This should enable you to get to grips with trickier areas.

- There can be considerable overlap in the individual fraud offences as the general offence of fraud is drafted widely, so you should consider all possibilities.

QUESTION | 5

Susan owns and runs a convenience store. May opens up a rival business in the same shopping precinct. Susan enters May's shop and, for fun, swaps price labels on two boxes of chocolates so that a £10 box is now priced at £2, and a £2 box is now priced at £10.

Stephen enters May's shop and, unaware of Susan's actions, selects the box of chocolates now (wrongly) priced at £2, knowing full well that it should be priced at £10. Stephen takes the box of chocolates to the counter and buys it for £2. The cashier, Gavin, does not realize that the item is wrongly priced.

Natasha goes to the delicatessen counter in May's shop and asks Joanne, the assistant, for six spicy sausages. The sausages cost 50p each. Joanne selects eight spicy sausages by mistake and wraps them up for Natasha. Joanne writes on the bag that it contains six sausages. Aware of Joanne's mistake, Natasha takes the bag to the counter where Gavin, unaware that the bag contains eight, not six, sausages, charges her £3.

Advise the Crown Prosecution Service of any criminal liability arising from these facts.

CAUTION!

- Make sure you do not fall into the trap of assuming that a defendant must have committed an offence. You should be prepared to advise that the prosecution may not, in some situations, be able to establish criminal liability for some incidents, especially where dishonesty is an issue.

- In this question, the facts involving each defendant are quite similar. Consequently, you will need to work through the elements of each offence of theft and fraud systematically.

DIAGRAM ANSWER PLAN

Identify the issues	■ Consider theft, fraud, burglary, and making off without payment.
Relevant law	■ Discuss **s 1** of the **Theft Act 1968**, especially appropriation and the dishonesty 'defences'; dishonesty in *Ivey v Genting Casinos*. ■ Discuss **ss 1, 2,** and **3** of the **Fraud Act 2006**. ■ Discuss **s 9(1)(a)** and **(b)** of the **Theft Act 1968**. ■ Discuss **s 3** of the **Theft Act 1978**.
Apply the law	■ Consider whether appropriation has taken place (switching labels) and whether there is dishonesty using the *Ivey* test. ■ Can fraud be said to have been committed given the gain/loss rule? ■ Consider the effect of *R v Hinks*.
Conclude	■ There is theft and possible fraud given the above discussion; as well as making off without payment in **s 3** of the **Theft Act 1978**.

When Susan enters May's shop and swaps price labels on two boxes of chocolates so that a £10 box is now priced at £2, and a £2 box is now priced at £10, she may have committed the offence of theft contrary to **s 1(1)** of the **Theft Act 1968**. The two boxes of chocolates are clearly property (see **s 4(1)**), and can be regarded as belonging to another as against Susan—see **s 5(1)** of the 1968 Act. Swapping the price labels over would be regarded as an appropriation of property belonging to another. On the basis of **s 3(1)**, an appropriation is any assumption of the rights of the owner. In *R v Morris* [1983] 3 All ER 288, this was interpreted as any assumption of any right of the owner. Swapping labels is effectively an assumption of the owner's right.[1] The live issue is dishonesty.[2] As this was a practical joke, it is unlikely that Susan can 'escape' liability under **s 2(1)(a)–(c)** of the **1968 Act**. Therefore, the issue of dishonesty will be a question of fact for the jury following the new test in *Ivey*:

- The court must determine the defendant's actual state of mind.
- The court asks whether, by the standards of ordinary people the behaviour of the defendant should be regarded as dishonest.
- There is no requirement that the defendant was aware that the defendant was dishonest according to the standards of ordinary people (the previous second limb of the *Ghosh* test).[3]

It is hard to tell how a jury might regard Susan's actions. As the value involved is small, and given that there is no direct personal gain for her, a jury might be reluctant to conclude that she was dishonest. This position should not change, even after *Ivey*.

In addition, Susan has no actual intention to permanently deprive. The issue is whether she can be deemed to have had this intent by virtue of **s 6(1)** of the **Theft Act 1968**.[4] Is it a situation where it was her intention to treat the property as her own to dispose of regardless of the other's rights? It could be argued that switching labels is evidence of her treating it as her own to dispose of, as she is creating the risk that someone might buy the goods at an undervalue.

There are two other possible offences to consider. The first is fraud by false representation contrary to **s 2** of the **Fraud Act 2006**. The offence requires proof that Susan dishonestly made a false representation, and intended by that representation to make a gain for herself or another,[5] or to cause loss to another or to expose another to a risk of loss. Switching price labels would constitute the false representation (**s 2(3)**). Susan is representing the selling price to be something other than the correct amount—this satisfies **s 2(2)**, which provides that a

Margin notes:

[1] Note here that the legal issue has been applied to the facts.

[2] In a criminal trial, several facts may be agreed. Facts which must still be argued are 'live' issues. Therefore, you can concentrate on these issues in a problem question, briefly mentioning the issues.

[3] When you have set this test out once, you do not need to repeat it later. You will use this test several times in an answer like this if there is more than one incident of the offence. Also, the different property offences have common elements.

[4] The point is that the court may regard her as having this intent, even if she does not have it on the face of it.

[5] Note that an actual gain need not be made.

representation is false if it is untrue or misleading. Obviously, the wrong price label is likely to mislead. As to *mens rea*, the prosecution will have to prove three elements: first, that Susan intended, by making the representation, to make a gain for herself or another, or intended to cause loss to another or to expose another to a risk of loss. The facts indicate that Susan swaps the price labels 'for fun'. Against this is the fact that she has a financial interest in May's business not doing well, and this may lead the jury to infer an intent to cause May loss. The second element of *mens rea* is that Susan must be shown to have known that the representation as to price was or might have been untrue or misleading. Her knowledge that the label indicated the wrong price is evident from the facts.

[6] Don't forget the dishonesty element in fraud. It isn't defined in the Act, so you need to use the reformulated common law test.

Third, it must be proved that Susan was dishonest.[6] Again, the jury would be asked to consider her actions in the light of a judicial direction under *Ivey*, as explained above.

If she had the intention to swap labels before entering the store, and if this could be equated with an intention to steal, she might be charged with burglary contrary to **s 9(1)(a)** of the **Theft Act 1968**. By entering intending to switch labels, even as a joke, she would be trespassing as per *R v Jones and Smith* **[1976] 3 All ER 54**.[7] Similarly, if she does commit theft in swapping labels, she could be guilty of burglary under **s 9(1)(b)** of the **1968 Act**.

[7] Trespass is a wide concept, and includes permission to enter.

At the time Stephen selects the box of chocolates, it is property belonging to another—see **ss 4(1)** and **5(1)** of the **Theft Act 1968**. Does he commit an offence of fraud by false representation contrary to **s 2** of the **Fraud Act 2006** when he offers to buy the chocolates for £2? The prosecution will argue that he is presenting himself as an honest shopper who believes £2 to be the correct price, and perhaps rely on **s 2(3)** of the **2006 Act**, which provides that a representation can include a representation as to the state of mind of the person making the representation. Even if this was the case, *mens rea* would have to be established and a jury might not regard his attempt to buy the chocolates at less than the normal selling price to be dishonest using the reasonable standards test under *Ivey*.

Section 3 of the **Fraud Act 2006** creates the offence of fraud by failing to disclose information. Liability would arise if it could be shown that Stephen dishonestly failed to disclose information that he was under a legal duty to disclose, and that he intended to make a gain for himself thereby. Stephen knew that the chocolates were mispriced, but he may not be under a specific legal duty to disclose this fact.[8]

[8] This would have to be a legal duty by contract or similar.

Turning to his possible liability for theft, did he appropriate the chocolates when he selected the box? As explained earlier, any assumption of the rights of the owner will suffice. Further, appropriation can be conduct to which the owner consents—see *Lawrence v*

Metropolitan Police Commissioner [1970] 3 All ER 933 and *R v Gomez* [1993] 1 All ER 1. The *actus reus* of theft is therefore made out when Stephen selects the chocolates. Was he dishonest? Stephen will rely on **s 2(1)(a)** of the **1968 Act**, contending that he appropriated the property in the belief that he had, in law, the right to deprive the store of it. Again, if the **s 2(1)(a)** argument does not succeed, the jury might not consider his actions as objectively dishonest.[9] The prosecution might seek to rely on the House of Lords' decision in *R v Hinks* [2000] 4 All ER 833, in which a majority of their Lordships held that a defendant could commit theft even where he acquired a valid title to property under a valid *inter vivos* transfer.[10] In other words, a defendant can steal property whilst becoming the owner of it. On this basis it could be argued that, notwithstanding that Stephen becomes the owner of the chocolates when he buys them, he nevertheless appropriates property belonging to another.

If fraud and theft charges fail, the prosecution might fall back on a charge of making off without payment, contrary to **s 3** of the **Theft Act 1978**. The offence requires proof that Stephen dishonestly made off without having paid as required or expected, that he knew payment was expected from him, and that he had intent to avoid payment of the amount due. The obvious problem is that he will argue that he did pay as required and expected—he paid the amount requested by the cashier.[11]

Does Natasha steal the sausages when she first takes possession of them? The sausages are property—see **s 4(1)**. Does property pass to her at the deli counter? Possibly not, as she has not yet paid—hence she appropriates by taking them. Does she have *mens rea* at this point? She may not be objectively dishonest, believing that it is her good luck that she has been given the extra sausages and that she has the legal right to keep them (see **s 2(1)(a)**). Would a reasonable person think this was dishonest in these circumstances? She does intend to permanently deprive. If property in the sausages does pass to Natasha at the deli counter, notwithstanding that she has not paid, **s 5(4)** of the **Theft Act 1968** (property got by mistake) cannot operate to prevent property passing here, as she is not under any legal obligation to make restoration of the sausages. Section 5(4) does not create the legal obligation to make restoration; it applies if there is, in civil law, a legal obligation to make restoration.[12]

Natasha may have committed a fraud offence at the checkout. She knows the bag is wrongly labelled, but says nothing. The prosecution may argue that her conduct amounted to an implied representation that she believed the bag to be correctly marked-up—see *DPP v Ray* [1974] AC 370 (an authority on the pre-**Fraud Act 2006** law, but still

[9] At times, you will need to consider both these tests, if the outcome is not clear.

[10] Set out the *ratio* of the case, then explain what it means in practical terms.

[11] Conclude by applying the law to the facts.

[12] There is no need to go into detail here, as it does not apply.

persuasive on this point). If her conduct can amount to a representation, it is clearly untrue or misleading. As the **s 2** offence does not require anything more by way of *actus reus*, liability would therefore hinge upon proof of *mens rea*. Natasha knows the price on the bag is too low—hence the jury would have to determine whether or not her actions were dishonest following a direction in accordance with *Ivey v Genting Casinos*. Some jurors might be minded to think that the mistake by the assistant is Natasha's good luck and that she ought to be allowed to benefit by it, especially as she did not induce it.

As with Stephen's liability, considered earlier, it is hard to see how there could be liability under **s 3 of the Fraud Act 2006** (fraud by failing to disclose information), the issue again being the absence of any legal (as opposed to moral) duty[13] on the part of Natasha to point out the shop assistant's error.

[13] This is an important distinction.

On a similar basis to Stephen, Natasha could be charged with making off without payment contrary to **s 3** of the **1978 Act**, and could also be charged with theft if *R v Hinks* was relied upon by the prosecution. In each of these offences, dishonesty might still prove the stumbling block for reasons outlined earlier.

LOOKING FOR EXTRA MARKS?

- One of the problems with theft and fraud offences is the overlap between them, and also the dividing line between civil and criminal law. A good discussion of *R v Hinks* in this question will add quality to your answer, as the point is not immediately obvious.

- An ability to focus on the 'live' issues for discussion will ensure that you stay relevant throughout the answer.

QUESTION | 6

Brian and Helen are neighbours. Brian agrees to keep an eye on Helen's house whilst she is away on holiday and she gives him a key to gain access. Whilst she is away, Brian goes into Helen's house to check that all is well. He thinks he might have a look around while he is there to see if there is anything worth taking. He helps himself to a £20 note he finds on the sideboard, as he had lent Helen £15 earlier that year and she had forgotten to pay him back. As he leaves, he notices that the milkman has left two pints of milk on the doorstep. Brian takes them home. That night, as he is lying in bed, Brian realizes that he may have forgotten to shut Helen's door properly, but decides not to worry about it until the following day. At 4 am, Charlie enters Helen's house through the unlocked front door and steals her DVD player. The next day Brian checks the house and notices

ⓟ

that the DVD player has gone. He does not report this to the police and leaves the house securely locked up. On her return, Helen calls on Brian before visiting her house. She gives him a £50 gift voucher, saying it is to make up for the money she owes him and to thank him for keeping her house safe. Brian says nothing about the DVD player or the £20 note. The next day, Charlie goes into a shop selling DVDs. As he wants some to play in his new DVD player, he puts several in his pocket. He is spotted by a security guard, Steve, and runs from the shop. On his way out, Steve confronts Charlie, who grabs his coat, forcing him to fall. Steve's wallet falls on the floor. Charlie takes £20 out of the wallet and runs out of the shop with the money and the DVDs.

Advise the Crown Prosecution Service as to the criminal liability of Brian and Charlie under the Theft Act 1968.

CAUTION!

- This question raises a number of different property offences, so ensure you deal with them separately, technically, and carefully.

- Remember not to jump to conclusions on issues such as trespass; this is a fluid concept.

DIAGRAM ANSWER PLAN

Identify the issues	■ Mention burglary, robbery, fraud, making off without payment.
Relevant law	■ Consider burglary contrary to **s 9(1)(a)** and **(b)** of the **Theft Act 1968**. ■ Consider fraud contrary to **s 3** of the **Fraud Act 2006**. ■ Discuss making off without payment contrary to **s 3** of the **Theft Act 1978**. ■ Consider robbery contrary to **s 8** of the **Theft Act 1968**.
Apply the law	■ Is Brian a trespasser given that he has permission to enter? ■ Discuss conditional intent and burglary. ■ Discuss robbery and force used in order to steal. ■ Consider *Hinks*/s 3 of the **Fraud Act 2006**.
Conclude	■ Charlie is guilty of robbery and burglary. ■ Brian is guilty of theft, fraud, and burglary.

This question raises issues of burglary, theft, and fraud. The first question is whether Brian has committed burglary when he enters the house. Burglary may be committed in two ways. Under **s 9(1)(a)**, a person is guilty of burglary if he enters any building or part of a building as a trespasser with intent to steal, inflict grievous bodily harm on any person therein, or commit criminal damage. Under **s 9(1)(b)**, a person is guilty of burglary if, having entered as a trespasser, he steals or inflicts grievous bodily harm on any person therein or attempts to commit any of these offences.[1] For burglary under **s 9(1)(a)**, the ulterior offences do not need to be committed, but there must be proof beyond any reasonable doubt of an intention to commit them. Under **s 9(1)(b)**, it must be proved that the defendant has committed one of the offences stated in the statute.

[1] It is a good idea to start with a definition of the offence. This gives you a ready-made structure.

The first element to prove is entry. Brian has entered the property with a key. The question is whether he can be considered to be a trespasser, even though he has Helen's permission to enter. In **R v Jones and Smith [1976] 3 All ER 54**, the court found that the defendants had entered as trespassers despite their previous permission, as they had entered for purposes beyond the scope of the consent given. Here, Brian will argue that he did not intend to steal when he entered, and that he could not be a trespasser because Helen had given him permission to enter. The prosecution will argue that if he enters in order to steal, he enters for a purpose in excess of his express or implied permission. Brian may further argue that a conditional intent to steal is insufficient for theft (**R v Easom [1971] 2 All ER 945**).[2] In the context of theft, a conditional intent is not sufficient. In that case, the defendant's conviction for stealing from a lady's handbag was quashed when there was nothing to steal. For the purposes of burglary, however, a conditional intent suffices, as the law recognizes the fact that most burglars do not intend to steal something specific.

[2] Note the different application of the rule for theft and for burglary.

We can probably assume that he does not have an intention to steal before he enters the property (he may have been simply checking on the property, as he was asked to do), but he takes the opportunity to take the property once he is inside. Therefore, if a charge of burglary is appropriate because trespass can be proven, it will be the second type of **s 9(1)(b)** burglary. There is also an intention to trespass in these circumstances.[3]

[3] Note that the *mens rea* for these offences is twofold—the intention (or recklessness) to commit the offence; and an intention to commit the ulterior offence.

If he has entered as a trespasser, then the next point to deal with is whether an ulterior offence has been committed for the purposes of **s 9(1)(b)**. He takes £20. Theft is the dishonest appropriation of property belonging to another with the intention to permanently deprive the owner of it (**s 1** of the **Theft Act 1968**). By removing the money from the sideboard, he has assumed one of Helen's rights (**s 3(1)**);

the money is property (**s 4(1)**) and it belongs to Helen (**s 5(1)**). The live issue here is dishonesty. The facts here suggest that Brian will argue that he was entitled to take the money. Dishonesty is not defined under the **Theft Act 1968** but **s 2(1)** sets out that a defendant is not to be regarded as being dishonest if the act was committed with any of the following beliefs: (i) a belief in a legal right to the property; (ii) a belief that the owner would consent; and (iii) a belief that the owner could not be traced by taking reasonable steps. In any of these situations, it is the defendant's personal belief which counts, even if this is unreasonable.[4] Does Brian genuinely believe that he has a legal right to the property? There is a debt here, but whether this argument works will depend on the jury. It might be reasonable to ask why Brian did not simply ask Helen for the money, as they were neighbours! The **s 2** argument may be more persuasive with regard to the milk. He may wish to argue that if Helen had realized that she had forgotten to cancel the milk, she may have given Brian permission to take it. It will have gone off by the time she gets home, so will be of no further use to her. He has appropriated it, it is property, and it belongs to another.[5]

When Helen returns, he accepts the £50 voucher from Helen. Two potential issues arise here. First, the prosecution might seek to rely on the House of Lords' decision in *R v Hinks* [2000] 4 All ER 833, in which a majority of their Lordships held that a defendant could commit theft even where he acquired a valid title to property under a valid *inter vivos* transfer.[6] In other words, a defendant can steal property whilst becoming the owner of it. The next question is whether he was dishonest in accepting the gift of the £50 voucher. The jury may well conclude that he is according to ordinary standards.

Second, he may have committed fraud by failing to disclose. **Section 3** of the **Fraud Act 2006** creates the offence of fraud by failing to disclose information. Liability would arise if it could be shown that Brian dishonestly failed to disclose information that he was under a legal duty to disclose, and that he intended to make a gain for himself thereby. The question is whether any legal duty to disclose the information arises, rather than a moral duty. In addition, the prosecution must prove dishonesty. The **Fraud Act** does not provide a definition of dishonesty, but the court will be likely to follow the principles set out in *Ivey v Genting Casinos*, discussed earlier. Would most people consider failing to mention what has happened to be dishonest? As he chooses not to reveal what has happened, it seems clear that Brian was doing something that most people would disapprove of.

Charlie may be charged with burglary contrary to **s 9(1)(a)** of the **Theft Act 1968**. He has entered the building without permission—therefore he is a trespasser. Whilst in the building, he steals the DVD player. He commits theft, the ulterior offence, by appropriating

[4] Note that this is a subjective test.

[5] Don't forget to deal with all the elements of theft for each incident.

[6] Set out the *ratio* of the case, then explain what it means in practical terms.

property belonging to another with an intention to permanently deprive Helen of the player. Charlie may also be liable for **s 3** of the **Theft Act 1978**. The offence requires proof that Charlie dishonestly made off without having paid as required or expected, that he knew payment was expected of him, and that he had intent to avoid payment of the amount due.

The elements of theft and burglary are made out in relation to the DVDs in the shop. As no force is used at this point, a charge of robbery is not appropriate. With regard to the money taken from Steve, however, a robbery charge may be appropriate. The last charge is robbery contrary to **s 8** of the **Theft Act 1968**. Robbery is defined as follows:

> A person commits robbery if he steals, and immediately before or at the time of doing so, he uses force on any person or puts or seeks to put any person in fear of force.

Theft is therefore an essential element of robbery, and the element of timing is crucial. The next element to consider is whether force was used and whether it was used in order to steal. The force need not be directed at a person, but can be directed to clothing. As Charlie grabbed Steve by the coat, there is evidence of his using force on Steve prior to stealing. The offence of robbery may be made out.

LOOKING FOR EXTRA MARKS?

- The issue of making off without payment will be spotted by stronger students and is an alternative.
- Dishonesty is not defined in the **Fraud Act 2006**, so the *Ivey* test will need to be applied carefully.

QUESTION | 7

To what extent has the Fraud Act 2006 improved the law?

CAUTION!

- Be careful that you do not stray into explanations which are overly descriptive. By all means explain the effect of the old and the new law, but keep this brief and concentrate on the flaws and criticisms.
- As there is still relatively little case law on this area, you will have to be specific on the statutory provisions.

DIAGRAM ANSWER PLAN

Explain the introduction of the **Fraud Act 2006** and its key provisions.

▼

Explain the previous law.

▼

Discuss causation and deception.

▼

Discuss dishonesty.

▼

Discuss overlap.

▼

Consider the width of the provisions, especially abuse of position and a failure to disclose.

▼

Conclude—despite the criticisms, the Act has simplified and consolidated the law.

A **SUGGESTED ANSWER**

The **Fraud Act 2006** was designed to replace many of the discrepancies and inconsistencies in the previous law of deception. These were spread over diverse provisions in the **Theft Acts 1968** and **1978**, and often related to very specific circumstances. Often, there was overlap with other property offences. The Act abolishes the deception offences in the **Theft Acts 1968** and **1978**.

[1] In discussing any piece of legislation, it is a good idea to think about the rationale for it.

Apart from the piecemeal nature of the previous law, there was a feeling that the existing legislation was not adequate to cope with increasingly complicated commercial fraud cases, or the internet age.[1] One of the problems surrounding this type of offence was the length, cost, and complexity of fraud trials. It might be argued that juries lack the specialist knowledge to deal with this type of complexity. Herring (2016) notes that:

there are special difficulties for jurors who have the task of determining the boundary between the hard nosed business person, the exciting entrepreneur and the dishonest criminal.

The problems of the previous law referred to above were well known, and acknowledged by Griew (1985) in his seminal work, *The Law of Theft*:

No one wanting to construct a rational, efficient law of criminal fraud would choose to start from the present position. The law ... is in a very untidy and unsatisfactory condition. The various offences are not so framed and related to each other as to cover, in a clearly organised way and without doubt or strained interpretation, the range of conduct with which the law should be able to deal.

A more modern law of fraud was needed in order to cope with these complexities and to bring the law up to date. Furthermore, the aim was to substantially simplify the law of fraud, thereby assisting juries in assessing guilt.

[2] Always set out what you are trying to achieve in the essay.

This essay briefly outlines the changes brought about by the Act, and identify some of the key criticisms of it, before drawing a conclusion in order to answer the question set.[2]

The **Fraud Act 2006** was designed to replace the complexities in the previous law of deception and creates an overarching offence of fraud. The Act received Royal Assent on 8 November 2006. It was based mainly on the recommendations in the Law Commission's *Report on Fraud* (Cm 5560) in 2002 and a Home Office consultation in May 2004 entitled *Fraud Law Reform*. It is worth noting that the Fraud Bill was remarkably well received in Parliament. For example, on the Second Reading in the House of Lords, Lord Lloyd of Berwick (*Official Report, House of Lords*, 22 June 2005; vol 672, col 1664) said:

My Lords, it seems to me that this is one of the best Bills to have come out of the Home Office for many a long year.

It had an ambitious remit:

The Fraud Bill is a small Bill [16 sections and three Schedules] but it is intended to do a big job. It aims to deliver an effective legal structure for tackling the growing threat posed by fraud. Fraud affects us all. It causes long-term damage to UK businesses, wrecks ordinary lives by destroying jobs, savings and pensions, and hits the pockets of every citizen of this country. An effective framework for tackling fraud is therefore crucial to citizens as well as to the economy. The Government's strategy is threefold:

- first, to modernise the law;
- secondly, to improve the investigation of fraud; and
- thirdly, to ensure that the prosecution and court procedures are efficient and effective.

[3] Now set out a brief summary of the law.

Section 1 creates a general offence of fraud; **s 2** creates an offence of fraud by false representation; **s 3** creates an offence of fraud by a failure to disclose; and **s 4** creates an offence of fraud by abuse of a financial position.[3] **Section 11** of the **Fraud Act 2006** creates an offence of obtaining services dishonestly. **Section 2** in particular would include, for example, the offence of 'phishing', in which claims are made on the internet, but it will also include the inclusion of false information on a mortgage or insurance premium application form, for example. The offence is triable either way, with the penalties on summary conviction reflecting the new sentencing regime (including imprisonment for a term not exceeding twelve months) or following conviction on indictment, to imprisonment for a term not exceeding ten years and/or a fine.

The sections have various points in common. The *mens rea* of the Act requires, first, that the defendant is dishonest. This is not defined in the Act and the common law test for dishonesty in *R v Ghosh* was adopted. There is some debate over whether the new test in *Ivey* will be adopted wholesale for fraud offences—the contention being that Parliament, having approved *Ghosh* implicitly, should really approve or put into legislative form any substantial change in the law. Second, it is necessary that the defendant has a 'view' to gain or to cause a loss to another. In addition, there must be an intent to falsely represent, to fail to disclose, or to abuse a financial position. These definitions, of themselves, provide a sharp contrast to the previous legislation on deception, where actual loss to the victim needed to be proved. There is no need to prove a causal link between the false representation and any loss caused to the victim. This simplifies matters for the prosecution and creates a more general offence. This made it difficult to prosecute anyone who 'deceived' a machine, for example. The Law Commission noted in 'Fraud' No 276 (2002):

a machine has no mind, so it cannot believe a proposition to be true or false, and therefore cannot be deceived. A person who dishonestly obtains a benefit by giving false information to a computer or machine is not guilty of any deception offence.

[4] In this essay, you can identify some of the things which have worked with the new Act, before moving on to the criticisms.

On this, undoubtedly the **Fraud Act 2006** has made the prosecution's job easier.[4]

On the other hand, a significant criticism of the Act is its width. David Ormerod (2007) argues that the offence of fraud does nothing more than to criminalize lying and is no more than an inchoate offence. He argues that **s 2** of the Act is overly broad, requiring as it does that the defendant makes a false representation. Ormerod states:

[5] By including some of the recognized critics of the Act, you are showing the examiner that you have not only studied the law, but that you have read around the topic.

[S]hould lying be a sufficient basis for criminal liability? What is the wrong which the defendant performs which warrants the criminal sanction?[5]

Ormerod further argues that the breadth of the Act means that there is no distinction between the fraudster who causes millions of pounds' worth of loss and the fraudster who does not. It is difficult to deal with sentencing of the offence if there is no distinction in terms of loss caused.

This uncertainty applies to the **s 2** offence of fraud by false representation, but also to fraud by a failure to disclose or fraud by an abuse of position. In the case of the former, the offence was said to be necessary to cater for a situation in which the victim may be ignorant of a loss, or where, according to the previous law, the effect of the deception would have had to be proven.

A further argument that the law is drafted too widely is acknowledged by Jennifer Collins (2011). Whilst Herring (2016) argues that the offence is potentially very wide (it can include, for example, employees making an unlawful profit from their position), Collins argues that because there is a moral reason for including it (avoiding disloyalty) and its inclusion is justified:

disloyalty is criminalised because it has a corrosive effect on an important basic value held by society … the importance of trust relationships.

The Law Commission in 'Fraud' No 276 (2002) made it clear that:

6 This definition was not translated into the Act itself, possibly leading to a lack of clarity.

The necessary relationship will be present between trustee and beneficiary, director and company, professional person and client, agent and principal, employee and employer, or between partners. It may arise otherwise, for example within a family, or in the context of voluntary work, or in any context where the parties are not at arm's length.[6]

This has now been confirmed in case law. In *R v Gale* **[2008] EWCA Crim 1344**, an office manager for DHL was convicted of this offence when he signed documentation stating that he could vouch for the contents of the cargo. In fact, this contained an illegal substance in the United States (khat). The court said that the defendant was in a position of trust as he could be exploited by those wanting to commit criminal offences. Similarly, in *R v Woods* **[2011] EWCA Crim 1305**, a deputy manager of a betting shop changed a customer's bet from £1 to £100, enabling her to collect £990 whilst giving the customer £10. It wasn't clear whether there was an abuse of position, but the court said that an employment situation was included. Ormerod (2007) holds that the range of defendants included in this offence is too wide.

Furthermore, the requirement for dishonesty is open to potential criticism. The definition of dishonesty can vary from defendant to defendant. The test has been criticized on the basis of its circularity; see Edward Griew (1985). A person who does not genuinely believe he is being dishonest according to ordinary standards, as opposed to his own value, is entitled to the defence. It is important to note that

7 A comparison to other property offences shows that you understand the law in context.

the **s 2** defences do not apply to the offence of fraud in the same way as they do to theft.[7] These criticisms may be addressed to some extent by the modifications following the decision in *Ivey v Genting Casinos*, which focuses on an objective standard for dishonesty, and will affect criminal cases.

In a similar way, the requirement for an intention to gain or cause loss is defined, broadly, in monetary terms. It also includes temporary deprivation, which neither theft nor the previous law of deception did.

Finally, it may be argued that there is substantial overlap in the different sections of the Act. A failure to disclose may also include a false representation or an abuse of position. It might be argued that this problem can be resolved with sensible prosecuting, but not all defendants will be confident to trust in this approach.

In conclusion, whilst the **Fraud Act 2006** has simplified the law and dealt with the piecemeal approach of the previous law of deception, it can be criticized on the basis of the width of its application, leading to uncertainty and possibly, therefore, unfairness.

LOOKING FOR EXTRA MARKS?

■ In a question like this, try to include some of the rationale behind the Act. Here, for example, we have included Law Commission Reports and Explanatory Notes to the Act.

■ A key concept in all of the property offences is dishonesty. This is largely defined at common law. It helps if you can explain and critique the problems this might create (such as overlap with existing offences or a circular definition).

TAKING THINGS FURTHER

■ Betts G, 'Robbery and the Principle of Fair Labelling' JCL 205.
Argues that given the breadth of the application of the offence, it should incorporate a minimum force threshold so that robberies of minor force can be reclassified as theft.

■ Collins J, 'Fraud by Abuse of Position: Theorising s 4 of the Fraud Act 2006' [2011] Crim LR 513–22.
Discusses the wide drafting of the section, arguing that the offence is 'undertheorized'. It explores the rationale for the offences, suggesting that it seeks to avoid exploitation and disloyalty and is akin to a fiduciary duty.

■ Dyson M and Jarvis P, 'Poison Ivey or Herbal Tea Leaf?' (2018) 134 LQR 198.
*Discusses the new test, arguing that Parliament has impliedly approved the **Ghosh** test by preferring its interpretation of dishonesty for use with the **Fraud Act 2006** and lamenting the loss of a clear mens rea element.*

■ Galli M, 'Oh My Ghosh: Supreme Court Redefines Test for Dishonesty in Ivey v Genting Casinos t/a Crockfords' (2018) 29(2) Ent LR 56.
Discusses the new test, arguing that it adds complication to a test which worked well despite its flaws.

■ Griew E, 'Dishonesty: The Objections to *Feely* and *Ghosh*' [1985] Crim LR 341.

Discusses the subjective and objective tests in the **Ghosh** *direction as to dishonesty and argues that the test leads to inconsistent verdicts and is difficult for juries to use.*

■ Herring J, *Criminal Law: Texts, Cases, and Materials* (8th edn, OUP 2016).

Texts, cases, and materials on criminal law.

■ Ormerod D, 'The Fraud Act 2006—Criminalising Lying?' [2007] Crim LR 193.

Provides an assessment of the **Fraud Act 2006** *and argues that its key concepts are drafted too widely.*

■ Shute S, 'Appropriation and the Law of Theft' [2002] Crim LR 445.

Provides an assessment of disagreements that **R v Hinks** *is the wrong decision in cases where the owner has consented to the appropriation.*

■ Simester A and Sullivan G R, 'The Nature and Rationale of Property Offences' in R A Duff and S Green (eds), *Defining Crimes* (OUP 2005).

A discussion of the rationale for the decision in **Gomez**.

■ Smith J C, '*R v Hinks*: A Case Commentary' [2001] Crim LR 162.

Criticizes the decision in **R v Hinks** *on the grounds that not even a civil right in property has been violated.*

■ Withey C, 'Comment—The Fraud Act 2006—Some Early Observations and Comparisons with the Former Law' (2007) 70 J Crim Law 220.

An assessment of whether the new provisions under the **Fraud Act 2006** *are an improvement on the previous law of deception.*

Online Resources   www.oup.com/uk/qanda/

For extra essay and problem questions on this topic, as well as advice on revision and exam technique, please visit the online resources.

7 Defences

ARE YOU READY?

In order to answer questions on this topic, you will need to understand the following:

- the test for insanity in the *M'Naghten* Rules 1843;
- the rules on automatism;
- the rules on voluntary and involuntary intoxication;
- duress, duress of circumstances, and necessity;
- public and private defence;
- consent as a defence;
- mistake.

KEY DEBATES

Debate: the 'defence' of necessity

Is there a defence of necessity in English law for the crime of murder? If a defendant is placed in an impossible situation, in which, for example, he must choose between killing or being killed, will the law show any sympathy? *Dudley and Stephens* [1884] would suggest not. However, in *Re A* [2000] the Court of Appeal agreed that the defence exists, albeit in very limited circumstances. Gardner has argued that to require a court to make an assessment of the lesser of two evils is an impossible task. Instead, one option is to frame the necessity of choice in terms of human rights (eg the right to life under **Article 2** of the **European Convention on Human Rights**).

Debate: intoxication as a defence

Strictly speaking, intoxication is not a defence, but a denial of *mens rea*. The courts have a balancing act to play, in that they need to perform a role of public protection as well as making sure that

⊙

no defendant is unfairly convicted. The law deals with this by distinguishing between the different types of *mens rea* (basic and specific intent). Virgo argues that this creates a type of 'rough justice' because defendants are convicted despite the fact that they do not have *mens rea* for the offence. Gardner disagrees, stating that advertence can count as a type of *mens rea* along with intention and, arguing along **Majewski** lines, that a defendant convicted in this way suffers no real injustice.

Ⓠ

QUESTION | 1

Gina took the tube to work. Whilst on the train, she started to feel dizzy. She noticed that one of the passengers, Bill, was staring at her. Gina shouted at Bill that if he did not stop staring, she would kick him in the head. Bill was quite frightened by this, and got up to move. As he did so, the train moved suddenly and he fell over, hitting his head on a metal pole. Gina got up from her seat in order to get off at the next station but was accidentally jostled by Stella. Gina pushed Stella over, causing bruising to Stella's arm. Gina then barged out of the train, thrusting people aside, including an old man, Tom. Bill received treatment from his doctor for concussion and depression as a result of this incident. Tom fell between the train and the platform and suffered two broken legs.

Advise the Crown Prosecution Service on Gina's criminal liability, including any defences she may have in the following alternative scenarios:

(a) **Gina is diabetic and took insulin before she left for work, but forgot to eat afterwards.**

(b) **It comes to light that Gina has stolen things from shops in the past when she has forgotten to eat after taking insulin.**

(c) **Gina had forgotten to take her insulin that morning.**

(d) **Gina is not diabetic but had been drinking heavily that morning.**

❗

CAUTION!

■ This topic is a good example of how criminal law is not easily separable into different topics, as every offence may give rise to a defence. Thus, you need to think about the effect of the defences on different crimes.

■ The difficulty with the mental defences is that there is some considerable overlap between the different categories. You should look carefully at the facts, as certain defences may be excluded due to the type of offence committed. Here, Gina has potentially committed non-fatal offences, therefore loss of control and diminished responsibility cannot be considered as they apply to murder only.

■ Check the rubric carefully, as you may not be asked to prove the substantive offence first.

DIAGRAM ANSWER PLAN

Identify the issues	▪ The legal issues are **s. 18, 20**, and **47** of the **Offences Against the Person Act 1861**. ▪ The defences are consent and self defence. ▪ Consider *mens rea* and intoxication.
Relevant law	▪ Discuss the *actus reus/mens rea* of the statutory offences, starting with the most serious. Define the offence first, then discuss the requirements of each. ‑ **R v Barnes** criteria. ‑ **Majewski** and specific/basic intent. ▪ Consider the duty to act.
Apply the law	▪ Discuss which defences apply, taking care to explain each requirement for them to apply. ▪ Does the intoxication matter? ▪ Conclude on the facts.
Conclude	▪ What is the effect of the defences discussed above? Consider the *Majewski* test.

SUGGESTED ANSWER

With regard to Bill, Gina may be guilty of common law assault or battery or of an offence under the **Offences Against the Person Act 1861**. She has committed an assault towards Bill. A common law assault can be committed contrary to **s 39 of the Criminal Justice Act 1988**. The *actus reus* of this offence requires that the defendant causes the victim to apprehend unlawful physical violence, and the *mens rea* that s/he intended or was reckless as to whether the victim apprehended the violence[1] (*Collins v Wilcock* **[1984] 3 All ER 374**). It is well established that words can be an assault, and Bill suffers depression as a result of this incident. Where an assault occasions actual bodily harm, the charge may be raised to **s 47** of the **Offences Against the Person Act 1861**. The assault requirement has been made out. As Bill is receiving medical treatment for the depression, this will be recognized as actual bodily harm, which requires an interference with the defendant's health or comfort: *R v Miller* **[1954] 2 QB 282**.

[1] The *mens rea* of this offence can be difficult to establish, but the courts tend to look at the reaction of the victim, and give this more weight.

[2] It must be medically recognizable to be counted as actual bodily harm.

Actual bodily harm can include psychiatric harm such as depression, as long as this is medically treatable. Mere emotions such as fear, distress, and panic do not fall into this category, but as Bill is receiving treatment for his concussion and his depressed state, the court is likely to find that he has suffered actual bodily harm.[2] The *mens rea* of this offence requires the *mens rea* of the initial assault. The prosecution need only show that the initial assault or battery caused the actual bodily harm.

Stella's bruising is likely to fall into the same category. Gina may argue that she has not caused this directly. **Section 47** of the **Offences Against the Person Act 1861** requires an assault or battery occasioning actual bodily harm. A battery is defined as an unlawful infliction of violence. The 'violence' can be direct or indirect. In *R v Martin* [1881] 1 QBD 54, the defendant was guilty of an unlawful and malicious infliction of harm when he barred the exits to a theatre, turned out the lights, and caused members of the public to panic and injure themselves. Gina pushes Stella, so there is an intentional (or at least reckless) infliction of harm. The fact that Stella falls and bruises her arm may prompt Gina to argue that she did not anticipate the resulting harm, but proof of this is not needed.[3]

[3] The *mens rea* of this offence is quite subtle. The prosecution does not have to prove that the outcome was foreseen by the defendant, just that the defendant is intentional or reckless as to the initial assault or battery.

With regard to Tom, Gina may have committed an offence either under **s 20** or **s 18** of the **Offences Against the Person Act 1861**. The first requires proof of either wounding or grievous bodily harm. There is no break in the skin, but broken legs amount to grievous bodily harm. This is a 'really serious injury' (*DPP v Smith* [1960] 3 All ER 161), particularly in light of Tom's age. The *mens rea* of **s 20** is intention or recklessness as to some degree of physical harm (*R v Mowatt* [1968] 1 QB 421). Gina acts recklessly here by barging him out of the way, with no regard to Tom. As proof of intention is required for **s 18**, this charge is unlikely to succeed.

(a) The fact that she is diabetic and has forgotten to eat after taking her insulin enables her to plead automatism. The courts divide this concept into non-insane automatism (which, when successful, is a valid defence) and insane automatism (which is not). This is due to the close relationship between insanity and automatism.[4] Automatism was defined by Lord Denning in *Bratty v Attorney-General for Northern Ireland* [1963] AC 386 as:

[4] In other words, a plea of automatism can result in a verdict of not guilty by reason of insanity. This may not be what the defendant is trying to achieve.

an act which is done by the muscles without any control by the mind such as a spasm, a reflex or a convulsion, or an act done by a person who is not conscious of what he is doing such as an act done whilst suffering from concussion or sleep walking.

For automatism to succeed, the court must accept that there is a total loss of control. In addition, the state of automatism must be caused by an external factor, and not an inherent state. When the condition is caused by an inherent condition, the courts will invoke the common law defence of insanity. The approach of the courts has not always been consistent, and this is especially true in diabetes cases. In *R v Quick* [1973] 1 QB 910, the defendant's conviction for assault occasioning actual bodily harm was overturned (and automatism accepted) when proof of a hypoglycaemic state (caused by taking insulin but failing to eat) at the time of the attack was accepted by the Court of Appeal. Lawton LJ observed that the defendant's mental capacity was not caused by the diabetes itself, but by the combination of the injection and the lack of food. In contrast, in *R v Hennessy* [1989] 1 WLR 297, the defence was not accepted, as the condition was caused by the disease itself (a failure to inject insulin, causing a hyperglycaemic state).

(b) Gina should be able to benefit from the defence of automatism. However, Gina has previously experienced similar incidents after failing to eat after her insulin shot. In *R v Bailey* [1983] 2 All ER 503, the court ruled that the defence would not be available in cases where the state of automatism could be regarded as 'self-induced' or where the defendant was at fault in becoming, say, hypoglycaemic.[5] The test here would be whether Gina was aware of the consequences of not eating after her shot. If she was reckless in taking the insulin and in not eating, this will provide the *mens rea* for offences she may commit whilst in that state. Gina may argue that she could not have foreseen that she might become violent. If the prosecution is successful in establishing this *mens rea*, then she will be guilty of the offence charged.

(c) On the basis of *R v Hennessy* [1989] 1 WLR 297, discussed in (a) above, the defence of automatism would not be available to Gina on these facts. The hyperglycaemia will be regarded as having been caused by an internal factor—here an inherent condition (the diabetes). If that disease causes a malfunction of the mind that manifests itself in violence, the courts will permit Gina to advance the defence of insanity. Under the *M'Naghten* Rules 1843 (*M'Naghten's Case* (1843) 10 C & F 200), everyone is presumed sane until the contrary is proved. However, it is a defence for the accused to show that he was labouring under such defect of reason due to disease of the mind as either not to know the nature and quality of his act or, if he did know this, not to know that what he was doing was wrong. The verdict will be not guilty by reason of insanity. The ambit of this offence was considered in the recent case of *Loake v CPS* [2017] EWHC 2855. The defendant, L, was convicted of an offence contrary to s 2(1) of the **Protection from Harassment Act 1997** on

[5] Effectively, this is a form of recklessness.

the basis that she had sent a large quantity of text messages to her estranged husband. She wished to use the defence of insanity, but the prosecution argued that the defence could only be used for an offence requiring proof of *mens rea*. As the offence in question could be proved objectively, insanity was not available. The defence argued that the *M'Naghten* Rules were not just applicable to the *mens rea* elements of the offence, but also to *actus reus*. The court agreed with the prosecution that insanity was not available in this instance. The High Court allowed the appeal:

At the heart of the rationale for the insanity defence is the principle that criminal punishment should only be imposed upon those who are responsible for their conduct … the defence of insanity operates so as to give effect to this principle, firstly by relieving the defendant of responsibility in cases where he did not know the nature and quality of his act. In modern terms, this simply means that the defendant literally 'did not know what he was doing'.

(d) The fact that Gina is intoxicated before she commits these offences allows her to argue that she did not, in fact, have the *mens rea* for them. This is a common law 'defence'. It is necessary to distinguish between crimes of specific intent and crimes of basic intent for this purpose. A further distinction is drawn between voluntary and involuntary intoxication. Crimes of specific intent may benefit from the defence; crimes of basic intent may not (*DPP v Majewski* [1977] **AC 443**). Put simply, crimes of basic intent are those for which recklessness may suffice for proof of the *mens rea*; those with basic intent are those for which actual intention is required (eg murder). The rationale expressed by the House of Lords in *Majewski* for denying the offence of intoxication in basic intent offences was that the drunkenness itself supplies the evidence of *mens rea*, since it is a reckless course of conduct. As the offences against the person of which Gina appears to be guilty are crimes of basic intent, intoxication will not afford a defence.

➕ LOOKING FOR EXTRA MARKS?

- The interplay between automatism and intoxication could be important here.
- A proper explanation of the rationale of *DPP v Majewski* will help to give your answer sufficient depth.
- Knowledge of debates in the area—such as the controversy over the issue of diabetes—will boost your mark.

If the defence of necessity is to form a valid and consistent part of our criminal law it must, as has been universally recognized, be strictly controlled and scrupulously limited to situations that correspond to its underlying rationale.

Discuss this statement with regard to duress and duress of circumstances, and necessity.

CAUTION!

- In addition to identifying the three defences and addressing any problems therein, it is important to address the rationale referred to in the question. To what extent are these defences 'controlled' or limited? Are these controls logical, given the expressed reasons for limiting the defences?
- Do not just describe everything you know about the defences—link to the question.

DIAGRAM ANSWER PLAN

Consider the three defences: duress, necessity, and duress of circumstances.

▼

Look at duress and the return to the objective test.

▼

Consider duress of circumstances.

▼

Discuss the limitations on the defences.

▼

Do the defences live up to their original rationale?

▼

Provide a conclusion-linking to the question set. Are the limitations on the defence(s) justified by their rationale?

SUGGESTED ANSWER

[1] Set out early on what you intend to achieve in the essay. You should address the question here specifically.

The three defences will be considered in turn, before their effectiveness is assessed according to their rationale.[1]

An accused may plead the defence of necessity where he has acted in an unlawful and criminal way to avoid a greater danger than that created by his unlawful conduct.

It has been doubted whether any defence of necessity is recognized in English criminal law and *R v Dudley and Stephens* [1881–85] **All ER Rep 61** is often cited in this context. This case was atypical in that it dealt with murder. For many years, the development of the defence of necessity (duress of circumstances) was hindered by the decision, in which two shipwrecked seamen killed and ate a cabin boy in order to survive. The court ruled that necessity could be no defence to murder and the accused were found guilty, and many commentators believed that the case was authority for the principle that necessity was not available as a general defence to other charges. It was thought that giving the defence a greater scope would 'open the floodgates' to spurious claims and that the difficulty in deciding whose life or property should be sacrificed outweighed the desirability of having the defence.

The point is further illustrated by *Southwark London Borough Council v Williams* [1971] **2 All ER 75**, in which Lord Denning said:

if hunger were once allowed to be a defence for stealing, it would open the way through which all kinds of disorder and lawlessness would pass.

[2] This case seems to widen the defence.	In *Re A (Conjoined Twins: Surgical Separation)* [2000] **4 All ER 961**, not only did the Court of Appeal agree that a defence of necessity exists, but two of the judgments thought that it could be used for murder, albeit in very limited circumstances.[2]

The Court of Appeal in *Re A* permitted a separation operation, recognizing the intentional nature of the killing of the weaker twin, and that it was necessary in order to save the life of the stronger twin. This was the case as otherwise it was inevitable that both would die. Lord Brooke gave several other examples: a parachutist may be justified in kicking away a victim clinging to his legs whose parachute has failed to open if both would die when they fall; a man may be justified in pulling a victim frozen with fear from an escape ladder in a capsized ship so that others may be led to safety. In these circumstances, an 'evil' is committed so that others' lives may be saved. Necessity may be characterized as a 'choice between evils'. The defendant is making a decision that one course of action is preferable to another. In *F v West Berkshire Health Authority* [1989] **2 All ER 545**, the action taken against the victim was considered to be in the victim's best interests and this formed a prominent part of the argument for the defence of necessity. In this case, a sterilization operation was carried out on a patient who lacked capacity to prevent the grave risk of pregnancy, which could have been psychologically harmful to her.

[3] Provide some critical commentary after each point you make—supported with evidence from academic articles.	However, *Re A* seems to widen the scope of the defence, even suggesting that a general defence exists.[3] The criteria applied were as follows:

- the act is needed to avoid inevitable and irreparable evil;
- no more should be done than necessary for the purpose to be achieved;
- the evil inflicted must not be disproportionate to the evil avoided.

Although the court stressed that the case was limited to its own facts, it could be argued that this is very wide indeed. In addition, it could be said that to open up the defence of necessity in this way could open up the prospect that there might be other instances where people would try to justify their actions.[4] It might further be argued that it would not be possible to say who should be the judge of the comparative value of lives. In this way, it might be said that the defence of necessity suggested by *Re A* is wider than it has been, and has lost sight of its original rationale.

Duress of circumstances has been developed by the courts in a series of cases which initially all involved driving offences committed while under some external threat.[5] The sequence began with *R v Willer* (1986) 83 Cr App R 225, where D's conviction for reckless driving (as it then was) was quashed because the jury refused to allow the defence of necessity. There was evidence that the defendant may have driven onto a pavement to escape from a gang of youths threatening violence to himself and his passenger. In *R v Conway* [1989] 3 All ER 1025, the defendant drove recklessly to escape from two men who had approached his car. There were similar results in *R v Martin* [1989] 1 All ER 652. The defendant's stepson was late for work. The defendant's wife, who had suicidal tendencies, threatened suicide if the defendant did not drive his stepson to work. D's conviction for driving while disqualified was quashed. In *R v Pommell* [1995] 2 Crim LR 607, the Court of Appeal made it clear that the defence was not limited to driving offences. In *R v Baker and Wilkins* [1997] Crim LR 497, the courts removed one of the remaining ambiguities of the defence by stating, confirming *Pommell*, that the defence is only available where the accused has acted to prevent death or injury to others. The defence seems very close to necessity. It is, however, restricted to threats of death or serious injury, whereas a general defence of necessity would simply weigh the harmful consequences sought to be avoided against the harm involved in the commission of the offence. In this sense, to avoid overuse, the limits are desirable.[6]

In *R v Petgrave* [2018] EWCA Crim 1397, D was in fear of gang violence, and on the night in question was in his car being chased by two men armed with a bat and a hammer. There was stationary traffic ahead. D mounted the pavement and his car injured two pedestrians, one seriously. The Court of Appeal upheld his conviction and

[4] This is the 'floodgates' argument and is closely linked to public policy arguments in the criminal law.

[5] This is a relatively new development.

[6] This sentence links the discussion back to the essay topic.

confirmed that both the subjective and objective questions had been rightly left to the jury. This case illustrates that the courts are reluctant to allow this defence easily.

The defence of duress is well established and provides that the defendant may be excused from liability where he engages in otherwise criminal conduct in circumstances where his will has been overborne by threats of death or serious injury designed to compel him to commit a criminal offence. He must reasonably have believed these threats to exist and to be inescapable except by compliance. The defence will only apply where a reasonable person of ordinary firmness would have done as he did.

Duress, however, cannot be used as a defence to murder. This was confirmed by the House of Lords in *R v Howe* **[1987] AC 417**. Lord Hailsham stated:

[7] A careful quote from a case can bolster the central argument. Here, Lord Hailsham's quote demonstrates the narrow approach of the law.

> I have known in my lifetime of too many acts of heroism by ordinary human beings of no more than ordinary fortitude to regard a law as either just or humane which withdraws the protection of the criminal law from the innocent victim and casts its cloak of protection on the coward and the poltroon in the name of a 'concession to human frailty'.[7]

The Law Commission (1993) has recommended that duress should be available as a defence to murder, but the courts still refuse to recognize it. In *R v Gotts* **[1992] 1 All ER 832**, Lord Keith stated: 'the complexities and anomalies involved in the whole matter of the defence of duress seem to me to be such that the issue is better left to Parliament to deal with'.

[8] Explain the law in outline.

There are two tests to be satisfied. First, the defendant must have been impelled to act as he did because he was in fear of death or personal injury to himself or a member of his family. Second, might a sober person of reasonable firmness, sharing the characteristics of the defendant, have responded to the situation as the defendant did?[8]

There appears to be a number of uncertainties emerging from these tests. The overlap with self-defence is one. A defendant can act in self-defence to protect anyone, but in duress the scope of potential victims is limited. The threat cannot pertain to, for example, financial loss.

The decision in *R v Hasan* **[2005] UKHL 22** has substantially narrowed the availability of the defence. The threat must now be immediate. Also, it was held that if a person becomes voluntarily associated with those involved in criminal activity in a situation where he knows or ought reasonably to know that he may be the subject of compulsion by them or their associates, he cannot rely on the defence.

These restrictions seem to be driven by public policy and are not entirely convincing. They do, however, remain restrictive. In *R v Van Dao (Vinh)* **[2012] EWCA Crim 1717**, three workers at a cannabis factory were convicted of cultivating cannabis and possession of criminal property. Two appealed against conviction on the grounds that they had been duped into believing that they were to have been cleaners, not cultivators, and that when they tried to leave, they were threatened with violence so that their will had been overcome. They were locked in with no means of escape, and their work had been under duress. Extending duress to a threat of false imprisonment would comply with **Article 26** of the **Council of Europe Convention on Action against Trafficking in Human Beings**: non-punishment of victims of trafficking for involvement in unlawful activities under compulsion. The Court of Appeal dismissed the appeal on the grounds that the defence of duress, on the facts, was fanciful. The defendants were found with mobile phones and keys to the building. But the view was expressed that a threat of imprisonment without an accompanying threat of serious harm would be insufficient, given the narrowness of the defence following *Hasan*.

The Law Commission has recognized that it is not fair to expect the standard of the reasonable person to be one of heroism, and it should be for the jury to decide whether the threat was one which the accused could reasonably expect to resist. Furthermore, it is worth noting here that the Law Commission in *Murder, Manslaughter and Infanticide 2006 Part 6: Duress* (LC 304, 2006) confirmed the view that *Martin* was correctly decided and, moreover, that *Hasan* cast no doubt upon it. The report stated that the particular circumstances of D should be taken into account in determining whether or not his or her belief was reasonably held. Thus, age, vulnerability, and recognized psychiatric conditions should all be allowed on the question of D's belief. In particular, psychiatric conditions such as learned helplessness in battered women syndrome could be included, as pointed out by Lady Hallett in *R v Brandford [2016] EWCA Crim 1794*:

Learned helplessness would be of particular relevance to a possible defence of duress. The term is used to describe the reaction of a victim to chronic and repeated abuse, whereby they feel that whatever they do nothing will change. They have no way of physically or emotionally breaking free from their abuser and the abuse. They cannot extricate themselves from the violent situation no matter how many cries for help they may make. They become increasingly passive. Traumatic bonding is the attachment that a victim has to their abusers which may make them supportive of the abuser and loyal to them. It may mean a victim will stay with their abuser through a variety of emotions but particularly through fear ... It is essential to analyse, with some care, the extent and timing of the domestic violence, the impact upon the person concerned and their presentation at the relevant time ...

In conclusion, the objective and restrictive nature of the tests may be unfair to some defendants accused of certain crimes. It is worth noting recent developments: in order to address the shortcomings of the duress defence in relation to victims of modern slavery, **s 45** of the **Modern Slavery Act 2015** creates a defence of compulsion. Unlike duress, it does not require a threat of immediate serious violence. However, it applies only in very limited circumstances.

LOOKING FOR EXTRA MARKS?

■ Make sure you refer to some critical arguments in addition to the judgments. Here, you could refer to the Law Commission's critique of Lord Hailsham's arguments in *R v Howe*.

■ A comment comparing the old law to the new will demonstrate that you understand not just the mechanics of the defence, but also its implications. *R v Hasan* has substantially tightened the operation of the defence, notably with regard to immediacy and the defendant's voluntary association with criminals.

QUESTION | 3

James was driving on a narrow mountain road. He came to a hairpin bend, where he saw Norma sitting in her parked car. Because the road was narrow, he could not go back or forward, or around the car. He saw a sign by the side of the road, 'Danger—serious risk of avalanche', and noticed small rocks coming down the mountainside. Fearing an impending avalanche and believing he had no alternative, he drove into the car in front, knocking it over the mountainside. He realized that this course of action was dangerous, and it resulted in Norma (the occupant of the car) being killed and the car being badly damaged. There was in fact no avalanche.

Discuss the criminal liability (if any) of James.

CAUTION!

■ This question involves a detailed consideration of the defence of necessity/duress of circumstances. There are many uncertainties concerning the defence, and this question should be attempted only by candidates confident in dealing with these issues.

■ In answering the question, candidates must, however, guard against the risk of dealing only with this defence, as due consideration must be given to the ingredients of the offences with which James could be charged. Thus, a full discussion of the concepts of intention and recklessness must be given in relation to murder, manslaughter, and criminal damage.

DIAGRAM ANSWER PLAN

Identify the issues	■ Consider murder and involuntary manslaughter—defences.
Relevant law	■ Consider murder and involuntary manslaughter—defences.
Apply the law	■ Discuss which defences apply, taking care to explain each requirement. Consider the conditions and each defence: *R v Graham*.
Conclude	■ What is the effect of the defences?

 SUGGESTED ANSWER

¹ Establish the key offences and defences first.

James could face charges involving unlawful homicide and criminal damage, but he may be able to raise the defence of necessity and/ or duress of circumstances.¹ The most serious offence to consider is murder. James has clearly caused Norma's death in fact—but for his actions she would not have died. There is no evidence to suggest that there has been any break in the chain of causation. The *mens rea* of murder is satisfied by the prosecution proving that James intended to kill or cause grievous bodily harm (***R v Moloney* [1985] 1 All ER 1025**). This is a question of fact for the jury. Although the general rule is that intention is a word in common use which is easily understood by the public, and therefore there is no need for the trial judge to embark on a detailed explanation of the concept, this case might require a further direction.

Whilst it is clear that foresight of consequence is evidence that can be used to contribute to proof of intention, it is not of itself conclusive evidence. Similarly, a judge cannot direct the jury that if James foresaw the consequence and the result was a natural consequence, James intended it. The trial judge would now use the direction suggested by the House of Lords in ***R v Woollin* [1998] 4 All ER 103** that the jury would not be entitled to find the necessary intention unless they felt sure that death or serious bodily harm was a virtually certain result of D's actions (barring some unforeseen intervention), and that D had foreseen death or grievous bodily harm as virtually certain.

James could argue that although he foresaw this possible consequence, death or grievous bodily harm was not his purpose, as his
motive was to save himself. Although this argument succeeded in *R
v Steane* **[1947] 1 All ER 813**, this was not a murder case, and it
is recognized that motive is not the same as intention. Motive is the
reason why one acts, whereas intention is the state of mind present
when the act is committed. In short, indirect intention will suffice.[2]

[2] Motive is not to be confused with
intent for the purposes of *mens rea*.

If the jury decided that James lacked the *mens rea* for murder, he
could still be found guilty of involuntary (constructive) manslaughter,
ie unlawful killing without intention to kill or do grievous bodily harm.
In order to establish liability for constructive manslaughter, the prosecution will have to prove that James committed a dangerous criminal
act that caused the victim's death. There are two possible bases for
such liability here.[3] The first is in relation to his driving of the vehicle.
There seems little doubt that the objective test for dangerousness
would be satisfied here. The test requires the court to consider whether
a reasonable and sober person would recognize that the defendant's
unlawful act subjected the victim to the risk of at least some physical
harm. Of course, James may argue that a driving offence is not of itself
sufficiently dangerous to be the ground for a conviction.

[3] You always need to be able to
identify an unlawful criminal act for
this type of manslaughter.

The alternative basis for constructive manslaughter could be for
the prosecution to rely on offences under the **Criminal Damage Act
1971** as the basis for an unlawful act manslaughter charge. It appears
that James committed criminal damage under **s 1(1)** of the Act when
he damaged Norma's car. Liability could be based on criminal damage
contrary to **s 1(1)** of the **1971 Act**, or on aggravated criminal damage
contrary to **s 1(2)**, ie damaging or destroying property either intending that or being reckless that the life of another would thereby be
endangered.

The second ingredient of constructive manslaughter is that the act
must be dangerous. It is enough that a sober and reasonable person
at the scene of the unlawful act would have been aware of the possibility of some physical harm occurring as a result of James's actions.[4]
Given the facts, it is submitted that the prosecution would have no
difficulty in satisfying this condition.

[4] This is an objective test, although
its interpretation now includes an
assessment of events as the defendant would have seen them.

There has always been uncertainty as to how the *mens rea* requirement for unlawful act manslaughter should be expressed. As Lord
Hope explained in *Attorney-General's Reference (No 3 of 1994)*
[1997] 3 All ER 936, the prosecution must prove that the defendant
intended to do what he did. It is not necessary to prove that he knew
that his act was unlawful or dangerous. It is unnecessary to prove
that he knew that his act was likely to injure the person who died as
a result of it.[5] All that need be proved is that he intentionally did what
he did—in practice, it will suffice if James was at least reckless as to

[5] Be careful with the *mens rea* of
this type of manslaughter. Any more
than this and it might be confused
with murder.

whether property would be damaged or destroyed; see *R v G* [2003] **4 All ER 765**.

On this basis, liability for constructive manslaughter should be made out.

It is worth noting that James could also incur liability for causing death by dangerous driving contrary to **s 1** of the **Road Traffic Act 1991**. The fault element is 'dangerousness', and this is assessed objectively.

[6] As the defences here do not negate an element of the defence but are defences of justification or excuse, the structure of your answer is important. Start by identifying the offences, and then outline the requirements for each defence.

What defences might be available to James?[6]

For many years, the development of the defence of necessity (duress of circumstances) was hindered by the decision in *R v Dudley and Stephens* [1881–85] All ER Rep 61, in which two shipwrecked seamen killed and ate a cabin boy in order to survive. The court ruled that necessity could be no defence to murder and the accused men were found guilty, and many commentators believed that the case was authority for the principle that necessity was not available as a general defence to other charges. It was not until the mid-1980s that the argument was renewed in a number of cases involving road traffic offences (*R v Willer* (1987) 83 Cr App R 225; *R v Conway* [1988] **3 WLR 1338**; and *R v Martin* [1989] 1 All ER 652) and the related defence of duress of circumstances was developed.

If the defence is raised, the prosecution retains the burden of proof, and according to the Court of Appeal in *R v Martin* (1988) **88 Cr App R 343** the jury will be directed to consider whether James acted reasonably and proportionately, in order to avoid a threat of death or serious injury. The direction should be in these terms:

(a) Was James, or may he have been, impelled to act as he did because, as a result of what he reasonably believed to be the situation, he had good cause to fear that otherwise death or serious physical injury would result? If so;

(b) Might a sober person of reasonable firmness, sharing the characteristics of James, have responded to that situation by acting as James did?

If both questions are answered affirmatively, James should be acquitted.

Note that the test applied to the defendant's belief in the reality of the threat is objective. This could be a problem for James as, although he believed there was an impending avalanche, this was not in fact the case.[7]

[7] Apply the law to the facts.

Although in *R v Williams* [1987] 3 All ER 411 it was recognized that for the defence of self-defence the accused should be judged on the facts as he believed them to be, and an honest but unreasonable mistake would not prevent the defence succeeding, the objective basis for compulsion defences, such as duress, was confirmed by the House of Lords in *R v Hasan* [2005] UKHL 22.

Assuming duress of circumstances is established, are there any policy reasons that would prevent the defence being available to James? Duress is not a defence to murder—that much is clear from *R v Howe* [1987] 1 All ER 771. *R v Dudley and Stephens* (see earlier in this section) provides that necessity is not a defence to murder, but *R v Dudley and Stephens* is actually a case involving duress of circumstance, hence directly applicable to James's case. James would have no duress-based defence to a charge of murder. *Re A (Children) (Conjoined Twins: Surgical Separation)* [2000] 4 All ER 961 does envisage necessity being available as a defence to murder, but the key distinguishing point is that the Court of Appeal was concerned with a situation where the doctors causing the death of one of the conjoined twins would not have been acting to save their own lives at the expense of another.[8] James is clearly acting to save his own life at the expense of Norma's, hence *Re A (Children) (Conjoined Twins: Surgical Separation)* is not applicable.

[8] You can distinguish your case from the authorities you are using.

If James is charged with unlawful act manslaughter, duress of circumstances could be available as a defence—his success will depend upon the extent to which the jury concludes that he acted as the reasonable person would have done.

LOOKING FOR EXTRA MARKS?

- Do not apply the rules from the cases in a blanket fashion. If you can distinguish the facts of the case in question from an established legal rule, do so.
- Make sure you know exactly what you are expected to cover by checking your syllabus carefully.

QUESTION | 4

Albert and John attend a party where they have some non-alcoholic drinks. It is known that Albert has recently been experiencing dizzy spells and fainting fits, but he has not sought medical treatment. At the party Albert becomes dizzy and is given six Valium tablets by an unknown person in an attempt to calm him down. Very shortly after taking the tablets Albert leaves the party with John. On the way home Albert repeatedly hits John over the head with a bottle, thereby killing him.

When arrested and charged with murder, Albert says: 'I cannot remember hitting him. I must have had a blackout.'

Discuss Albert's possible defences.

CAUTION!

- Questions on mental abnormality are quite common in examinations. They are often in essay form, but this problem does require the student to take into account the alternative reasons why Albert acted as he did. If a murder has taken place and insanity is an obvious issue, a consideration of the defences of automatism and diminished responsibility—and how they are related—is required.

- The ingredients of all three defences must therefore be covered in detail, with a clear demonstration of the differences between them. Sometimes voluntary intoxication must also be considered.

DIAGRAM ANSWER PLAN

| Identify the issues | ■ Consider murder and diminished responsibility.
■ Mention automatism, insanity, and intoxication. |

| Relevant law | ■ **Section 2** of the **Homicide Act 1957** as amended by **s 52** of the **Coroners and Justice Act 2009**.
■ *Bratty v AG for NI/M'Naghten/DPP v Majewski*. |

| Apply the law | ■ Discuss which defences apply, taking care to explain each requirement. |

| Conclude | ■ What is the effect of the defences? |

SUGGESTED ANSWER

Albert has caused the death of John in fact and in law. There is no evidence of anything that would suggest a *novus actus interveniens*. In order to support a charge of murder, the prosecution will have to establish that Albert intended to kill John, or intended to do him some grievous bodily harm.[1] If Albert's evidence is plausible, it may be that he will successfully defend a murder charge by relying on one of a number of defences involving a partial or complete denial of *mens rea*, such as automatism, insanity, or diminished responsibility.

[1] The first thing you should do is identify what he may be guilty of—even if that is not the conclusion.

Diminished responsibility is a partial defence that reduces the defendant's liability from murder to manslaughter. The defence is contained in **s 2(1)** of the **Homicide Act 1957** amended by **s 52** of the **Coroners and Justice Act 2009**. Defendants charged with murder tend to rely on diminished responsibility rather than insanity, and it has succeeded in a wide variety of circumstances, including mercy killings, and killings as a result of an irresistible impulse. Professor Andrew Ashworth (2013) has pointed out that in 80 per cent of cases in which it is raised the prosecution are prepared to accept the plea.

[2] The key is that the defendant must have a recognized medical condition. This is an improvement on the previous law, but also may be narrower.

Albert will have to prove that, at the time of the killing, he was suffering from an abnormality of mental functioning arising from a medical condition.[2] The facts indicate that Albert has been suffering from some symptoms suggesting he was unwell, but the difficulty he will encounter in discharging the legal burden of proof is the fact that there appears to be no expert medical evidence to support the defence. Simply having dizzy spells will not, of itself, discharge the legal burden of proof on Albert as regards establishing the defence, neither will the transient effect caused by the taking of Valium suffice. Voluntary intoxication is not, of itself, to be regarded as a recognized medical condition for the purposes of **s 52** of the **2009 Act**; see *R v Dowds* **[2012] EWCA Crim 281**.

Even if he were able to provide the necessary expert medical evidence, Albert would have to go on to establish that this abnormality of mental functioning caused a substantial impairment in: (i) his understanding of the nature of his conduct; (ii) his ability to form a rational judgement; or (iii) his ability to exercise self-control. The Court of Appeal has confirmed that, for the purposes of the **Coroners and Justice Act 2009**, the concept of substantial impairment should be approached in the same way as was the case under the **Homicide Act 1957**. Hence, there should be evidence of more than some trivial degree of impairment, but there does not have to be evidence of total impairment; see *R v Lloyd* **[1967] 1 QB 175**. Of these three, the lack of understanding of the nature of his actions is likely to prove the most fruitful for Albert (note that he claims to have been unaware of his actions), provided the jury is satisfied that the impairment is substantial and, further, that the abnormality of mental functioning provided an explanation for Albert's actions in the sense that it was the cause or a contributory factor in

[3] It is essentially a case of a causative link.

making Albert act as he did. In summary, therefore, there are grounds for this defence succeeding, provided some expert medical evidence is available to establish the requirements of **s 52**.[3]

Prima facie, the most attractive defence to Albert is automatism, as this is a complete defence to murder and the burden of proof is on the prosecution to disprove the existence of the defence. Albert simply has to provide an evidential basis for reliance on the defence.

Automatism was defined by Lord Denning in *Bratty v Attorney-General for Northern Ireland* [1963] AC 386 as 'an act which is done by the muscles without any control by the mind such as a spasm, a reflex or a convulsion, or an act done by a person who is not conscious of what he is doing such as an act done whilst suffering from concussion or whilst sleep-walking'.

Albert will argue that he did not know what he was doing and therefore his act was involuntary. The prosecution must prove that the act was voluntary, but it is entitled to rely on the presumption that every man has sufficient mental capacity to be responsible for his act; and if the defence wishes to displace this presumption it must give some evidence from which the contrary may reasonably be inferred. Much will therefore depend on the expert medical evidence.

[4] Set out the requirements for the defence of automatism to succeed.

For automatism to succeed, the court must accept that there was a total loss of control.[4] In *Attorney-General's Reference (No 2 of 1992)* [1993] 4 All ER 683, the Court of Appeal ruled that the trial judge was wrong to direct the jury that a syndrome known as 'driving without awareness' could amount to automatism. Impaired, reduced, or partial control is not enough. The prosecution could argue that Albert had enough control to pick up a bottle and repeatedly hit John over the head, and therefore that automatism should not apply.

A second problem concerns the fact that Albert had not sought medical treatment for his condition. The prosecution could argue that the automatism was therefore self-induced and that Albert was blameworthy in not seeking treatment. Further, if Albert had taken alcohol or non-prescribed hallucinatory drugs, automatism will not succeed (*R v Lipman* [1969] 3 All ER 410)—but see later in relation to consumption of Valium tablets. Notwithstanding these two issues, if the Valium had the effect of completely destroying Albert's self-control, and he was unaware that this would be the consequence of taking the drug, he may succeed with the defence of automatism.

Where, however, there is evidence that Albert actually suffered from some inherent medical condition that, in conjunction with the Valium, had the effect of causing him to lose his self-control, the prosecution may seek to lead evidence suggesting that insanity is a more appropriate defence.

[5] Set out the requirements for the defence to succeed.

Under the *M'Naghten* Rules (1843) 8 ER 718,[5] everyone is presumed sane until the contrary is proved. However, it is a defence for the accused to show that he was labouring under such defect of reason due to disease of the mind such that either:

(a) he does not know the nature and quality of his act; or

(b) if he does know the nature and quality of his act, he does not know that what he was doing was wrong (in the sense of contrary to law, as opposed to morally wrong).

The trial judge must first decide if Albert was suffering from a disease of the mind, and if so, the jury will then decide if the other ingredients of the defence have been satisfied. The judicial pronouncements on insanity are certainly at variance with medical practice, and the question of public safety is a factor that the judiciary obviously takes into account. In *Bratty*, Lord Denning stated that 'any mental disorder which has manifested itself in violence and is prone to recur is a disease of the mind' and this was reiterated by Lord Diplock in *R v Sullivan*, where the House of Lords upheld the trial judge's decision to label epilepsy 'a disease of the mind',[6] when he stated:

6 Essentially, this is a public policy argument.

> if the effect of a disease is to impair these facilities [of reason, memory, and understanding] so severely as to have either of these consequences referred to in the latter part of the rules, it matters not whether the aetiology of the impairment is organic, as in epilepsy, or functional, or whether the impairment itself is permanent or is transient and intermittent, provided that it subsisted at the time of the commission of the act.

Thus, arteriosclerosis and violent sleepwalking have all been deemed diseases of the mind. In the latter case, the Court of Appeal held that many people sleepwalk, but that if an accused uses violence while sleepwalking, the condition would have to be regarded as being due to a disease of the mind. So the accused in *R v Burgess* **[1991] 2 All ER 769**, who while sleepwalking violently assaulted the victim, was found 'not guilty by reason of insanity' as he was plainly suffering from a defect of reason from some sort of failure of the mind causing him to act as he did without conscious motivation. The Court of Appeal upheld the trial judge's decision to label the condition as a disease of the mind, on the basis that it was due to an internal factor that manifested itself in violence.

Albert may seek to rely on the common law defence of intoxication. There is little doubt that, if his loss of awareness was caused by the consumption of the Valium tablets, he could be regarded as having been in a state of intoxication. Murder is a specific intent crime, hence on the basis of *DPP v Majewski* **[1976] 2 All ER 142**, self-induced intoxication can be raised as a defence. If it succeeds, it will reduce Albert's liability to manslaughter.

7 Note that this is not strictly speaking a defence but a denial of *mens rea*.

There may be an argument that Albert might escape liability altogether on the basis of the intoxication.[7] Even in respect of basic intent crimes such as manslaughter, there must be evidence that the defendant was reckless in consuming the intoxicant. In the case of alcohol or Class A drugs, this is rarely an issue. In the case of Valium, there may be some debate as to whether Albert was aware of the risk of what side effects there might be. *R v Hardie* **[1984] 3 All ER 848** provides that if there is evidence that the self-administration of drugs may not have been reckless, the issue ought to be left to the jury. In short, if it was not Albert's fault that he lost consciousness, he should be acquitted.

LOOKING FOR EXTRA MARKS?

- You need to develop a sense of the areas the examiner is going to give credit for, rather than writing about everything you think may be relevant. Here, automatism is likely to be more successful—this is a good reason to plan your answer carefully.
- Be ready to explain the role of recklessness and basic/specific intent.

QUESTION | 5

A group of friends are on a Thames cruise. One of the doors has been left open by Sam, a member of the crew, and when they are on their way, the boat starts to sink. Panic ensues, and the friends realize that the only way to escape will be to jump off. Sue and Graham run to the edge, where there is a convenient place to jump. When they get there, they see that Pete is trying to climb down but is frozen with fear. Sue pushes him away. Pete drowns, and Sue and Graham manage to escape.

Graham punches his colleague, Rob, when Rob suggests that he could have done more to save Pete. Rob falls unconscious and Graham, feeling guilty, calls an ambulance. At the hospital, he is left unattended when Annie, the doctor on duty, wrongly concludes that he does not need immediate treatment. Rob dies from his injury. Graham says that he was acting out of character as he is diabetic and although he had taken his insulin injection that morning, he had not had time to eat. As a result, he had been experiencing some dizzy spells. He had also had several glasses of wine the night before in order to cope with the stress of the boat accident. It transpires that this is not the first time that Graham has felt dizzy at work, but it has always passed within a few minutes, so he didn't think anything of it.

Discuss any criminal liability arising from these facts. Do not discuss inchoate offences.

CAUTION!

- You need to work through the requirements of any potential offences before you consider which defences might apply. Do not make the mistake of discussing the defences straight away.
- The rubric makes it clear that you should not discuss inchoate offences. Make sure you do not fall into this trap. This is the examiner's way of making sure that you do not have too much to write about.

DIAGRAM ANSWER PLAN

| Identify the issues | ■ Include murder, involuntary manslaughter, defences. |

| Relevant law | ■ Discuss causation in fact and in law, common law defences of insanity and automatism, *M'Naghten* Rules and internal and external factors. |

| Apply the law | ■ Consider whether there is a *novus actus interveniens* on the medical treatment.
■ Consider whether the act is dangerous.
■ Discuss necessity—*Re T* [1990] Crim LR 256. |

| Conclude | ■ What is the best possible defence? |

SUGGESTED ANSWER

This question concerns murder, manslaughter, and the defences. Murder is defined at common law as the unlawful killing of a human being under the Queen's Peace. The *mens rea* requires that the defendant has an intent to kill or to cause grievous bodily harm. In order to establish the *actus reus*, the prosecution must show that the defendant has caused the death. Pete's death has been caused by being pushed off the ladder. Sue has not done anything to try to prevent him from falling. He would not have died if he had not been pushed (*R v White* [1910] 1 QB 410).[1] The next question is whether this is a substantial and operating cause of death. There is no evident *novus actus interveniens* here. Sue will argue that she was forced to push Pete out of the way, and it was necessary to do so in order to save themselves. Where the defendant is presented with two harms and decides to avoid the greater and accept the lesser by means of committing a crime, he may have the defence of necessity. It is a complete defence, being a justification for the defendant's conduct, thereby negating any unlawfulness in the crime. The feared harm that the defendant chooses to avoid must be serious personal injury or death. Sue will argue that if she had not pushed him off, she and Graham would have died themselves. Historically, necessity was not available

[1] Also known as the factual causation test.

² Note how a direct quote from the case bolsters the point.

as a defence to murder (*R v Dudley and Stephens* [1884] LR 14 QBD 273). Lord Coleridge stated, 'the broad proposition that a man may save his life by killing certainly is not law in the present day'.² In *Re A (Children) (Conjoined Twins: Surgical Separation)* [2001] 2 WLR 480, the court accepted that there might be exceptions to the rule. This case is similar to the situation in the *Herald of Free Enterprise*. This was not a murder case, but this situation would

³ This was a key part of the *ratio* in *Dudley*. You can show the examiner how you can use your powers of legal reasoning by distinguishing the facts of our case.

be different to the situation in *Dudley and Stephens* because the man had effectively chosen to put himself in danger by not moving, so that in theory a defence of necessity could be available.³ In *Dudley and Stephens*, the victim was 'chosen' to die, by the other defendants. In *Re A* [1990] **Crim LR 256**, Lord Brooke gave this example as a case in which the defendant would be able to benefit from necessity. As long as it could be said that Sue and Graham were 'designated for death' and that Pete was impeding their escape, they will probably be able to benefit from the defence.

The punch which results in Rob's death may be the basis of unlaw-

⁴ Clearly set out the requirements of this new offence.

ful act manslaughter. The problem here is causation. Graham has committed an unlawful act, which is dangerous.⁴ The act is at least a battery, and probably the infliction of at least actual bodily harm—a punch is likely to 'interfere with the health and comfort' of Rob. He might argue that he does not have *mens rea*; however, this is satisfied on proof of intention or recklessness as to the unlawful act. The

⁵ It is important to discuss this here. Students often forget to discuss this element of involuntary manslaughter.

unlawful act must be dangerous. Dangerousness is defined objectively in *R v Church* [1966] 1 QB 59:⁵

the unlawful act must be such as all sober and reasonable people would inevitably recognize would subject the other person to at least the risk of some physical harm.

Most people would recognize that a punch like this could be dangerous. The next question is whether Graham can argue that the chain of causation was broken. Medical evidence will not generally break the chain of causation unless it is 'palpably wrong' (*R v Jordan*

⁶ Note that they nearly always do, unless the facts are very similar indeed to *Jordan*.

(1956) 40 Cr App R 152). The cases of *R v Smith* [1959] 2 QB 35 and *R v Cheshire* [1991] 1 WLR 844 are likely to prevail here.⁶ In the former case, it was held that the defendant's act had to be a substantial and operating cause of the victim's death and in the latter, the Court of Appeal held that even though medical negligence was the immediate cause of the victim's death, it did not exclude the defendant's responsibility. It is unlikely that Annie's treatment of Rob in the hospital will break the chain of causation, even if it is negligent.

Graham will try to raise a defence on the basis of automatism on the basis of the insulin he has taken. Automatism is a plea that the link between mind and body is missing, resulting in a lack of voluntary

[7] A proper case definition.

control over one's actions. In *Bratty*, Lord Denning defined the offence as 'an involuntary act done by the muscles … without control of the mind'. If successful, it provides a complete acquittal.[7] In order to be successful, it must be shown that the defendant experienced a complete loss of control, and that that loss of control was caused by an external factor, such as medication. Medication in respect of an underlying internal disease can provide the necessary external source. The use of insulin by a diabetic defendant, causing hypoglycaemia, would fall into this category. However, if the prosecution can show that the defendant was reckless in taking the insulin (eg by failing to eat, knowing that particular behaviour would ensue) then the defence cannot usually succeed. Whether it succeeds will depend on the type of crime with which the defendant is charged. If it is a crime of basic intent, then it is likely to prevent the defence from succeeding, as there is already an element of recklessness. In this situation, we know that Graham has experienced some dizzy spells in the past after taking insulin but failing to eat. However, we do not know that these spells have resulted in violence. The result, here, is therefore uncertain.[8] As alcohol is a factor here too, the court will need to consider whether this is a crime of specific or basic intent (manslaughter is a crime of basic intent as it can be established via proof of recklessness). If it is basic intent, the usual rules on intoxication will apply.

[8] Apply the law to the facts, as best you can.

Graham may be able to plead, in relation to his plea of automatism, that his emotional state triggered these events. In *Re T* [1990] **Crim LR 256**, the defendant suffered from post-traumatic stress disorder as a consequence of being raped. Later, the defendant stabbed the victim during a robbery. If the internal/external factor had been strictly applied, then automatism would not have been available, but the rape was considered to be the external factor needed for proof of the defence. The traumatic event of the boat sinking might be considered to be in this category.

If not, Graham can be considered to be insane. This will lead to a verdict of not guilty by reason of insanity, with disposal ranging from indefinite detention in a mental hospital to an absolute discharge (**Criminal Procedure (Insanity and Unfitness to Plead) Act 1991** and the **Domestic Violence, Crime and Victims Act 2004**). The defence is defined according to the *M'Naghten* Rules[9] as a defect of reason due to a disease of the mind so as to deprive the defendant of either knowledge as to the nature and quality of his actions or knowledge that the act is legally wrong. The concept of disease of the mind is wide enough to include physical as well as mental disorders. Diabetes would fall into this category.[10] If Graham wants to raise this defence, he will have to do so on the balance of probabilities. It may be easier for him to prove automatism, as he can raise medical evidence (on an evidential burden only) of his condition.

[9] You can summarize the definition before applying it.

[10] As we explained earlier in *R v Quick* in Question 1.

It is possible that Graham may be able to show (although this will be difficult/unlikely) that he was suffering from a form of post-traumatic stress as a result of the accident. Furthermore, as the incident seems to be temporary, it may be difficult for him to show insanity.

LOOKING FOR EXTRA MARKS?

■ These defences are similar—as such you should make an effort to evaluate them and advise your client on the best way forward. Note that the practical effects may be an important consideration.

■ Although necessity is difficult to show, it may now be accepted in certain circumstances. You can show your legal analysis by outlining these circumstances.

QUESTION | 6

Pat lost all his savings deposited with DSC Bank after it ceased trading. He joined a campaign group called Action against Avarice (AAA) whose mission was to make bank managers accountable for the global financial crisis 'by any means'. Greg, recently released from prison for armed bank robbery, was the leader of AAA. Greg approached Pat and told him that in order to be accepted as a member of the group he must attack Fred, the manager of Floyds Bank, outside the local branch and take photographs of his injuries. AAA would release these to the press to raise awareness of their cause, without identifying Pat. If he completed this task, he would be paid £2,000. Pat, anxious to recoup some of his savings, but also fearful of Greg's reputation for violence, agreed.

A few days later, Pat loitered outside the local branch of Floyds until he saw a man in a pinstriped suit leaving the bank. Pat assumed this was Fred, but in fact it was Humphrey, the manager of Barking Bank, who had just been to Floyds for a meeting with Fred. Pat threw an egg at Humphrey, hoping to then wrestle him to the ground. When the egg shattered on Humphrey's face, a piece of shell entered his eye, scratching his eyeball. Unable to see properly, Humphrey tripped over a loose paving stone, falling into the road, where he was hit by an oncoming car. Humphrey suffered a broken pelvis but eventually made a full recovery.

When the incident was reported in the press, Greg realized that Pat had attacked the wrong man and was furious. He went straight to Pat's house to confront him. He slapped Pat's face, unaware that Pat had a loose tooth. The tooth was dislodged, got stuck in Pat's windpipe, and had to be surgically removed.

Discuss the liability, if any, of the parties involved, including any defences they may have.

CAUTION!

■ Note that you are not required to discuss any inchoate offences arising in this question.

■ Note that the *mens rea* for s 47 of the **Offences Against the Person Act 1861** only requires the prosecution to prove intention or recklessness as to the initial assault or battery.

DIAGRAM ANSWER PLAN

Identify the issues	■ Consider non-fatal offences against the person (common law and **Offences Against the Person Act 1861**). ■ Discuss the defence of duress. ■ Discuss transferred malice.
Relevant law	■ Consider **s 47** of the **Offences Against the Person Act 1861** and the meaning of actual bodily harm. ■ Discuss causation. ■ Discuss the meaning of grievous bodily harm. ■ Consider the definition of duress (*Graham*).
Apply the law	■ Verify that a scratch clearly interferes with comfort. ■ Mistaken identity is irrelevant. ■ Is there an intention to cause grievous bodily harm? ■ Discuss the objective test in duress—G's reputation for violence.
Conclude	■ As there are several offences of the **Offences Against the Person Act 1861**, defence of duress is unlikely to succeed.

SUGGESTED ANSWER

This question concerns non-fatal offences against the person and the defence of duress.

Pat's first offence against Humphrey occurs when he threw an egg at him, which shattered on Humphrey's face, a piece of shell scratching his eyeball. Assuming that the scratch was minor, P may have committed assault occasioning actual bodily harm (ABH) contrary to **s 47** of the **Offences Against the Person Act 1861**. If it was more serious, then P has possibly committed an offence of malicious wounding or malicious infliction of grievous bodily harm (GBH) contrary to **s 20.** There is nothing in the question to suggest that the injury was anything more than minor.[1]

Section 47 of the **Offences Against the Person Act 1861** consists of two *actus reus* elements, and two possible *mens rea* elements. The *actus reus* consists of proof of an assault or battery which *in*

[1] It is important that you do not 'invent' facts in the question. Unless the facts suggest the injury is more serious, or are really ambiguous, stick to what is suggested. You won't lose marks for choosing one offence over the other unless there is a real error (eg failing to mention a wound when blood is drawn).

addition occasions or causes ABH. ABH is defined according to *Miller* [1954] 2 All ER 529 as 'any interference with the health or comfort of the victim'. It can include both physical or psychiatric harm (*Chan-Fook* [1994] 1 WLR 689, as confirmed by *Burstow* [1834] EWHC Exch J79 [1977] UKHL 34) and must be more than trifling or transient (*Chan-Fook*), but *T v DPP* [2003] EWHC 266 held that one of these requirements will suffice (momentary loss of consciousness). A scratch to the eye is clearly uncomfortable. Note that it will not count as a wound for the purposes of s 20 of the **Offences Against the Person Act 1861**, for a scratch which does not break the inner skin is not a wound (*Moriarty v Brookes* (1834)).

[2] A common mistake is to forget all the elements of the *actus reus* of the relevant offence.

In order to successfully prove the offence of ABH, the prosecution must first prove all the elements of either an assault or battery.[2] Both have common law definitions but were considered to have been statutory offences since s 47 of the **Offences Against the Person Act 1861** in *DPP v Little* [1992] QB 645. The penalties for each are defined according to s 39 of the **Criminal Justice Act 1988**. Clearly, by hitting Humphrey in the face with an egg, Pat has committed the *actus reus* of battery (defined at common law as any act by which D inflicts unlawful personal violence upon the victim). The violence need only be as minor as non-consensual touching (*Faulker v Talbot* [1981] 3 All ER 468) and need not consist of an injury. It will be unlawful if it is without consent or lawful excuse. A battery can be committed in the absence of an assault, defined as any act by which D causes V to apprehend immediate, unlawful person violence (*Venna*[1975] 3 WLR 737). Whether Humphrey had time to apprehend immediate violence is unknown, but it would certainly seem that he has suffered a battery. The *mens rea* of battery consists of the intentional or reckless infliction of violence, recklessness being defined subjectively in accordance with *Cunningham* [1957] 2 QB 396 as the conscious taking of an unjustified risk of harm. There seems little doubt that Pat threw the egg at Humphrey intending to hit him with it, and therefore the battery will have been directly intended. It is important to note that Pat (P) intended an offence against Fred, whereas his offences were mistakenly aimed at Humphrey (H). The doctrine of transferred malice will apply so as to transfer any intention aimed at one victim over to another within the same type of offence (*Latimer* [1886] 17 QBD 359; *Pembliton* (1974) (1874) LR 2 CCR 119). Therefore, provided the relevant *mens rea* for any offence can be proved beyond all reasonable doubt against Pat, the mistaken identity of the victim will be irrelevant.

Having established both the *actus reus* and *mens rea* of battery, it is necessary to prove an unbroken chain of causation between that offence and the ABH (*Roberts* [1971] EWCA Crim 4; *Savage, Parmenter* [1991] 94 Cr App R 193). There is no issue in relation to

[3] The *mens rea* of the non-fatal offences can be tricky. Remember that the *mens rea* does not extend to the full *actus reus* except in the case of **s 18** of the **Offences Against the Person Act 1861**. Therefore, it is likely that the defendant will be convicted even where he argues that he did not intend the full gravity of the offence committed.

causation here and so this should not be difficult to establish. No *mens rea* is necessary in relation to the harm sustained by a victim of ABH (*Roberts*). Therefore, it is not necessary to prove that P intended or foresaw any injury to H, simply that he caused it. The only *mens rea* that does need to be established is in relation to the initial assault or battery, which has already been established as set out above. Therefore, P seems to have committed assault occasioning ABH against H.[3]

However, Humphrey then trips over a loose paving stone, falls into the road, and is hit by an oncoming car, breaking his pelvis. This more serious injury would amount to GBH, defined according to *DPP v Smith* [1961] AC 290 as 'really serious harm'. It need not be life threatening. Two potential offences are designed to deal with defendants committing GBH: the malicious infliction of GBH contrary to **s 20** mentioned above and **s 18 of the Offences Against the Person Act 1861**—maliciously causing GBH with intent to cause GBH or to resist arrest. It does not appear from the question as though P intended to cause GBH to Humphrey. The chain of events began when he threw an egg at him, 'hoping to wrestle him to the ground', presumably in order to take photographs of him, as agreed with Greg. Wrestling someone to the ground does not indicate an intention to cause GBH. Therefore, the relevant offence would be **s 20**—the malicious infliction of GBH. Infliction no longer implies that there needs to be a prior assault, as was once the case (*Clarence* (1989) 22 QB 23), or that harm be directly inflicted (*Salisbury* [1976] VR 452) provided it is caused by D. Here, Pat might argue that he was not the legal cause of H's broken pelvis because it was the result of an unforeseeable *novus actus interveniens*, ie Humphrey tripping over the loose paving stone, which resulted in his falling into the road and being hit by a car. A chain of causation will exist where the result is the natural and probable consequence of D's act or omission. To establish a break in the chain of causation, Pat will need to satisfy the court that the intervention was free, deliberate, and informed (*Pagett* (1983) 76 Cr App R 279; *Rafferty* [2007] EWCA Crim 1846), in other words, that it was unforeseeable. Otherwise, provided his initial offence can be regarded as the substantial and operating cause of H's eventual injuries (*Smith* [1959] 2 QB 35; *Malcherek and Steel* [1981] 2 All ER 422), or the significant cause of the result (*Cheshire* [1991] 1 WLR 844), the chain will be unbroken and he will be regarded as the legal cause of H's injuries. It would not be unforeseeable that Humphrey (or anyone else) might trip over a loose paving stone, having just been hit in the face with an egg. Neither would it be unexpected therefore that he might fall into the road and into the path of a vehicle. Presumably the incident occurred on a pavement next to a road. Even if one were to apply the 'victim escape' rules, the only sort of 'escape' which might break a causal chain is one which is

[4] At each stage, make sure you apply the law to the facts, reaching a reasoned conclusion.

'unreasonable' given the circumstances and characteristics of the victim (*Williams and Davis* [1992] **Crim LR 198;** *Marjoram* [2000]). It would not be unreasonable for H to attempt to escape from P, and tripping over a paving stone is not exceptional. Therefore, P would appear to be the legal cause of H's broken pelvis and to have committed the *actus reus* of **s 20**.[4]

The appropriate *mens rea* for **s 20** is 'malicious', being defined as either intention or subjective *Cunningham* recklessness. However, it is not necessary for the prosecution to prove either intention or foresight as to GBH, merely as to some harm (*Mowatt* [1972] [1968] 1 QB 421, confirmed by *Savage and Parmenter* [1992]). Therefore, provided it can be proved that Pat foresaw some lesser injury to Humphrey (ie ABH) over and above the initial battery, he can be convicted of this offence. Pat intended to wrestle Humphrey to the ground and then photograph him. He must have realized that this conduct might result in some sort of injury, albeit minor. If so, he will have the necessary *mens rea* for **s 20**.

[5] With defences, as with offences, ensure that you set out the tests necessary to prove the defence. Here the prosecution will have to disprove the defence as a defence, in addition to proving that Pat has committed the *mens rea* and *actus reus*. This will need to be done to the criminal standard.

Pat may have a complete defence of duress in relation to the offences against Humphrey if they were committed as a result of fear due to threats of serious physical harm from Greg. There are two tests: subjective and objective.[5] Regarding the subjective test, the threats do not need to be the sole reason for acting (*Valderrama-Vega* [1985] **Crim LR 220**), but the harm feared must be immediate or almost immediate, as opposed to imminent or in the future (*Hasan* [2005] 2 **WLR 709** overruling *Hudson and Taylor* [1971] 2 **WLR 1047**). Pat's fear would need to be reasonable and any mistake in that respect would probably now also need to be reasonable (*Hasan*, cf *Martin* [2000]). On the question of the objective test, Pat will want to show that a sober person of reasonable firmness, sharing his characteristics, would have responded to the threats in the same way (*Graham* [1982] 1 **WLR 294;** *Howe* [1987] **AC 417**). The problems in the way of this defence are, first, that there was no express threat against Pat by Greg, although it might have been implied given Greg's propensity for violence. There would be no problem with nomination of the crime since Greg specified exactly what offence he expected P to commit. The fact that Pat was to receive £2,000 would not negate the defence if he genuinely acted through fear of serious physical violence.

However, the second problem is that any violence which P might have feared was not immediately or almost immediately threatened, and it appears that he 'agreed' to commit the crime, although this might have been with reluctance. The third problem relates to the objective question. A reasonable person would probably leave the organization in question, rather than commit an offence. Moreover, the defence will fail where D has voluntarily associated with criminals he knows or ought to know are violent, whether he foresees they might put him under coercion or not (*Hasan*). This test is very strict, and on this basis alone, therefore, the defence will probably fail because Pat is fully aware of Greg's reputation for violence.[6]

[6] The case of *R v Hasan* has substantially narrowed the test for duress. In particular, it precludes its use where there is an association with a known criminal.

The next offence was committed by Greg against Pat when he slapped his face. A slap is a battery, as described above. Pat must have apprehended immediate unlawful violence from Greg, and so there may also have been a prior intentional assault. No injury arises on the facts and so there can be no question of ABH in respect of this initial offence. Both assault and battery can be regarded as 'common assault' contrary to **s 40** of the **Criminal Justice Act 1988**. However, the common assault was committed by Greg, unaware of the fact that Pat had a loose tooth, which subsequently became lodged in his windpipe. This might or might not have been serious enough to amount to 'really serious harm'. Much would depend on the facts. The appropriate offence is difficult to discern without further information but it must be at least **s 47** ABH and possibly even **s 20** GBH. (Both of these have been explained earlier.) There is no doubt that in either case, Greg's initial assault or battery was the legal cause of the harm sustained by Pat. His lack of awareness of the tooth problem would be no barrier to finding an unbroken chain of causation on the principle that 'you take your victim as you find him' or the 'thin skull' rule (*Blaue* **[1975] 1 WLR 1411**).

Regarding *mens rea* for **s 47**, the fact that he did not intend or foresee any harm greater than a battery would not preclude conviction of **s 47** provided the initial assault/battery was accompanied by *mens rea* and there existed an unbroken chain of causation in relation to the ABH. However, in order to be convicted of **s 20**, he needs to have at least foreseen some harm, although not really serious harm. Whether or not he did is unclear and would need to be ascertained before attempting to convict him of this crime.

Therefore, to conclude, it seems likely that both Pat and Greg will have committed several offences against the person. It is unlikely that P will be able to defend himself on the basis of duress.

 LOOKING FOR EXTRA MARKS?

■ An ability to untangle the *mens rea* in a question like this and apply them properly to the facts will earn you marks, as the difficulty of *mens rea* in the non-fatal offences is well recognized by examiners.

- Show the examiner that you are aware of the development of the law, even in a problem question. Here, the law on duress and its development in *R v Hasan* is a good opportunity to demonstrate your awareness of this development. Prior to *Hasan*, the rule on voluntary association would not on its own have prevented Pat from using the defence.

TAKING THINGS FURTHER

- Ashworth A, *Principles of Criminal Law* (OUP 2013).
  Seminal textbook on the criminal process.

- Bleasdale-Hill L, '"Our Home is Our Haven and Refuge—a Place Where We Have Every Right to Feel Safe": Justifying the Use of Up to "Grossly Disproportionate Force" in a Place of Residence' [2015] Crim LR 407.
  Discusses the lack of clarity in the proportionality test in self-defence and explores the intention of Parliament in drafting the new 'householder' provisions.

- Child J and Sullivan G R, 'When Does the Insanity Defence Apply? Some Recent Cases' [2014] Crim LR 788–801.
  Summarizes some case law on the insanity defence and focuses on the definition of disease of the mind.

- Collins J and Ashworth A, 'Householders, Self-Defence and the Right to Life' (2016) 132 LQR 377.
  *Analyses the compatibility of the householder provision with **Article 2** of the **European Convention on Human Rights (ECHR)**.*

- Gardner S, 'The Importance of Majewski' (1994) 14 OJLS 280l.
  Discusses the fairness and basis of this key decision.

- Gardner S, 'The Domestic Criminal Legality of the RAF Drone Strike in Syria in August 2015' [2016] Crim LR 35.
  Discusses whether a fatal drone strike carried out by UK forces in Syria was lawful under English criminal law.

- Law Commission, Legislating the Criminal Code; Offences Against the Person and General Principles (LC 218, 1993).
  *Report on the reform of non-fatal offences, some of which were implemented in the **Domestic Violence, Crime and Victims Act 2004**.*

- Manwaring J, 'Windle Revisited' [2018] Crim LR 12, 987–92.
  Questions the decision in Windle and the requirement for the defendant to know what he was doing as legally rather than simply morally wrong.

- Robinson P, 'A Brief Summary and Critique of Criminal Liability Rules for Intoxicated Conduct' (2018) 82(5) J Crim Law 381–7.
  Discusses the impact of intoxication on criminal liability generally and whether addiction should cause voluntary intoxication to be regarded as involuntary.

■ Samuels A, 'The Diabetic Driver' (2017) 33 CL&J 181.
Discusses the difficulties in proving non-insane automatism and insanity when a driver blames his diabetes for a collision.

■ Virgo G, 'The Law Commission Consultation Paper on Intoxication' [1993] Crim LR 415.
An assessment of the reform proposals in the above consultation paper.

Online Resources   www.oup.com/uk/qanda/

For extra essay and problem questions on this topic, as well as advice on revision and exam technique, please visit the online resources.

8

Secondary Liability and Inchoate Offences

ARE YOU READY?

In order to answer questions on this topic, you will need an understanding of the following:

- the idea of secondary liability;
- encouraging and assisting crime;
- the doctrine of joint enterprise;
- the *mens rea* of the secondary participant following the judgment in *R v Jogee* [2016] **UKSC 8** and the effect on the 'fundamental difference' rule;
- the provisions of the **Serious Crime Act 2007** relating to inchoate liability;
- conspiracy under the **Criminal Law Act 1977**;
- attempts under the **Criminal Attempts Act 1981**.

KEY DEBATES

Debate: the *mens rea* of the accomplice

The *mens rea* of the accomplice has been the subject of considerable debate. Following *R v Powell and Daniels* [1997] 4 All ER 545 and *R v Chan Wing-Siu* [1985] AC 168, a defendant could be convicted as an accomplice to murder, provided he merely foresaw the possibility that the principal offender might kill or cause grievous bodily harm with intent to kill or cause grievous bodily harm.

The question of the level of foresight has now been settled by the Supreme Court decision in *R v Jogee* [2016] **UKSC 8**, which held that the courts in *Chan Wing-Siu* and *Powell and English* 'took a wrong turn', and that the mental element of intent to assist or encourage should be intention, not

○

simply foresight. In doing so, it has apparently abolished the separate category of joint enterprise liability and has substantially revised the effect of the 'fundamental difference' rule.

Debate: rationale for the Serious Crime Act 2007

The previous common law offence of incitement was replaced by the provisions in this Act in the form of three new offences which concentrate on the facilitating of another's offence. Wilson and Ormerod (2015) argue that the new offences are too complicated, particularly in the verbal definitions. Child (2012) argues that the *mens rea* elements in these offences are not clear, leading to further uncertainty.

QUESTION | 1

Alvin contacted Bernard, suggesting that they kill Zac because he had refused to pay them a debt. After hearing Alvin's proposals, Bernard secretly decided that he would not do anything to help Alvin, but he told Alvin that he would do anything he could to assist. Their conversation was overheard by Ceri and Desmond, who both agreed to help. Ceri obtained a loaded revolver and gave it to Alvin, and Desmond agreed to drive them in his car to Zac's house.

On the appointed day, Bernard failed to arrive; and after Desmond had taken them to their destination, he telephoned the police in time to stop Alvin shooting at Zac.

Discuss the criminal responsibility of the parties.

CAUTION!

- This is a relatively straightforward question concerning the inchoate offences and accessorial liability. These must be dealt with separately.

- All points in problem questions like this relating to accomplice liability will need to be considered in the light of the decision in *R v Jogee*.

DIAGRAM ANSWER PLAN

Identify the issues	▪ Consider encouraging the commission of crime, conspiracy to murder, attempted murder, and accomplice liability.
Relevant law	▪ Outline the relevant law: the **Serious Crime Act 2007, Criminal Law Act 1977**, and **Criminal Attempts Act 1981**.
Apply the law	▪ Is the withdrawal effective? Consider the *mens rea* aspect for conspiracy.
Conclude	▪ Draw a conclusion on the parties' liability.

SUGGESTED ANSWER

There is now a number of inchoate offences with which Alvin could be charged. His initial action in contacting Bernard suggesting that they kill Zac could amount to the crime of encouraging murder, contrary to **s 44** of the **Serious Crime Act 2007**.[1] Alvin clearly intends that the offence of murder should be committed and that the necessary course of conduct should be followed with the requisite fault element for murder. Liability is inchoate, so the fact that the killing never takes place is irrelevant. The offence focuses on Alvin's state of mind—hence the fact that Bernard does not want to go through with the plan will be no bar to liability.

All four participants could be charged with conspiracy to murder under **s 1** of the **Criminal Law Act 1977**. In order to establish a statutory conspiracy, it must be shown that two or more persons agreed that a course of conduct should be pursued which, if the agreement were to be carried out in accordance with their intentions, either:

(a) would necessarily amount to or involve the commission of any offence or offences by one or more of the parties to the agreement; or

(b) would do so but for the existence of facts which render the commission of the offence or any of the offences impossible.

The prosecution must prove that an agreement existed between the parties.[2] It is submitted that there is an agreement on the facts and,

[1] Under **s 47(5)** of the **2007 Act**, it suffices if Alvin believed that, were the act to be done, it would be done with the *mens rea* for murder, or that he was reckless as to whether or not this would be the case, or that his state of mind was such that, were he to have done what was encouraged or assisted, he would have acted with the fault required.

[2] If they are still in the course of negotiations, this would not be sufficient.

as they intend that death will result, the parties could be guilty of conspiracy to murder. However, Bernard will argue that as he had no intention to assist, and did nothing to assist, he cannot be guilty. The key case on this point is the House of Lords' decision in *R v Anderson* [1985] 2 All ER 961. In this case, the accused was convicted of conspiring with a number of people to help one of them escape from jail. He had agreed to supply wire to cut the prison bars, but said he never intended the plan to be put into effect and believed that it could not possibly succeed. However, his conviction was upheld as he had agreed that the criminal course of conduct should be pursued, and it was not necessary to prove that he intended that the offence be committed. In this case, Lord Bridge also stated (at p 965) that the *mens rea* of conspiracy is established 'if and only if it is shown that the accused when he entered into the agreement, intended to play some part in the agreed course of conduct in furtherance of the criminal purpose which the agreed course of conduct was intended to achieve'. On this basis, Bernard would have a defence, but Lord Bridge's *dictum* was clarified by the Court of Appeal decision in *R v Siracusa* (1989) 90 Cr App R 340, where O'Connor J stated that, 'participation in a conspiracy is infinitely variable: it can be active or passive. There is no need for the prosecution to prove an intention on each accused's part in the carrying out of the agreement.' Bernard would therefore be found guilty of conspiracy to murder.[3]

[3] These two cases clarify the *mens rea* for conspiracy.

Desmond may also be able to argue that he lacked the *mens rea* for conspiracy to murder, as his informing the police demonstrated that he had an intention to frustrate the intention of the conspiracy. In *R v McPhillips* [1990] 6 BNIL, Lord Lowry CJ in the Court of Appeal of Northern Ireland held that an accused who had joined in a conspiracy to plant a bomb, timed to explode on the roof of a hall of a disco, was not a party to a conspiracy to murder because he intended to give a warning in time for the hall to be cleared. However, in *Yip Chiu Cheung v R* [1994] 2 All ER 924, the Privy Council held that an undercover police officer posing as a drug dealer would have the necessary *mens rea* for conspiracy when he deliberately carried drugs to entrap other drug dealers. Neither his good motive nor the instructions of his superiors would have been a valid defence.[4]

[4] This case is also good authority for the proposition that motive should not be confused with intention.

Bernard may incur liability under **s 45** of the **Serious Crime Act 2007** on the basis that he does encourage Alvin by saying he would assist in the murder. The question for the jury will be whether or not there is evidence that Bernard believed that the offence would be committed, and that his actions would encourage or assist its commission. The fact that he did not intend to help does not necessarily mean that his apparent enthusiasm was not capable of encouraging the others.[5] As to *mens rea*, it would suffice that Bernard believed

[5] Apply the law to the facts, distinguishing if necessary.

that, were the killing of Zac to take place, it would be done with the fault required for murder.

As withdrawal is recognized as a defence for an accomplice, it is submitted that a conspirator should have a similar defence, if only to provide an incentive for a conspirator to make efforts to stop the conspiracy succeeding. Desmond should not be found guilty of conspiracy. Perhaps the Crown Prosecution Service would decide it is not in the public interest to prosecute Desmond.

Alvin may also be guilty of attempted murder. Clearly, he has the necessary *mens rea*, an intention to kill (*R v Whybrow* **(1951) 35 Cr App R 141**), but has he committed the *actus reus* of attempt? The test the prosecution must satisfy under **s 1(1)** of the **Criminal Attempts Act 1981** is that the accused has done an act that is more than merely preparatory to the offence. This is a question of fact for the jury after the trial judge has decided that there is sufficient evidence to be left to them to support such a finding. Thus, in *R v Jones* **(1990) 91 Cr App R 356**, the Court of Appeal upheld the jury's decision that the accused had done more than a merely preparatory act for attempted murder in pointing a sawn-off shotgun at the victim, even though he had still to remove the safety catch.

⁶ No further information is given on these facts.

Whether Alvin would be guilty of attempted murder would therefore purely depend on what precise point the plan had reached before he was stopped.[6]

Bernard, Ceri, and Desmond may also face charges under the **Accessories and Abettors Act 1861** of counselling, procuring, aiding, and abetting. It is often difficult to identify precisely the specific involvement (see *R v Richards* **[1974] 3 All ER 1088**), but counselling and procuring are acts done before the principal offence, whereas aiding and abetting take place at the time of its occurrence. Clearly, as they intended to assist and contemplated the type of crime (*Chan Wing Siu v R* **[1984] 3 All ER 877**), they appear to have the necessary *mens rea*. Desmond would argue that he validly withdrew by contacting the police in time for them to stop the murder (*R v Becerra* **(1975) 62 Cr App R 212**), and Bernard would contend that his failure to arrive constituted a withdrawal. It is submitted that whereas Desmond's argument would succeed, Bernard's would fail as in *R v Rook* **[1993] 2 All ER 955** the Court of Appeal held merely not turning up to be insufficient, suggesting that a positive act may be required. As was confirmed in *R v O'Flaherty* **[2004] Crim LR 751**, whether or not withdrawal is effective is a matter of fact and degree. The later it is left, the more is required by way of positive action.

Ceri does not appear to have any defence available, and his act of giving Alvin a loaded gun satisfies the ingredients of this offence.

Thus, Ceri and Bernard could be found guilty of abetting an attempted murder. Although the offence of attempt to aid and abet was abolished by **s 5** of the **Criminal Law Act 1977**, there is an offence of attempting to abet.

Ceri and Desmond could also incur liability under **s 45** of the **Serious Crime Act 2007** on the basis of their offering to help Alvin. Again, this would be seen as committing acts capable of encouraging murder, intending that Alvin should commit murder.

LOOKING FOR EXTRA MARKS?

- A really good understanding of the statutory provisions will make all the difference in this question.

- Be sure to apply the legal principles to the facts throughout, distinguishing if necessary.

QUESTION | 2

Amy, Betty, Claire, and Debbie plan to break into X's warehouse in order to steal. Amy, Betty, and Claire know that there will be a nightwatchman on the premises, but Debbie does not know this fact. Amy gives Betty a loaded revolver, telling her not to hesitate to use it if the occasion should so require. When they set off to X's warehouse, Debbie knows that Betty has a revolver in her possession, but Claire does not. Once inside the warehouse, the four are interrupted by the nightwatchman, Victor. As Betty is about to fire the revolver at Victor, Amy, recognizing Victor as her cousin, knocks Betty's hand to one side, crying out 'Don't shoot'. Amy's act causes the bullet to miss Victor, but it strikes and kills Peter, a police officer who is entering the room.

Advise the Crown Prosecution Service on any criminal liability arising from these facts.

CAUTION!

- You may often find that the facts presented to you feature a conspiracy before the commission of the subsequent completed offence. It is tempting to advise on the criminal offences in the order in which they are presented by the question, but it is usually best to leave inchoate offences until the end and present them as alternatives to other forms of accessorial liability.

- This is a detailed scenario, so some of the detail has been curtailed to represent what a candidate could reasonably expect to achieve in an examination. The problem of the foresight of the defendants has been made somewhat more straightforward with the decision in *R v Jogee*.

DIAGRAM ANSWER PLAN

Identify the issues	■ Mention murder, transferred malice, involuntary manslaughter, and attempts.
Relevant law	■ Consider causation in murder and intent and *mens rea*. Set out the inchoate offences.
Apply the law	■ Use the decision of *R v Jogee* on foresight and intent to assist and encourage.
Conclude	■ Conclude using accessorial liability for murder and manslaughter.

SUGGESTED ANSWER

Betty kills Peter by causing his death in fact and in law. The fact that Amy grabs her arm to stop her firing at Victor does not amount to a *novus actus interveniens.* Even though her gun points at Peter not Victor, her pulling the trigger is still a voluntary act. The *mens rea* of murder is satisfied by the prosecution proving that Betty intended to kill or intended to cause grievous bodily harm (*R v Moloney* [1985] 1 All ER 1025).[1] Following *R v Woollin* [1998] 4 All ER 103, the jury should be directed that they will be entitled to infer that Betty intended to kill if there is evidence that she foresaw death or grievous bodily harm as virtually certain to result from her actions. Given that Betty was intending to fire the revolver at Victor, foresight of some grievous bodily harm on her part seems evident.

Betty may argue that, as she intended to fire the gun at Victor, she did not intend to harm Peter. The court will apply the doctrine of transferred malice. Thus, if the accused has the necessary *mens rea* of the offence but the actual victim is different from the intended victim, the *mens rea* will be transferred and the accused will be guilty; see *R v Mitchell* [1983] 2 All ER 427.

Betty might argue that she was simply firing a warning shot in Victor's direction, and that it was Amy's act of hitting her arm which caused her aim to alter, resulting in Peter's death. In the event of this argument being accepted, Betty would still be guilty of involuntary

[1] Start by identifying the offence, before considering accessorial liability.

(unlawful act) manslaughter on the constructive basis. The prosecution would need to prove that Betty intended to do an act that was unlawful and dangerous (*R v Newbury and Jones* **[1976] 2 All ER 365**). Simply drawing and pointing a gun at someone would be unlawful, ie assault; and as the test for dangerous is objective ('the unlawful act must be such as all sober and reasonable people would inevitably recognise must subject the other person to at least the risk of some physical harm resulting therefrom, albeit not serious harm' per Edmund Davies J in *R v Church* **[1965] 2 All ER 72**, reaffirmed in *R v JM* **[2012] EWCA Crim 2293**), this element of the offence would be made out. The intention to assault is evident.[2]

In light of the above, it should be noted that Betty might also have incurred liability for attempting to murder Victor, contrary to **s 1(1)** of the **Criminal Attempts Act 1981**. There is evidence to support the assertion that she takes steps more than merely preparatory to killing Victor (indeed, she seems to have committed the 'last act' within her power). The *mens rea*, however, requires proof that she intended to kill Victor—intention to cause grievous bodily harm will not suffice for a charge of attempted murder; see *R v Walker and Hayles* **(1989) 90 Cr App R 226**. For reasons outlined earlier, proof of this might be doubtful unless she confesses that killing him was her intention.

Amy will, in all likelihood, be guilty of **s 9(1)(a)** of the **Theft Act 1968** burglary. She could also be charged with counselling Betty's offence of aggravated burglary under **s 10** of the **Theft Act 1968**. Amy encourages Betty to go armed with the gun and it is her intention that Betty should do so. The **Serious Crimes Act 2007** applies here.

Turning to Amy's liability in relation to the death of Peter, it could be argued that she incurs liability as a principal offender, as she does contribute to causing his death: but for her pushing Betty's hand to one side, Peter would not have been killed. Her actions in causing the gun to be fired at Peter are the operating and substantial cause of his death. *Mens rea* would be problematic, however, as her intention when she pushes Betty's hand is to prevent harm. There is no evidence that she intends any harm to occur to Peter as opposed to Victor. Indeed, it might be impossible to identify any fault that would suffice for her to be convicted of a form of manslaughter as principal offender. There is no obvious dangerous criminal act as is required for unlawful act manslaughter, and it is far from obvious that the duty of care and grossly negligent breach of duty of care needed for killing by gross negligence can be identified.[3]

The prosecution will almost certainly seek to charge Amy with either the murder or manslaughter of Peter as an accomplice to Betty's actions. Amy supplies Betty with a loaded gun, knowing that there is a nightwatchman on the premises. There is compelling evidence on these facts that she contemplates a scenario in which the gun will be discharged by Betty—especially given the evidence that she told Betty to use the gun if necessary. However, the position has now changed. This will be discussed below. At the very least, Amy contemplated that Betty might kill or do grievous bodily harm either with intent to kill or with intent to do grievous bodily harm. In *R v Powell; R v Daniels; and R v English* [1999] 1 AC 1,[4] the House of Lords had held that, to found a conviction for murder, it was sufficient for a secondary party to have realized, in the course of a joint enterprise, that the primary party might kill with intent to do so or with intent to cause grievous bodily harm. Following the decision in *R v Jogee* [2016] UKSC 8, the mental element for secondary liability is an intention to assist or encourage the crime. In the absence of an actual agreement, mere contemplation that Betty might kill will be insufficient. Where a defendant departs from the agreed plan, he is only guilty as an accomplice if he intended to commit the crime, or if he intended to assist or encourage the principal to commit it. Previously, intention was not required. The second defendant was guilty if he had foresight.

If Betty was found guilty of manslaughter, Amy might contend that she could not be found guilty as an accomplice to murder. This point arose in the Privy Council case of *Hui Chi Ming v R* [1991] 3 All ER 897, where the court upheld the conviction of the accused for murder even though the principal offenders had in an earlier trial been found guilty of manslaughter only. The principle is that if the *actus reus* has been committed, the court will look at the *mens rea* of the individual participants in order to ascertain their criminal responsibility.

In the event that there is any difficulty in establishing the *mens rea* of Amy as an accomplice to murder, the prosecution is most likely to contend that Amy incurs liability as an accomplice to the manslaughter of Peter by Betty on the basis that his death was an unforeseen and accidental consequence of the common design (committing a burglary armed with a loaded weapon) being carried out. Both *R v Betts and Ridley* (1930) 22 Cr App R 148 and *R v Baldessare* (1930) 22 Cr App R 70 support the conclusion that an accomplice will be a party to the accidental consequences of the principal offender's acts, provided the principal offender's actions were within the scope of what the accomplice contemplated or agreed. In *R v Baldessare*, the court held that an accused who agreed to take and drive away a car was guilty of abetting manslaughter when the principal offender drove so negligently as to cause a pedestrian's death, as although this consequence was unforeseen, it arose when the principal offender was acting within the scope of the agreement.

[4] As *R v Jogee* is such a recent decision, it is a good idea to explain exactly what has changed with regard to the defendant's *mens rea*.

Betty could be charged with the attempted murder of Victor. Similarly, Amy could be charged as an accomplice to the attempted murder—for an example of accessorial liability for attempt, see **R v Dunnington [1984] 1 All ER 676**.

The facts indicate that Amy does try to stop Betty firing at Victor. Hence Amy may argue that, notwithstanding her supply of the gun, she had, at the last minute, withdrawn from the joint enterprise, and should not incur any liability as an accomplice to the attempted murder. The key case on withdrawal is **R v Becerra and Cooper (1975) 62 Cr App R 212**, where before the principal offender in the course of a burglary killed the victim, the accomplice had said 'Come on, let's go', and had left the building. The Court of Appeal, in upholding his conviction for murder, held that something vastly more substantial and effective was required to constitute a valid withdrawal, such as shouting a warning or physical intervention. Amy would argue that in shouting 'Don't shoot' and knocking Betty's hand, she had done all that she reasonably could to prevent the crime. It will be a question of fact for the jury to determine whether or not this is the case.[5] As was confirmed in **R v O'Flaherty [2004] Crim LR 751**, whether or not withdrawal is effective is a matter of fact and degree. The later it is left, the more is required by way of positive action.

As with Amy, Claire could be charged under **s 9(1)(a)** of the **Theft Act 1968** as a principal offender. As she does not know Betty had the gun, the prosecution would not charge her as an accomplice to Betty's offence of aggravated burglary under **s 10** of the **Theft Act 1968**.

Claire knew that there was a nightwatchman on the premises, providing evidence that she did contemplate some harm being caused to him if the burglary was to succeed. For her to be convicted of murder, however, there would have to be evidence that she intended to assist or encourage the crime.[6] The key point for Claire would be the use of the weapon. Provided she did not intend the death of any person, she could avail herself of the 'fundamentally different' rule, under which even an accomplice who contemplates that death or serious injury might occur can escape liability if the principal offender causes death by the use of a fundamentally different (more dangerous) modus operandi—such as the use of a gun instead of a cosh.

If Claire contemplated some harm being caused to a person, not amounting to actual bodily harm, she could be convicted as an accomplice to manslaughter on the given facts, but again, she would escape liability if she was able to avail herself of the 'fundamentally different' rule; see **Attorney-General's Ref (No 3 of 2004) [2005] EWCA Crim 1882**.

It is relevant in these circumstances to ask whether there was a shared criminal purpose—there does not appear to have been here.

[5] The roles of the judge and jury in this type of case were confirmed in **R v Jogee**. It is the role of the jury to determine this on a question of fact.

[6] This was explained earlier.

Debbie could be charged with offences contrary to **s 9(1)(a)** of the **Theft Act 1968** burglary, as outlined earlier, and as an accomplice to Betty's offence of aggravated burglary under **s 10** of the **Theft Act 1968**.

Regarding accessorial liability for homicide, Debbie's position is slightly different from Claire's. Debbie knows about the gun, but not that there will be a nightwatchman. It is submitted that her knowledge regarding the gun will put her in a much worse position than Claire, however. The prosecution will argue that as she knew about the gun, she contemplated its use—why else did she think Betty was taking it? Following the decision in *R v Jogee* (see earlier), it will no longer be possible to convict her, even if she contemplated or foresaw it—only an intention will suffice.[7] Regarding her liability both as an accomplice to the attempted murder of Victor and the murder of Peter, in order to escape liability Debbie would be forced to use the weak argument that although she knew that Betty had a gun, she did not think that Betty would actually use it. Debbie could be held to have had sufficient *mens rea* to be an accomplice to the murder of Peter and the attempted murder of Victor.

Even before the four parties enter the warehouse, they would be guilty of the crime of conspiracy to burgle under **s 1** of the **Criminal Law Act 1977**, as they have agreed to pursue a course of conduct which would necessarily involve a criminal offence. Amy would also be guilty of encouraging and assisting Betty to commit burglary, assault, and possibly murder when supplying her with the gun and encouraging her to use it; see **s 46** of the **Serious Crime Act 2007**.

[7] Foresight will no longer be sufficient *mens rea* for accessorial liability.

LOOKING FOR EXTRA MARKS?

- This question requires you to show your knowledge of recent legal developments. You can do this by contrasting with the previous law.
- Accessorial liability and principal offences are difficult to structure in the same question—keep these issues separate.

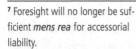

QUESTION | **3**

Kirk hires Miles and Chaka to attack Patti, a business rival. Kirk makes it clear that he wants Patti frightened off so that she will no longer be a threat to Kirk's business. One evening, Miles and Chaka follow Patti as she leaves her office to go home at the end of the day. Miles picks up a large stone from the gutter, grabs Patti from behind, and beats her on the head with the stone. Patti dies of a brain haemorrhage. Chaka is standing close to Miles as he carries out the attack and does not take steps to intervene and stop him.

Kirk, Miles, and Chaka are subsequently arrested in connection with Patti's death. Under questioning, Chaka admits that she knew Miles had a history of violent behaviour and previous convictions for grievous bodily harm, but claims that she had no idea Miles had a stone in his hand when he hit Patti. Kirk admits hiring Miles and Chaka to frighten Patti but denies any intention that Patti should be physically harmed.

Advise the Crown Prosecution Service as to the criminal liability of Kirk, Miles, and Chaka in respect of the death of Patti.

CAUTION!

- Consider what Chaka may have contemplated—this is crucial to the *mens rea*.

- Good fact management is key to providing a clear and concise answer. Always start by dealing with the liability of the principal offender. Once you have established what s/he has done, you can see what accessorial liability of other parties might be derived from this.

DIAGRAM ANSWER PLAN

Identify the issues	■ Consider murder and unlawful act manslaughter; accomplice liability and joint enterprise; conspiracy and assisting or encouraging crime.
Relevant law	■ Discuss the *actus reus* and *mens rea* of murder. ■ Discuss liability for manslaughter by an unlawful and dangerous act. ■ Discuss liability under the **Serious Crime Act 2007**.
Apply the law	■ Consider the liability of Kirk as an accomplice to Miles. ■ Consdier whether Miles goes beyond what was contemplated by Chaka.
Conclude	■ Draw a conclusion on the above.

SUGGESTED ANSWER

[1] In a case like this, it is always important to show that you have identified the primary offence and the principal offender. You can then start to see what secondary liability might apply.

The prosecution will need to prove that Miles was the cause in fact and in law of Patti's death.[1] As for causation in law, the application of the 'but for' test would suggest that but for his having attacked Patti with the stone, she would not have suffered the injury resulting in her death—see *R v White* [1910] 2 KB 124. The facts provide that Patti dies of a brain haemorrhage. Miles may argue that Patti had a 'thin skull' and was more prone to serious injury as a result of the attack than would have been the case with the average person. It is unlikely that such an argument would succeed. *R v Blaue* [1975] 1 WLR 1411 provides that Miles must take his victim as he finds him or her. The fact that Patti might have been more susceptible to injury will not be relevant in law.

Assuming causation can be established, the question arises as to whether or not Miles had the *mens rea* for murder. The prosecution would have to prove that he intended to kill Patti or intended to cause her grievous bodily harm. Alternatively, it would suffice for the prosecution to prove that Miles foresaw her death, or her suffering grievous bodily harm, as being a virtually certain consequence of his actions; *R v Woollin* [1998] 4 All ER 103. On the one hand, beating a person on the head with a large stone suggests evidence of at least an intention to do some grievous bodily harm. On the other hand, the jury would need to review the evidence indicating the force used and Miles's own direct testimony. Although not relevant to the issue of causation, evidence that Patti was more susceptible to this type of harm might influence a jury in concluding whether or not Miles did foresee death or grievous bodily harm as virtually certain.

Given the uncertainty regarding the *mens rea* for murder, Miles's potential liability for unlawful act manslaughter must be considered. The attack on Patti is clearly an unlawful (ie criminal) act—specifically, an assault. It should not be too difficult for the jury to apply the test for dangerousness here in relation to the unlawful act; see *R v Church* [1965] 2 All ER 72 as developed in *R v Dawson* (1985) 81 Cr App R 150. The prosecution would have to prove that a sober and reasonable bystander, at the scene of the attack on Patti, would have foreseen the risk of her suffering some physical harm. This should be self-evident on the facts, as should the *mens rea* for the unlawful act—ie Miles being at least reckless as to whether Patti suffers a battery or actual bodily harm.

[2] Now you can deal with the secondary liability—in this case, joint enterprise.

The prosecution will allege that Chaka was party to a joint enterprise in the attack on Patti—see *R v Petters and Parfitt* [1995] **Crim LR 501**. Chaka is at the scene of the crime acting in concert with Miles.[2]

A number of issues arise for consideration. First, can Chaka argue that by not physically participating in the attack she played no part in it? Mere presence at the scene of a crime will not normally result in accessorial liability. Chaka's case is hardly that of an innocent bystander happening to witness a crime, however. She set out with Miles to carry out some sort of unlawful attack on Patti that would result in Patti being frightened off. Indeed, the prosecution will in all likelihood rely upon her failure to prevent Miles from carrying out the attack as evidence that she passively adopted his actions in hitting Patti with the stone.[3]

[3] Note this application of the law to the facts.

Second, if Chaka is to be convicted of murder as a party to a joint enterprise, what *mens rea* has to be proved on her part? On the basis of *R v Powell*; *R v Daniels*; *and R v English* **[1999] 1 AC 1**, Chaka could have been convicted of murder if she intended the death of Patti (unlikely on the facts); or intended that Patti should suffer grievous bodily harm (doubtful on the facts); or where she realized that, in the course of pursuing the joint enterprise, Miles might have killed or caused grievous bodily harm with intent to produce either of those consequences (possible, given the facts). Chaka confessed that she knew Miles had a history of violent behaviour and previous convictions for grievous bodily harm. This would have helped to prove that she foresaw death or grievous bodily harm as possible consequences of an attack by Miles.[4]

[4] The *mens rea* is foresight, not intention.

The issue will now be dealt with differently by the courts, following the decision of *R v Jogee* **[2016] UKSC 8**. The prosecution will have to be satisfied that Chaka intended to encourage or assist Miles in the commission of the offence. Simple foresight on Chaka's part that Miles might commit the offence will not suffice.

The third issue is as to whether or not Chaka can argue that Miles's deliberate use of the large stone as a weapon amounted to a conscious departure from the joint enterprise. In *R v Powell*; *R v Daniels*; *and R v English* **[1999] 1 AC 1**, the House of Lords had held that where a party to a joint enterprise 'only' foresaw the principal offender causing grievous bodily harm, and the principal offender in fact killed the victim by using a 'fundamentally different' act, the accomplice could escape liability on the basis that the principal had exceeded the scope of the joint enterprise.

[5] This last case clarified the House of Lords approach in *Rahman*, however.

In *R v Rahman and Others* **[2008] UKHL 45**, the House of Lords was willing to extend the scope of the 'fundamentally different' rule to the benefit of an accomplice who foresaw that the principal *might* kill with intent to kill or with intent to some grievous bodily harm.[5]

The use of the knife to cut the victim's throat rather than the gun to kneecap the victim is a fundamentally different modus operandi—one that carries with it a much more obvious risk of death. Hence

Chaka may argue that she foresaw grievous bodily harm (especially in light of her knowledge of Miles) or even that she foresaw Miles causing death as a result of his intentionally inflicting grievous bodily harm, but that she did not foresee the use of a weapon. In the light of the decision in *R v Jogee*, it is clear that the rule has lost much of its significance. Knowledge of a particular weapon only has significance in the context of the court's assessment of *mens rea*. It could be evidence of intention to assist, but this will not be a foregone conclusion.

A fourth point is that Chaka may argue that she did not even contemplate grievous bodily harm being caused. She would cite in support of this the fact that Kirk asked them simply to frighten Patti. If this is the case, Chaka clearly cannot be guilty as an accomplice to murder. The prosecution may, however, argue that she should be convicted as an accomplice to manslaughter. Before the decision in *R v Jogee*, if Chaka only contemplated some harm falling short of grievous bodily harm, it was possible she could be convicted as an accomplice to manslaughter, provided the actions of Miles were not a deliberate departure from the conduct that she contemplated.[6] Now, actual intention will be needed. Hence if she contemplated the use of a weapon, Miles's use of a stone will not amount to a departure from the joint enterprise. If Chaka did not contemplate the use of any weapon, she may escape liability altogether. It seems that Chaka's liability will derive from what she foresaw Miles doing, not the intent with which she foresaw him acting.

Note that the prosecution will also have the option of charging Chaka with encouraging the commission of the offence by Miles on the basis that she was supporting him at the scene of the crime by her presence—see ss 44–46 of the **Serious Crime Act 2007**. There will still be an issue here regarding which crime Chaka was encouraging Miles to commit—but at the very least she can be said to have encouraged him to commit an assault, and to have believed that her encouragement would lead to the commission of the offence.[7]

Kirk was not present at the scene of the attack on Patti, hence he would be regarded as a secondary party—an accomplice involved prior to the commission of the offence. Hiring Miles and Chaka to carry out the attack on Patti would amount to counselling (*R v Calhaem* [1985] 2 All ER 266). The problem lies in whether or not Kirk could be charged with counselling murder or manslaughter. As noted earlier in this section, *R v Powell; R v Daniels; and R v English* [1999] 1 AC 1 provided that an accomplice could be guilty of murder provided he at least contemplated that the principal might kill the victim or cause him grievous bodily harm. Kirk will say that he only intended that Patti should be frightened and that he did not contemplate any serious harm, or possibly that he did not contemplate any harm at all.

[6] This is quite a fine point, and illustrates the difficulties facing the courts in situations of accessorial liability.

[7] Again, ensure you apply the law to the facts carefully.

The court will want to be satisfied that he did much more than merely contemplate harm, but that he actually intended that harm to result. Again, foresight or contemplation will not be sufficient for the prosecution to discharge their burden of proof.

Kirk, Miles, and Chaka could be charged with conspiring to cause Patti actual bodily harm, or even grievous bodily harm, contrary to **s 1(1)** of the **Criminal Law Act 1977**. The fact that Kirk intended to play no active part in the attack is no bar to liability—see **R v Siracusa (1989) 90 Cr App R 340**. It would be enough that he agreed with others that the course of conduct should be pursued.

Finally, Kirk could be encouraging Miles and Chaka to assault (in the narrow sense) Patti—the fact that they act on the encouragement would be no bar to his liability for the offence created by **s 44** of the **Serious Crime Act 2007**. He encourages the commission of the offence of (narrow) assault and intends that it should be committed.

LOOKING FOR EXTRA MARKS?

- As the law is still finding its feet in this area, a discussion of how the recent changes impact on the defendant's liability, and an acknowledgement that the position under the previous law would be very different, will show that you are aware of the practical operation of the changes.

- A detailed and forensic application of the law to the facts will help your analysis in a question like this—especially with regard to balancing both the prosecution and the defence arguments.

QUESTION | 4

Discuss and analyse the decision of the Supreme Court in the case of **R v Jogee [2016] UKSC 8** on secondary party liability for murder.

CAUTION!

- This is a complicated area of law, given clarity in this recent case. Note that you are being asked to comment on the scope of this case, so make sure you only deal with joint enterprise, rather than secondary party liability as a whole.

- It is essential to avoid simply describing the legal position—make sure you find room to comment on how and why the judges reached their decision.

DIAGRAM ANSWER PLAN

> Give an explanation of secondary liability and joint enterprise.
>
> ▼
>
> Consider the decision in *R v Jogee* and the previous law.
>
> ▼
>
> Consider the impact and assessment of the decision.
>
> ▼
>
> Discuss blameworthiness in the criminal law.
>
> ▼
>
> Come to a conclusion on the effectiveness of the decision.

SUGGESTED ANSWER

Secondary liability for a criminal offence arises where the person who did not commit the *actus reus* of the crime (the secondary party) encourages or assists the person who does commit it (the principal offender). If the encouragement or assistance was intentional, then the secondary party is guilty of the same offence.[1] The encouragement or assistance forms the *actus reus*; the intention to encourage and/or assist the principal forms the *mens rea*.

[1] Set out in summary form the general area of law you are going to discuss.

A particular problem arises, however, when the principal offender departs from the agreed crime, or commits another crime entirely, in the course of the planned criminal activity. The court must then assess the correct level of *mens rea* for the secondary participant. This type of liability became known as joint enterprise. The question is whether the secondary participant must intend the other to commit the crime, or whether he must simply be aware of the possibility that it might be committed. Until recently, foresight was sufficient to convict the secondary participant of murder.

[2] Set out your plans for the essay, with reference to the question set.

This essay analyses this problem, with reference to the landmark Supreme Court decision of *R v Jogee* [2016] UKSC 8, which reverses the previous common law position.[2] This had stated that the secondary participant could be convicted of murder where he merely had foresight of the crime committed by the principal. The legal position is now that in order to be convicted of murder, the secondary participant must intend to assist or encourage the commission of the offence in order to be found guilty of murder. The Supreme Court essentially abolished the previous category of joint enterprise liability.[3]

Two House of Commons Justice Committee reports recommended that the Law Commission review the law (see *Joint Enterprise, House of Commons, Justice Committee, Report 1957* (January 2012) and *Joint Enterprise: Follow Up* (HC Paper No 310, 2014). It was against this background of widespread criticism of joint enterprise that the Supreme Court decided *Jogee* in 2016.

In this way, it has effectively abolished joint enterprise liability, and has substantially reduced the significance of the fundamental difference rule. The law prior to this recent decision was contained in two key cases: *R v Powell and English* **[1997] 4 All ER 545** and *R v Chan Wing-Siu* **[1985] AC 168**. These cases held that the mental element required of the secondary party was simply that he *foresaw* the possibility that the principal defendant might commit another crime. If the defendant did foresee this possibility, the courts treated this as sufficient *mens rea* for the crime, and as tantamount to authorizing

the principal to commit it. The effect of this was that the secondary party was guilty of the crime even though he did not intend to commit it. Thus, a lower *mens rea* threshold was set for the second defendant, but the outcome was the same. In other words, this basis for liability in cases of joint enterprise is reflected in the following statement of Sir Robin Cooke in *Chan Wing-Siu*:[4]

Where a man lends himself to a criminal enterprise knowing that potentially murderous weapons are to be carried, and in the event they are in fact used by his partner with an intent sufficient for murder, he should not escape the consequences by [relying on a belief that their use was unlikely] ... that there is such a principle is not in doubt. It turns on contemplation or, putting the same idea into words, authorization, which may be express but is more usually implied ... the criminal liability lies in participating in the venture with that foresight.

The Court of Appeal has considered this issue of departure recently: in *R v Tas* **[2018] EWCA Crim 2603**, A had acted as getaway driver for what he claimed to believe would be an attack on V using fists; in fact, P fatally stabbed V. In *R v Harper* **[2019] EWCA Crim 343**, A intervened to assist P in a fight at a club using fists (and possibly a glass), but P fatally stabbed V. The Court of Appeal held in both cases that the use of a knife was not an overwhelming supervening event. What mattered was not the type of weapon but whether A had the necessary *mens rea*.

The approach in *Chan Wing-Siu* was criticized in various quarters on the grounds that it was fundamentally unfair to convict a defendant of a crime which they did not commit personally.[5] It meant, for example, that a young person in a gang (D1) would be guilty of murder where one member of that gang (D2) killed, and D1 knew that it was a possibility, even though D1 was elsewhere at the time. It meant that the scope of liability for murder was extremely wide, a surprising consequence given the insistence on the high threshold for intention in murder elsewhere. It was also unfair between defendants, of course, because it meant that the secondary party could be convicted of the same crime as the person who actually caused the death on the basis of a much lower level of mental culpability.

In *R v Powell; R v Daniels; and R v English* [1999] 1 AC 1, the court followed the approach in the earlier case, dealing particularly with the problem of the first defendant using a particular weapon. The court recognized the problem of convicting merely on foresight, but cited the need to prevent crime. Both of these cases, it is submitted, were decided on the basis of public policy and the need to balance the prevention of harm to the public with any potential danger of wrongly convicting an offender. The court in *R v Jogee* held this approach to be incorrect.

As stated earlier, the recent decision in *R v Jogee* has completely changed this position. It declared that the law had taken a wrong turn in *Chan Wing-Siu* [1985] and in *Powell and English*. On the one hand, it can be argued that the secondary defendant's *mens rea* need not be of the same level as that of the principal; on the other hand, it can be argued that it is unfair to convict a defendant of murder on the basis of anything less than intent. If foresight is not sufficient *mens rea* to convict a single defendant, it should also not be sufficient to convict a secondary participant.

In the case in question, the appellant, Jogee, was convicted of the murder of Paul Fyfe, the boyfriend of Naomi Reid. Paul Fyfe was stabbed to death by Mohammed Hirsi in the hallway of her home. Hirsi was convicted of murder, having been encouraged to 'do something to Fyfe' by Jogee, who was outside with a broken bottle. The fatal stabbing was done by Hirsi with a knife which he took from the kitchen.

The trial judge directed the jury that the appellant was guilty of murder if he took part in the attack on Mr Fyfe and if he realized that it was possible that Hirsi might use the knife with intent to cause grievous bodily harm.

⁶ Key reasons for the decision should be explained here.

The court concluded that this decision was incorrect. The decision did not take account of other important cases on secondary participation, and departed from the basic rule that the mental element is an intention to participate, not simply foresight. Henceforth, the secondary party will only be guilty of the crime if he intended that the crime be committed or if he intended to encourage and assist in its commission.⁶ Their Lordships acknowledged the problems that the previous law had created, stating (at para 81):

it cannot be said that the law is now well-established and working satisfactorily. It remains highly controversial and a continuing source of difficulty for trial judges.

To rely on these two cases (**Chang Wing-Siu** and *Powell; Daniels; English*) was to rely on cases which were in fact only part of the history of this area. In this way, the *mens rea* required of the secondary party is more or less the same as that required of the principal offender. The fact that the secondary participant was aware of the possibility that such a crime might be committed might be evidence, even strong evidence, of authorization or intent to commit it, but it was not equivalent to it. Foresight and authorization are not the same. As a result, the Supreme Court concluded that the law had taken a wrong turn. The law should, therefore, be returned to the position it was in before those two cases.

The dangers of a threshold 'too low' for secondary liability were explained by Lord Hughes and Lord Toulson (at para 83):

murder already has a relatively low *mens rea* threshold because it includes an intention to cause serious injury, without intent to kill ... the *Chan Wing-Siu* principle extends liability for murder to a secondary party on the basis of a still lesser degree of culpability, namely foresight only of the possibility that the principal may commit murder.

The danger of having such a low threshold is that it contradicts the rule that a defendant must be blameworthy to be convicted.[7]

This position, following this landmark judgment, is therefore that the mental element for the secondary participant is an intention to assist or encourage the crime (at para 79):

in plain terms, our analysis leads us to the conclusion that the introduction of the principle was based on an incomplete, and in some respects erroneous reading of the previous law, coupled with generalised and questionable policy arguments.[8]

Further support for the rectitude of the decision is that it is very similar to Parliament's intention in the enactment of the **Serious Crime Act 2007** when it created the new offences of intentionally encouraging or assisting the commission of an offence. It was argued in the case that it was not the role of the courts to address this issue, but that legislation should deal with it. In fact, as the law in this area is predominantly common law, it was right that the courts should consider it.

One of the problems in the previous law was that too many convictions arose from it, and that, in particular, young people were unfairly convicted and a disproportionate number of black males were convicted. A defence argument defence arguments put forward in the case is that teenagers in particular find it difficult to foresee the behaviour of others. The judgment may be reflecting the importance of protecting

[7] In this context, the reference to constructive refers to interpretation—the court would interpret that one crime had necessarily been committed through the commission of a crime committed by someone else.

[8] The *ratio* of the case.

[9] In fact the judgment made a reference to the subjective landscape of the criminal law.

[10] This is important as it is one of the main reasons for the decision in this case.

[11] Conclude on the main points you have raised and offer a comment yourself.

children's rights as protected in the **United Nations Convention of the Rights of the Child,** an argument previously considered in other important cases involving *mens rea*, such as *R v G and Another* **[2003] UKHL 50.**[9] It is important not to over-criminalize children, which is what the previous law on joint enterprise may have been doing. In considering the fairness of the previous law, the Supreme Court in *R v Jogee* stated that previous judgments could have, but did not, consider these consequences in making the decisions they did:[10]

there was no consideration in *Chan Wing-Siu* or in *Powell and English* of the fundamental policy question of whether and why it was necessary and appropriate to reclassify such conduct as murder rather than manslaughter. Such a discussion would have involved, among other things, questions about fair labelling and fair discrimination in sentencing.

The law relating to secondary participation and particularly joint enterprise was unfair, and as such it is submitted that in overturning it, the Supreme Court has made the right decision.[11] To allow a defendant to be convicted of such a serious offence, when he only foresaw the possibility of death or injury but did not intend it, undermines essential principles of *mens rea*. The decision of the court in *Chan Wing-Siu*, which had decided that foresight was sufficient, caused a wrong principle to become embedded in the law. It is now necessary, in order for a secondary party to be found guilty of murder, that he must intentionally assist or encourage the principal to act. The ruling in *R v Jogee* has not been without criticism. There has not been a flurry of appeals and relatively few have been successful. In *R v Crilly* **[2018] EWCA Crim 168**, specific facts were emphasized by the Court of Appeal: A had taken part in a burglary of what he believed were empty premises; when he discovered they were occupied, he tried to persuade his co-defendants to leave; there was only a very short time between the discovery of the occupant and the infliction of fatal violence by P; and death was possibly caused by a single punch. In *R v Dreszer* **[2018] EWCA Crim 454**, there was insufficient evidence from which inferences of intention could be drawn: there was no witness to the killing and no evidence of the cause of V's death or where it had occurred. The Court in *Crilly* approved *R v Johnson (Lewis)* **[2016] EWCA Crim 1613**, which made it clear that 'substantial injustice' is a more stringent requirement than the usual test of whether a conviction is or may be unsafe. It is deliberately so, given the public interest in legal certainty and the interests of the victim (or their family).

The true effect of *R v Jogee* remains to be seen. It has been criticized on the basis that the decision in *Chan Wing-Siu* was a development to the law, rather than a change to it. Other cases could be read in this light. Ormerod and Laird (2016) argue that the ruling in *Jogee* has sidestepped the important question of whether the principal and the accessory should have the same *mens rea* at all:

One of the main criticisms leveled at the law on joint enterprise was the fact a lower threshold of *mens rea* applied to the accessory as opposed to the principal, which meant that he was convicted despite not necessarily having demonstrated any of the culpability or wrongdoing of the principal. Although the judge would be directing the jury that the same *mens rea*, i.e. intention, applies to both the principal and the accessory, as a matter of substance a different threshold of foresight would suffice for guilt, depending upon whose liability was being considered. There could be those who argue that this approach means that the accessory would once again be liable to conviction despite the fact he lacks the same level of culpability as the principal.

Given the outstanding questions and the criticisms of *Jogee* which have already emerged, it is likely that there will be further developments in this area of law. Its practical impact will also depend upon prosecutorial decision making, and the Crown Prosecution Service launched a consultation in 2017 on its Legal Guidance on Secondary Liability (http://www.cps.gov.uk/consultations). 'Joint enterprise' may be gone, but this area of accessorial liability remains controversial.

LOOKING FOR EXTRA MARKS?

- Make sure your answer to this question is not too descriptive, either of the area of law or the case. In other words, it is important to make some critical comment about the new development. Here, the answer referred to unfairness.
- Key quotes from the judgment can give extra quality to your answer.

TAKING THINGS FURTHER

- Buxton R, 'Joint Enterprise: *Jogee*, Substantial Injustice and the Court of Appeal' [2017] Crim LR 123.
  *A brief commentary on **Jogee**, arguing that the test for historic appeals should be that the conviction was unsafe, rather than the higher standard of 'substantial injustice'.*
- Child J, 'Exploring the Mens Rea Requirements of the Serious Crime Act 2007 Assisting and Encouraging Offences' (2012) 76 J Crim Law 220–31.
  Explores the mens rea requirements in the new provisions.
- Dyson M, 'Principals without Distinction' [2018] Crim LR 296.
  Considers the principles underlying accessorial and joint venture liability and the extent to which they are addressed by the current law.

- Jarvis P and Bisgrove M, 'The Use and Abuse of Conspiracy' [2015] Crim LR 261.

  Discusses the problems of charging a defendant with conspiracy when there is a number of substantive offences. Proposes that the charge should focus on a single agreement instead.

- Mirfield P, 'Intention and Criminal Attempts' [2015] Crim LR 142–8.

  Discusses changes in the courts' approach to mens rea in attempts.

- Ormerod D and Laird K, '*Jogee*: Not the End of a Legal Saga but the Start of One?' [2016] Crim LR 539.

  Considers the various legal questions which **Jogee** *still leaves unresolved and argues that the Court of Appeal needs to address them swiftly.*

- Ormerod D and Wilson W, 'Simply Harsh to Fairly Simple: Joint Enterprise Reform' [2015] Crim LR 3–27.

  Discusses criticisms of the law of joint enterprise/parasitic accessorial liability. Argues for reform along the lines of the decision in **R v Jogee**.

 Online Resources www.oup.com/uk/qanda/

For extra essay and problem questions on this topic, as well as advice on revision and exam technique, please visit the online resources.

Mixed
Questions

9

ARE YOU READY?

In a way, all criminal law questions are mixed, in the sense that knowledge of the pervasive and fundamental principles of *actus reus*, *mens rea*, and the defences are essential. In addition to this, you may find that some examination questions cover a number of different offences/defences. You should not let this faze you, but adopt the same structured approach that you would in dealing with one offence. Structure is important in all types of criminal law questions, but this is especially true with mixed topics. Essay questions on mixed topics are rarer, but will be discursive questions in which you are asked to critically evaluate or compare common concepts in the criminal law. Some common areas for combination are listed below, but of course this list is not exhaustive. The following combinations will be discussed in this chapter:

- sexual offences and burglary;
- offences against the person, self-defence, and consent;
- murder and manslaughter;
- theft, fraud, and other property offences;
- secondary participation and offences against the person;
- subjective and objective approaches to liability.

QUESTION 1

The criminal law can sometimes produce inconsistent decisions, leading to uncertainty and unpredictability.

Critically assess the extent to which you believe this statement to be true of the criminal law.

CAUTION!

■ This question requires you to take a wider policy view of the development of the criminal law. Try to think of examples throughout your syllabus that can be used in your arguments to answer the question.

■ Avoid the common mistake of interpreting the question to read 'Choose one area of the criminal law where there are difficulties and write all about it.' This question has been included as it enables you to think more widely about the role of the criminal law within the legal system and society as a whole, and any contradictions within it. It does not really matter which aspects you cover, as long as you assess the impact on the criminal law as a whole.

DIAGRAM ANSWER PLAN

Introduce the problem by referring to the changing nature of the criminal law.

▼

Discuss constant change—*R v R*.

▼

Look at lack of code—*Metropolitan Police Commissioner v Caldwell* and *DPP v Morgan*.

▼

Consider logic, policy, and the subjective/objective approaches.

▼

Consider the role of the House of Lords—*R v Clegg*.

▼

Draw a conclusion. addressing whether the criminal law remains inconsistent.

SUGGESTED ANSWER

[1] This statement acknowledges the problem set out in the question. You should then set out how you plan to answer it.

The development of many areas of law follows a consistent and logical course. The basic foundations, their concepts, and their application are accepted by the vast majority, and only fine-tuning or adjustments of these principles are required to meet new situations.[1] This cannot always be said about the criminal law, where the debate about fundamental concepts—such as whether recklessness should be interpreted subjectively or objectively; whether a mistake of fact relied upon by a defendant should have to be one that a reasonable person would have made; whether duress should be a defence to a charge of murder—is still ongoing. In this essay, we attempt to identify some of the reasons for this, and propose some solutions.

One of the problems is that the criminal law is subject to constant change. It has to adapt to cover new phenomena, such as stalking, drug abuse, and internet fraud, and to reflect society's changing social and moral standards. As the House of Lords stated in *R v R* [1991] **4 All ER 481**, abolishing the husband's marital rape exemption, the common law is capable of evolving in the light of social, economic, and cultural developments.[2] In that case, the recognition that the status of women had changed beyond all recognition from the time (*Hale's Pleas of the Crown* (1736)) when the husband's marital rape exemption was initially recognized was long overdue. Similarly, the criminal law once reflected the moral position that it was a crime to take one's own life. Failure in such an enterprise was prosecuted as attempted suicide and could be punished. However, attitudes softened and it was recognized that such a person needed help and not a criminal trial. As a result, the law was consequently amended by the **Suicide Act 1961**. The 1960s saw similar changes in respect to the laws relating to homosexuality and abortion. Changes in the law can also result from a shift in ideology on the part of an elected government, or as a response to new threats to the safety and stability of society—for example, legislation to combat terrorism.[3]

There is no doubt that the development and application of the criminal law would be more consistent and predictable if the courts exhibited a more uniform approach to its development. This is especially true when the courts consider subjective and objective tests in assessing liability. The problem is illustrated by two House of Lords decisions: *Metropolitan Police Commissioner v Caldwell* [1981] **1 All ER 961**, where an objective approach to recklessness was used, and *DPP v Morgan* [1975] **2 All ER 347**, where a subjective approach to mistake was applied. Why was it that liability for recklessness was imposed on an objective basis, but where a defendant made a mistake of fact he was entitled (subject to any statutory provision to the contrary) to be judged on the facts as he honestly believed them to be? It might be argued that two different areas of the criminal law were being considered (criminal damage and rape), but the inconsistency is still stark. At least in so far as recklessness is concerned, the House of Lords embraced the notion of subjectivity again in *R v G* [2003] **4 All ER 765**, but the very fact that the legal definition of such a basic concept could change so much in the space of twenty years is itself startling. The problem in *DPP v Morgan* has been dealt with by incorporating it into the mainly objective stance in the **Sexual Offences Act 2003**. The defendant must now have a reasonable belief in consent. This demonstrates inconsistency even

[2] You will not have room here to discuss all the possible examples of the law's stance on social change, so choose one or two examples.

[3] This, of course, is related to the point about social change, discussed earlier. More recently, this legislation has attracted criticism on the grounds that it is too draconian.

in the context of the change. In the case of *R v G* (above), the courts were prepared to adopt a subjective standard, but in the context of sexual offences, an objective standard has been adopted. Changes to the defences to murder adopted in the **Coroners and Justice Act 2009** also demonstrate this approach. The Act requires that in deciding whether the defendant should be able to benefit from the defence of loss of control, s/he should be assessed according to the standards of a person with 'a normal degree of tolerance and self-control'. This leaves little room for consideration of a defendant's personal characteristics, which may have influenced their behaviour when committing the crime.

Often the criminal law follows a logical approach in its application; but as it does not exist in a vacuum and is not simply the application of academic principles, policy considerations sometimes have to prevail. As Lord Salmon stated in *DPP v Majewski* **[1976] 2 All ER 142**, regarding the defence of intoxication:

the answer is that in strict logic the view [intoxication is no defence to crimes of basic intent] cannot be justified. But this is the view that has been adopted by the common law which is founded on common sense and experience rather than strict logic.

This may demonstrate the balancing act the courts have to play between preventing crime and protecting the public and ensuring that the defendant's rights in the criminal trial are not compromised. Policy considerations[4] are also behind **s 1(3)** of the **Criminal Attempts Act 1981**, [5] whereby in the offence of attempt, the facts are to be as the accused believes them to be. Thus, an accused, objectively viewed, may appear not to be committing a criminal act but because they believe they are, they can be guilty of attempting to commit that criminal act, as in *R v Shivpuri* **[1986] 2 All ER 334**.

There is often no means of predicting which approach will prevail. In *Jaggard v Dickinson* **[1980] 3 All ER 716**, the accused, who had been informed by her friend X that she could break into X's house to shelter, mistakenly broke into V's house while drunk. She was charged with criminal damage under **s 1(1)** of the **Criminal Damage Act 1971**, but argued that she had a lawful excuse under **s 5(2)** of the Act as she honestly believed that she had the owner's consent. Although the prosecution contended that this was a crime of basic intent and therefore drunkenness was no defence (citing the House of Lords' decisions of *Metropolitan Police Commissioner v Caldwell* and *DPP v Majewski* in support), the Court of Appeal quashed her conviction, giving priority to the statutory provision of **s 5(2)** of the **1971 Act**.

One important aspect of the criminal law process in recent years, which has caused uncertainty, is the role of the Supreme Court in

[4] Because criminal law often deals with social issues, policy must play a key part.

[5] Try to give concrete examples of statutory provisions or cases which illustrate the points you are making.

changing the criminal law. Clearly, judges are there to say what the law is, not what it should be; but Lord Simon in *DPP for Northern Ireland v Lynch* [1975] 1 All ER 913 said:

I am all for recognising that judges do make law. And I am all for judges exercising their responsibilities boldly at the proper time and place ... where matters of social policy are not involved which the collective wisdom of Parliament is better suited to resolve.

Thus, in *R v R*, the House of Lords changed the law of rape by abolishing the husband's defence of marital rape immunity without waiting for Parliament to implement the Law Commission's recommendations. However, their Lordships took the opposite view in *R v Clegg* [1995] 1 All ER 334, where they refused to follow the Law Commission's suggestion that a person who was entitled to use force in self-defence but who used unreasonable force, thereby killing the victim, would be guilty of manslaughter, not murder. Lord Lloyd stated:

I am not adverse to judges developing law, or indeed making new law, when they can see their way clearly, even where questions of social policy are involved. [A good example is *R v R*.[6]] But in the present case I am in no doubt that your Lordships should abstain from law making. The reduction of what would otherwise be murder to manslaughter in a particular class of case seems to me essentially a matter for decision by the legislature.

⁶ It's a good idea to link this back to the earlier part of your essay.

It is difficult to appreciate the essential difference in issues in these two cases, despite Lord Lowry's justifications in *R v Clegg* that '*R v R* dealt with a specific act and not with a general principle governing criminal liability'. Clearly, there is a difference in opinion amongst the Law Lords as to the correct application of these principles. This is well illustrated by the House of Lords' decision in *R v Gotts* [1992] 1 All ER 832. The majority decision not to allow duress as a defence to attempted murder was on the basis that duress was no defence to murder. The minority view to the contrary revealed a different analysis. They argued that duress is a general defence throughout the criminal law, with the exceptions of the offences of murder and treason. It is for Parliament, and not the courts, to limit the ambit of a defence; and as attempted murder is a different offence to murder, duress must therefore be available.

It is submitted that these are the main reasons why the development and application of the criminal law is often uncertain and unpredictable. There are other factors, such as whether an issue is a question of law for the judge or fact for the jury, for example the meaning of 'administer' (*R v Gillard* (1988) 87 Cr App R 189);[7] the difficulty in ascertaining the *ratio decidendi* of many cases, for example *R v Brown* [1993] 2 All ER 75 (consent); and the possible effect of the decisions of the European Court of Human Rights. But it

⁷ This is a good illustration of the point made in Chapter 1 on the importance of statutory interpretation.

is the lack of a uniform principle that is the main factor causing the inherent uncertainty.

The general principles of criminal law are often the subject of discussion by academic commentators, who look for inconsistencies and conflicts within the law. A critical and historical analysis of the criminal law is offered by A Norrie in *Crime, Reason and History* (Weidenfeld and Nicolson 1993), arguing that the criminal law is the product of historical social class contradictions. Legal principles reflect the interests of the economically powerful middle class. The law may appear class-neutral, but liability is construed from so-called 'voluntary' individual actions, removed, abstractly, from surrounding social and political forces. At p 23 he says:

In place of real individuals belonging to particular social classes, possessing the infinite differences that constitute genuine individuality, the reformers proposed an ideal individual living in an ideal world. 'Economic man' or 'juridical man' were abstractions from real people emphasising one side of human life—the ability to reason and calculate—at the expense of every social circumstance that actually brings individuals to reason and calculate in particular ways. Crime was a social problem. It arose out of particular social conditions and was brought into being in the midst of struggles between social classes over definitions of right and wrong.

Norrie argues here that fundamental principles of the criminal law such as blameworthiness are flawed and lead to contradiction and inconsistency. The solution is to make more moral, political, and social factors available to decision makers in order to reach just decisions, rather than them deciding on the basis of the ideal individual.

On a practical note, the Law Commission has long argued that the solution lies in codifying the law (see Law Com No 143) on the basis that 'the criminal law could then exhibit a uniform approach to all crimes and defences'.

Other major European countries (France, Germany, and Spain) have a detailed criminal code, with a uniform approach providing a starting point for interpreting the law. The criminal law in England and Wales has developed in a piecemeal fashion, with one offence's development showing little consistency with another's. So, often it is difficult to say what our law actually is, even before lawyers start to debate how it should be applied, for example *R v Savage*; *R v Parmenter* **[1992] 1 AC 699**, interpreting (after more than 130 years of use) the provisions of the **Offences Against the Person Act 1861**. A code could be expressed in clear language with definitions of fundamental concepts such as intention and recklessness, as suggested by the Law Commission's Draft Criminal Code; although, the former chairman of the Law Commission Justice Henry Brooke stated (**[1995] Crim LR 911**): 'Nobody in their right mind would want to put the existing criminal law into a codified form.'

LOOKING FOR EXTRA MARKS?

■ This is a difficult question in which you really have to determine your own parameters. If you can choose some good examples in case law of the inconsistency of the criminal law, your essay will be of better quality than if you make sweeping statements.

■ The structure of an essay like this is very important, so make your points and back them up with evidence and analysis. Deal with one point at a time, and make sure the examples you give are linked back to the original question.

QUESTION | 2

One night, Betty joins her neighbour Ron for a drink. Betty would have been happy with just one or two glasses of wine but Ron insists that she drink more to accompany him. Ron dishonestly tells her that he is compiling a medical database of women's breast sizes and asks if she will agree to his measuring her. She agrees. Unknown to Betty, Ron has spiked the wine with a tranquilizer. Betty becomes so drunk she hardly knows what she is doing. He leads her to the bedroom and suggests they have sex. Betty refuses. Ron then threatens her with violence. She passes out just as he pushes her onto the bed and has sexual intercourse with her. After a few weeks Betty learns that she is not only pregnant but also HIV+. She sends Ron an email giving him a week in which to agree to marry her, failing which she will break his legs. She hears nothing and so bombards him with threatening emails and telephone calls. Ron becomes so concerned that he obtains anti-depressants from his doctor. Betty sees him coming home from work one day. She rushes at him with a penknife, and cuts his head. Ron later asserts he believed Betty had consented to being measured and to having sex with him. He claims he did not know he was HIV+. As a result of these incidents, Betty now suffers nightmares in which she is being attacked by strange men.

Advise Betty and Ron.

CAUTION!

■ This question contains both sexual and non-sexual offences against the person—be careful that you do not muddle the idea of consent as a defence to the statutory assaults, and consent as a key element in a sexual offence charge. Deal with the two issues separately. See *R v B* [2007] 1 WLR 1567.

■ Consider each defendant separately, then look at all possible offences, starting with the most serious in the hierarchy of non-fatal offences. If actual harm is caused, the statutory assaults must be considered.

DIAGRAM ANSWER PLAN

Identify the issues	■ Mention rape, sexual assault, statutory assaults under the **Offence Against the Person Act 1861**, and defences.
Relevant law	■ Use the **Offences Against the Person Act 1961**, and consider consent obtained by fraud and the meaning of actual bodily harm/grievous bodily harm. ■ Discuss the evidential presumptions in **s 75** and reasonable belief.
Apply the law	■ Does Betty lack capacity? Discuss the case law on fraud and consent. ■ Will the court presume lack of consent in these circumstances? ■ Discuss the boundaries between actual bodily harm and grievous bodily harm and the *mens rea* of the respective offences.
Conclude	■ Draw a conclusion, including any defences.

SUGGESTED ANSWER

This question raises issues of non-fatal offences and sexual offences.

In relation to Ron, the first charge will be a sexual assault contrary to **s 3** of the **Sexual Offences Act 2003**. Under this provision, a person commits an offence if he intentionally touches another person, the touching is sexual, the complainant does not consent to the touching, and the defendant does not reasonably believe that the victim consents. It is clear from these facts that Ron touches Betty, and that she agrees.[1] The question for the court will be whether Betty has been deceived into agreeing. The defendant must reasonably believe in consent. Ron's belief in Betty's consent is to be determined having regard to all the circumstances, including any steps he took to ascertain whether she consented. In *Tabassum* **[2000] 2 Cr App R 328**, the defendant asked several women to take part in what he said was a survey for cancer research involving him feeling their breasts. The court held that there had been no true consent, since the women were consenting in the belief that the touching took place for medical purposes. As Betty believes that Ron is compiling a medical database, and consents on this basis, the court is likely to decide that consent was obtained fraudulently.[2]

[1] Do remember to apply the law to the facts of the problem question, even where it seems obvious. You need to demonstrate that you are able to break an offence down in terms of *actus reus* and *mens rea*.

[2] It is a good idea to come to a mini conclusion at each stage of the problem.

The other issue here is that of Betty's capacity. Consent is defined in **s 74**, which provides that a person consents if he agrees by choice, and has the capacity to make that choice. Betty's consumption of alcohol may mean that she has lost this capacity. In *R v Bree* **[2007] EWCA Crim 256**, the Court of Appeal overturned the rape conviction of the lower court and noted that the capacity of an individual to cope with alcohol (and therefore to give or withhold consent when having consumed it) varied between individuals and day-to-day and, as such, was a matter 'inapt for detailed legislative structures'. However, it endorsed academic commentary on the **Sexual Offences Act 2003** by Professors Temkin and Ashworth ('The Sexual Offences Act 2003: (1) Rape, Sexual Assaults and the Problems of Consent' [2004] Crim LR 328–46), as well as taking note of a proposed change to **s 75** of the **Sexual Offences Act 2003**, which would have included a clause covering instances where the victim was too intoxicated (through alcohol or drugs).

The concept of reasonable belief for the sexual offences is supported by the provisions in **ss 75** and **76**. **Section 76** provides for some conclusive presumptions about consent. Where the defendant did the relevant act, and intentionally deceived the victim as to the purpose or nature of the act, it is to be conclusively presumed that the victim did not consent. Given the above provisions, it seems likely that Betty's consent to being touched is invalid and that Ron will be found guilty of sexual assault.

The next issue to consider is whether Ron is guilty of rape.

Under **s 1(1)** of the **Sexual Offences Act 2003**, rape is committed when a person (A) intentionally penetrates the vagina, anus, or mouth of another person with his penis, B does not consent to the penetration, and A does not reasonably believe that B consents. It is clear here that sexual intercourse has taken place, therefore the key fact in issue here is that of consent.

To turn to *mens rea*, the prosecution must show that the defendant intended to have sexual intercourse and that he did not reasonably believe that the victim was consenting. In other words, where the defendant claims he believed that the victim was consenting, if such a belief is proved to be unreasonable, the jury should convict. This is the case even where that belief is held honestly. In deciding whether the defendant's belief was unreasonable, the jury should have regard to all the circumstances, including any steps the defendant could reasonably have taken to ascertain whether the victim consented (**s 1(2)** of the **Sexual Offences Act 2003**). This provision places an onus on the defendant to ascertain whether or not there is consent in situations where there might be doubt. In some circumstances, the Act provides for certain evidential presumptions to be raised against consent. These include a situation where the victim may be in fear and a situation in which the victim is not acting in full capacity due to ingesting a substance. If it is proved that the defendant did the relevant act and one of the circumstances existed at the time, it will be presumed that the complainant did not consent to the act, and the defendant did not reasonably believe that the complainant consented unless the defendant adduces sufficient evidence to raise an issue to the contrary. Betty's consent here will not be valid.

Her capacity to agree by choice (**s 74**) is affected by alcohol. In any event, Ron has threatened Betty with violence. As a result, the evidential presumptions in **s 75(2)(a)** will apply unless Ron can adduce evidence to the contrary. This seems unlikely, when there is evidence of violence.[3]

[3] The presumption is rebuttable, but in this instance, it will be difficult for Ron to do this. The threat of violence is clear.

The last issue to consider with regard to Ron is his potentially reckless transmission of HIV, giving rise to a charge of **s 20** of the **Offences Against the Person Act 1861**. The transmission of a sexually transmitted disease can be grievous bodily harm, so the question is whether Ron can be convicted, given that he claims he did not know that he had HIV. In *R v Dica* **[2004] QB 1257**, the defendant, knowing that he was HIV+, had sexual intercourse with two women who were both diagnosed as being HIV+. He was charged with offences under **s 20** of the **Offences Against the Person Act 1861** on the basis that he had recklessly transmitted the disease to the women when they had not known of the risk of infection. In this scenario, the *mens rea* element is missing and therefore the prosecution will not succeed on this charge.

The fact that Betty is now suffering from nightmares may give rise to a charge of one of the statutory assaults in addition to the sexual offences already established. Ron may be charged with assault under **s 47** of the **Offences Against the Person Act 1861**. The *actus reus* of this charge is an assault occasioning actual bodily harm. Actual bodily harm can include psychiatric harm as long as this is medically treatable and does not simply amount to emotional distress (see *R v Chan Fook* **[1994] 2 All ER 452**).[4] If Ron raises the common law defence of consent to this charge, the argument of *Tabassum* (see earlier) will apply—fraud or deceit as to the nature or purpose of the act will nullify consent.

[4] Actual bodily harm is defined as harm which interferes with the health or comfort of the victim. This may include psychiatric harm, which must be medically recognized. This may even extend to grievous bodily harm if it is sufficiently serious.

Betty may be charged with various non-fatal offences against the person. She sends emails and makes phone calls which cause Ron to ask his doctor for anti-depressants. If Ron's state of mind is sufficiently serious to warrant medical treatment and goes beyond mere emotional distress (see *R v Chan-Fook*, discussed earlier in this question), then Betty may be charged with an assault occasioning actual bodily harm. An assault is defined as an act which causes the victim to apprehend the immediate application of unlawful violence (*Venna* **[1975] 3 WLR 737**). The *mens rea* aspect is intention or recklessness—the latter being defined subjectively (*R v G* **[2003] 4 All ER 65**). In this scenario, it seems clear that Betty intended to worry Ron—and, in any event, her messages contain a threat of violence. The assault causes him to visit his doctor to ask for anti-depressants. There seems to be no problem with causation—the messages have prompted him to do so.

Betty's physical assaults on Ron will be met with the more serious charges under the **Offences Against the Person Act 1861.** There is no doubt that Betty intended to commit at least a battery.[5]

[5] Note that under **s 47** Betty need not have the *mens rea* for the actual bodily harm—she only needs the *mens rea* for the assault.

However, the cut to Ron's head is a wound. Thus, the appropriate charges are **ss 18** or **20** of the **Offences Against the Person Act 1861.** A wound requires the rupture of both the dermis and the epidermis. It is, in other words, a breaking of the skin (*C v Eisenhower* **[1984] QB 331**). The wound is sufficient to establish the *actus reus*; there is no need to prove that this was grievous bodily harm. Under **s 20**, the grievous bodily harm must be inflicted, which will be satisfied here in the fact that Betty rushes at Ron with a penknife, which causes the wound. The *mens rea* for **s 20** is satisfied by proof that Betty was malicious. This means that she inflicted the wound either intentionally or recklessly, ie she was at least aware of the possibility of causing some physical harm. It seems clear that she intended to hurt Ron with the penknife.

LOOKING FOR EXTRA MARKS?

■ A really good understanding of the development of case law in this area will help you to achieve high marks. The definition of the word 'inflict' in the context of **s 20** of the **Offences Against the Person Act 1861** in particular is significant. A full discussion of *R v Clarence* (1888) 22 QB 23, *R v Tabassum* [2000] 2 Cr App R 328, and *R v Dica* [2004] QB 1257, and, applying the law to the facts in a reasoned way, will help you achieve high marks in this answer. *Tabassum* was approved in *Dica*, so that *Clarence* is effectively regarded as bad law on this topic.

■ Few students explain *all* the requirements of the *actus reus* and *mens rea* in answer to this type of question, or understand the subtleties of the *mens rea* differences between **ss 20** and 47. In order to understand this area fully, you should read in full the judgment in *R v Savage; R v Parmenter* [1992] 1 AC 699.

QUESTION | 3

Justin and Tintin, having been partners for several years, split up when Tintin discovers that Justin is having a relationship with Roger. Tintin, incensed by what Justin has done, decides to seek revenge.

Tintin enters Justin's flat, using the front door key that he still has, armed with a pair of scissors that he intends to use to stab Justin. Tintin goes into Justin's bedroom and finds him asleep in bed.

ⓘ

Instead of stabbing Justin, Tintin decides to use the scissors to cut off Justin's ponytail whilst he is asleep, so without waking Justin. Tintin rummages through the drawer of Justin's bedside table and removes some nude photographs that he took of Justin in the shower.

As he is about to leave the flat, Tintin is confronted by Roger, who is just arriving. Tintin, who is still holding the scissors, fears that Roger is about to attack him. He pushes the scissors into Roger's arm, causing a deep cut, and runs off. Tintin subsequently writes to Justin, telling him that if he does not return the ring he gave to Justin to celebrate the fifth anniversary of their being partners, he intends to put the nude photographs of Justin on the internet. Justin, who is a secondary school headmaster, is worried that if Tintin carries out his threat he might have to resign from his job.

Discuss any criminal liability arising from these facts.

 CAUTION!

- Note the possibility of aggravated burglary, as well as burglary.
- You need to address the issue of whether this is a householder case in the terms of **s 43** of the **Crime and Courts Act 2013**.

DIAGRAM ANSWER PLAN

Identify the issues	■ Discuss burglary, statutory assaults, and wounding or grievous bodily harm.
Relevant law	■ Use **s 10** aggravated burglary. ■ Discuss **s 9** of the **Theft Act 1968** and the meaning of trespass; self-defence; and blackmail. Consider **s 21** of the **Theft Act 1968** and **s 20** of the **Offences Against the Person Act 1861**.
Apply the law	■ Consider whether Tintin is a trespasser, whether he can benefit from self-defence, and whether he has the *mens rea* for wounding.
Conclude	■ Conclude on the facts.

SUGGESTED ANSWER

When Tintin enters Justin's flat armed with the scissors he may have committed burglary contrary to **s 9(1)(a)** of the **Theft Act 1968**, or aggravated burglary contrary to **s 10** of the 1968 Act. Was he a trespasser when he entered?[1] He may have had express or implied permission to enter the flat when he was in a relationship with Justin, but as the relationship has now ended, it could be argued that the permission has been expressly or impliedly revoked. In any event, if he enters intending to stab Justin, or even simply armed in order to do some physical harm, the prosecution will argue that this is entry in excess of any implied permission Tintin may have had: see *R v Jones and Smith* [1976] 3 All ER 54. Under **s 9(1)(a)**, Tintin can be convicted of burglary if he entered as a trespasser with intent to do some grievous bodily harm on a person in the building.[2] Grievous bodily harm for these purposes means 'serious' harm. Liability under this limb of **s 9(1)(a)** would require more evidence as to Tintin's precise intentions. The alternative formulations under **s 9(1)(a)** are that Tintin entered as a trespasser intending to steal, or that he intended to cause criminal damage. Again, the evidence as to his state of mind at the time of entry is inconclusive.[3] If it can be shown that he intended to steal photographs or human hair, or indeed commit criminal damage to Justin's hair, a **s 9(1)(a)** charge might be sustainable—but it is submitted there is no direct evidence of this.

Burglary contrary to **s 9(1)(a)** could be based on Tintin's entry into the flat with a key, or indeed his entry into Justin's bedroom as a trespasser, given that burglary can be committed by a defendant entering part of a building as a trespasser. The prosecution would be advised to base liability on the act of trespass that carried with it the strongest evidence of the necessary ulterior intent to steal or cause grievous bodily harm or criminal damage.

Under **s 10** of the **1968 Act**, a person is guilty of aggravated burglary if he commits any burglary and at the time has with him any weapon of offence.[4] The scissors could constitute a weapon of offence for these purposes.

Once inside Justin's bedroom, Tintin decides not to stab Justin. Has Tintin nevertheless gone far enough to be charged with attempting to commit wounding contrary to **s 1** of the **Criminal Attempts Act 1981** and **s 20** of the **Offences Against the Person Act 1861**? Under the **1981 Act**, the prosecution will have to prove that Tintin has taken steps more than merely preparatory to wounding Justin. Whether or not entering Justin's bedroom armed with scissors is sufficient to satisfy this requirement will be a question of fact to be determined by the jury—*R v Gullefer* (1990) 91 Cr App R 356.

[1] This is a key issue for the burglary charge and depends on the meaning of trespass.

[2] The intention must be formed at the point of entry.

[3] You do not have to reach a definite conclusion, and in fact should try to incorporate both the prosecution and defence arguments in your answer.

[4] This interesting case shows the scope of the meaning of actual bodily harm.

In cutting off Justin's ponytail, Tintin will have committed the offence of causing actual bodily harm contrary to **s 47** of the **Offences Against the Person Act 1861**. *DPP v Smith* **[2006] All ER (D) 69 (Jan)** establishes that cutting off another's hair without consent amounts to actual bodily harm.[5] There is no doubt that Tintin intended to cause this result and there would appear to be no defence available (revenge not being a defence at common law—perhaps not even a mitigating factor in sentencing). A burglary charge could be sustained if Tintin entered the bedroom intending to do grievous bodily harm. Entering intending to cut hair would not suffice for these purposes.[6] The facts here indicate that he only decided to cut Justin's hair once he had entered the bedroom. For the same reason, a charge of burglary contrary to **s 9(1)(b)**, alleging that Tintin, having entered Justin's bedroom as a trespasser, committed grievous bodily harm would not be sustainable, as the cutting of the hair would only be actual bodily harm.

[6] If you consider theft in a case like this, also consider burglary.

The prosecution may consider charging Tintin with theft of the photographs of Justin. The photographs are clearly property; see **s 4(1)** of the **Theft Act 1968**. The facts indicate that the photographs were taken by Tintin—hence he may argue that they still belong to him. The prosecution may need to clearly establish that Tintin made Justin the owner of the photographs, but in any event **s 5(1)** of the **1968 Act** extends the concept of 'belonging to another' to encompass situations where, even though the defendant is the legal owner of the property in question, it can still be deemed to be property belonging to another as against the defendant if the property is in the possession or control of another. On the facts, the photographs would clearly be regarded as having been in Justin's possession or control; see further *R v Turner (No 2)* **[1971] 1 WLR 901**.

Tintin's removal of the photographs would constitute an appropriation—see **s 3(1)** of the **Theft Act 1968**. Hence the live issues will be those relating to *mens rea*. The prosecution must prove that Tintin's appropriation of the pictures was dishonest. Under **s 2(1)(a)** of the 1968 Act, Tintin will not be dishonest if he can show that he honestly believed he had the right in law to take the photographs. He does not have to show that any such right exists in law, simply that he believed he had the right. The fact that he was the photographer may be supportive evidence here. It is also significant that he does not appear to have had the intention to use the pictures for blackmailing purposes (considered later) until after he removed them. Tintin could cite this as evidence that he had an 'honest' motive in his initial removal of the pictures. It is submitted that **s 2(1)(b)** (honest belief in the owner's consent) and **s 2(1)(c)** (honest belief that the owner cannot be found) have no application on these facts. If, therefore, Tintin cannot rely on **s 2(1)(a)**, he will have to rely on the jury and its view following a direction in terms laid down in *R v Ghosh* [1982] QB 1053. The jury must first decide whether, according to the ordinary standards of reasonable and honest people, what Tintin did was dishonest. If it was not dishonest by those standards, he is not guilty of theft. If he was, the jury must go on to consider whether Tintin himself must have realized that what he was doing was by those standards dishonest. Given the facts, it is almost impossible to tell how a jury would determine this, although it may well take a dim view of a defendant who, having entered a flat without permission, armed with a weapon, subsequently threatens to embarrass the victim by publishing the pictures.

If dishonesty is established, the prosecution will have to prove the second element of *mens rea*, namely an intention on the part of Tintin to permanently deprive Justin of the photographs. It should be noted that the intention to permanently deprive must exist at the time of appropriation. Tintin's intentions in this regard are not clear at the time he removes the pictures from Justin's bedroom. It subsequently becomes clear that he intends to use the pictures for what may be blackmailing purposes. The prosecution could argue that even if Tintin lacked the necessary intention to permanently deprive in relation to the pictures when he was in the bedroom, it is later evidenced by his threats to publish them. Tintin will argue that he did not intend to keep the photographs, but was simply using them as a bargaining factor in respect of the ring. Under **s 6(1)** of the **1968 Act**, in cases where the defendant does not actually have an intention to permanently deprive, he can nevertheless be deemed to have such an intent if he intends ' … to treat the thing as his own to dispose of …'. In *R v Raphael and Another* [2008] EWCA Crim 1014, the appellant took P's car and then told P that it would be returned to him provided he paid £500. The Court of Appeal had little hesitation in concluding that the taking of property in such circumstances could amount to theft— the requirement that money be paid by the owner for the return of his property falling very much within the scope of **s 6(1)**.

In the present case, Tintin is seeking the return of a ring as exchange for the photographs—essentially the same issue as in *R v Raphael*. Assuming, therefore, that the photographs are property belonging to another, and assuming Tintin is dishonest, theft should be made out.

If Tintin did commit theft when he removed the pictures from Justin's bedroom, he may also be guilty of burglary contrary to **s 9(1) (b)** of the **Theft Act 1968**—having entered the bedroom as a trespasser he therein stole.[7]

[7] The offences under **s 9(1)(a)** and **(b)** are different—ensure you apply each to the facts carefully.

In cutting Roger's arm, Tintin caused a wound—see *C v Eisenhower* [1983] 3 WLR 537. Thus, Tintin may have committed an offence under either **s 18** ('wounding with intent …') or **s 20** ('maliciously wound') of the **Offences Against the Person Act 1861**.

[8] Be careful with the *mens rea* of these offences—explain them carefully.

The key factor will be *mens rea*.[8] More evidence is needed on the type of harm Tintin intended to cause. If he intended to cause serious harm, an intention to do some grievous bodily harm could be established, thus making out a case under **s 18**. It is submitted that there should be ample evidence to sustain a charge under **s 20**. Malicious wounding requires evidence that Tintin was at least aware that his actions created the risk of causing some physical harm, albeit slight.

Tintin will presumably argue that, in attacking Roger, he acted in self-defence, using reasonable force to protect himself. The fact that Tintin may have been 'in the wrong' inasmuch as he was trespassing in Justin's flat does not remove his right at common law to act in self-defence if threatened with unlawful violence from Roger. The facts

[9] This is a subjective test.

indicate that Roger had not actually attacked Tintin, hence Tintin will have to provide evidence that he honestly believed Roger was about to use unlawful violence on him. *R v Williams* **[1987] 3 All ER 411** and subsequent cases make clear that Roger is entitled to be judged on the facts as he honestly believed them to be, a position now confirmed by **s 76** of the **Criminal Justice and Immigration Act 2008**.[9] Assuming Tintin did honestly believe he was about to be attacked by Roger, was the force he used reasonable in the circumstances as he believed them to be? On the basis of **s 76(7)**, the jury should be directed to take into account the fact that Tintin may not have been able to weigh to a nicety the exact measure of any necessary action. Under **s 43** of the **Crime and Courts Act 2013**, a householder relying on self-defence is given greater latitude in terms of the degree of force permitted. Provided the terms of the provision are met, he will be acting lawfully unless his actions were a grossly disproportionate

[10] It's wise to explain, when discussing the defences, the final outcome for the defendant.

response to the perceived threat. If self-defence is made out, Tintin will have a complete defence. If the jury conclude that there was a basis for Tintin acting in self-defence but he used more force than was reasonable, he will have no defence at all.[10]

When Tintin subsequently wrote to Justin telling him that if he did not return the ring, he would put the nude photographs of Justin on the internet, Tintin may have committed blackmail contrary to **s 21** of the **Theft Act 1968**. There is clearly a demand. The accompanying threat would amount to the required menaces. The test is essentially objective—what would the effect be on the reasonable person? See *R v Clear* **[1968] 1 QB 670**. In cases where the reasonable person would not be threatened, the menaces can still be made out where the defendant has knowledge of the victim that indicates a particular sensitivity to the threats. The fact that Justin would be particularly embarrassed because of his job may be a factor here. The demand must be made with a view to gaining property or causing loss to another. In this respect, the obtaining of the ring would constitute the gaining of property (even if

Tintin is getting back something he thinks belongs to him anyway—see s 34(2) of the **Theft Act 1968**). The most difficult aspect of establishing blackmail may lie in showing that the demand was unwarranted. Under **s 21**, the prosecution must prove that Tintin had no belief that he had reasonable grounds for making the demand; and that he had no honest belief that the use of the menaces was a proper means of reinforcing the demand. Tintin will argue that he honestly believed he had a reasonable basis for making the demand as the relationship with Justin was over, and that he had no, or perhaps only doubtful, recourse to law in order to get the ring back.

LOOKING FOR EXTRA MARKS?

- The offences and defences contain a certain amount of overlap. It is a good idea to explain exactly what will happen in court to each defendant. This will give clarity to your answer.
- Do not assume that violence always results in injury—look carefully at the facts of the question.

QUESTION | 4

Anne took her father's car without his knowledge, picked up her friends Barbara and Christine, and drove to the seaside. On the way, they were involved in an accident with another car, which was being driven erratically. Both cars were damaged. Anne, Barbara, and Christine booked into a hotel room and then went drinking. By the end of the evening, they had all drunk a great deal of wine. When they got back to the hotel, they began re-enacting scenes from famous boxing matches. Barbara tried to land a blow on Anne's face but completely misguided her punch and knocked Anne down. Barbara was wearing a ring and this caused a bad cut over Anne's eye. Anne and Barbara then hurled themselves at Christine and pushed her out to the balcony. During this time, Christine was laughing but was also trying to suggest that she was tired and wanted to stop. Anne and Barbara picked Christine up and held her over the edge of the balcony. Thinking that they were going to let her fall, Christine pulled violently on Barbara's arm. Barbara overbalanced and fell to the ground, breaking her leg.

Discuss the criminal liability of Anne, Barbara, and Christine. How would your answer be different if Barbara had been killed as a result of the fall?

CAUTION!

- This question raises a number of offences. Deal with them all separately.
- The consent issue, and any other defences, should be dealt with once liability has been established.

DIAGRAM ANSWER PLAN

Identify the issues	■ Discuss criminal damage; assault; assault occasioning actual bodily harm; wounding; and involuntary manslaughter.
Relevant law	■ Is it a wound? Check **s 20** of the **Offences Against the Person Act 1861**. ■ Is there consent?
Apply the law	■ Use intoxication as a defence or a denial of *mens rea*.
Conclude	■ Consider involuntary manslaughter.

SUGGESTED ANSWER

¹ Identify the relevant offences.

This question raises the possibility that a number of crimes have been committed, including criminal damage (**Criminal Damage Act 1971**), assault under **s 39** of the **Criminal Justice Act 1988**, assault occasioning actual bodily harm, and potentially involuntary manslaughter.¹

The damage to the cars would amount to criminal damage if Anne was subjectively reckless, but there is nothing in the facts to suggest that Anne's driving was at fault.

When Barbara knocked Anne down and inflicted the cut over her eye, prima facie she committed offences of common law battery, assault occasioning actual bodily harm, and unlawful and malicious wounding under **ss 47** and **20** of the **Offences Against the Person Act 1861**.

² A common law battery might lead to the more serious offence. You should always look to the level of harm.

Battery requires proof that Barbara intentionally or recklessly inflicted force on Anne, whilst **s 47** requires that the infliction of force led to actual bodily harm.² This must be more than merely trivial injury. Clearly, the blow amounted to a battery.

³ Be careful with the *mens rea* here.

The wounding offence requires proof of a break in both layers of the skin (*C (A Minor) v Eisenhower* [1984] QB 331) and the cut described is clearly sufficient to satisfy this requirement. It is arguable that Barbara intended some injury, though it is more likely that she would merely have been aware of the risk of injury in trying to land the light blow.³ Similarly, Anne and Barbara committed battery on Christine when seizing her and holding her over the balcony and, in turn, Christine committed the offence of the unlawful and malicious infliction of

grievous bodily harm when pulling violently on Barbara's arm and causing her to fall and break her leg. The likelihood is that Christine did not
intend any such injury but certainly saw the risk of some injury.

Barbara will argue that Anne was consenting to the risk of injury
arising out of her rough behaviour, and Anne and Barbara will argue
that Christine was consenting to the risk of injurn out of their rough
behaviour. The general rule is that the victim cannot consent to injury
which amounts to actual bodily harm or worse. This is the principle in
R v Brown **[1993] 2 WLR 556**.[4] However, there is a number of recognized exceptions to this rule, including one for rough, undisciplined
horseplay. The defence was successfully raised in *R v Aitken* **[1992]
1 WLR 1066** by an RAF officer when he set fire to the flying suit of one
of his colleagues, who was badly burned. Likewise, in *R v Richardson
and Irwin* **[1999] Crim LR 494**, the defence was successfully used by
some students who dropped one of their friends from a balcony when
engaged in drunken behaviour. The defence will be successful when
the defendant did not intend to inflict the serious injury and where
the victim was genuinely consenting.

Generally, intoxication will not be a valid plea where the defence
is one of basic intent. According to *DPP v Majewski* **[1977] AC 443**,
any attempt to introduce evidence of intoxication in such an offence
will inevitably result in a conviction. Remarkably, the court did hold
in *Richardson and Irwin* that the defendant could rely on a drunken
mistake as to consent. Though all the defendants were probably
drunk to some extent, there is every reason to suppose that Anne
was consenting to the minor risks involved in the mock boxing and
that Barbara meant nothing more than to inflict a small slap.[5] Equally,
Christine was probably consenting to the rough horseplay, at least
until she was held over the balcony.

Christine will argue that she genuinely believed that Anne and Barbara were going to let her fall and to cause her serious injury. Her
defence will be one of self-defence. This requires proof that the use of
force was necessary and that the force used was proportionate to the
harm threatened. If there was no risk that Christine would be injured,
then she will be entitled to be judged on the facts as she believed
them to be (*R v Gladstone Williams* **[1987] 3 All ER 411**). There
is no reason to doubt that Christine genuinely believed that she was
about to suffer serious injury.

If Barbara had died as a result of the fall, then the appropriate
charge would be involuntary manslaughter. This is likely to be of the
gross negligence type evidenced in *R v Adomako* **[1994] 3 WLR 288**
and constitutes a killing by the defendant in circumstances where the
defendant is under a duty of care, that duty is breached, and there
is a risk of death. In addition, the conduct must be so bad in all the
circumstances as to amount to a criminal act or omission.[6]

[4] Public policy determines this
decision.

[5] You need to apply these arguments to the facts in question.

[6] The duty here is creating a dangerous situation.

LOOKING FOR EXTRA MARKS?

- The consent issue is dealt with on the basis of public policy. This can make it difficult to predict what the outcome will be. You should draw attention to this issue. This is especially true with rough horseplay.
- This is a short question, which must be tightly argued.

QUESTION | 5

Joe, Tim, and Mike go out one night, intending to meet some girls and have sexual intercourse. They meet Sue, Helen, and Jane in a local wine bar. Tim tells Jane that he is the famous footballer Tim Jenkins, whom Jane has always admired. He tells her that he wants to start a relationship with her, and will take her to see him play. None of this is true. After two hours, the women decide to go home, but invite the men back to their house for a cup of tea. Tim and Jane go into her room and have sexual intercourse. Joe and Helen had started kissing on the sofa while Mike and Sue were chatting in the kitchen. While Helen was not looking, Joe slipped a sedative into her tea. Helen became very drowsy and Joe carried her into the bedroom, where he had sex with her. Sue walked back into the lounge and saw a packet of pills on the table. She guessed what had happened and told Mike to leave. Mike refused and told Sue she had better not start or she would get what was coming to her. He took a knife from his pocket and placed it on the sideboard. Sue was extremely frightened and allowed Mike to have sex with her. After the men had left, Sue called the police. Joe and Mike said that they had honestly believed that the girls had consented to sex. Jane discovers that she has contracted herpes, a sexually transmitted disease.

Discuss the liability of Joe, Tim, and Mike under s 1 of the Sexual Offences Act 2003.

CAUTION!

- Do not be tempted to allow your own views of the defendant's behaviour to interfere with your legal advice.
- When dealing with the evidential presumption under **s 75**, remember that it does not necessarily mean that the victim has or has not consented.

DIAGRAM ANSWER PLAN

Identify the issues
- Identify the legal issues—rape (**s 1** of the **Sexual Offences Act 2003**), submission, and consent: *R v Olugboja* and **s 74**.
- Identify evidential presumptions as to consent under **s 75 (2)(a)** and the conclusive presumption in **s 76**.
- Consider **s 20** of the **Offences Against the Person Act 1861**— reckless transmission of a sexually transmitted disease.

Relevant law
- Start with the *actus reus* and *mens rea*—the sexual intercourse, the meaning of consent, and the defendant's belief in consent. Then explain the *actus reus* and *mens rea* of the offence of reckless GBH under **s 20** of the **Offences Against the Person Act 1861**. Discuss the concept of reckless transmission in *R v Dica*.

Apply the law
- Discuss the meaning of recklessness in the context of biological grievous bodily harm.
- Discuss the court's presumptions as to consent.

Conclude
- What offences are they guilty of? Conclude.

SUGGESTED ANSWER

This question raises issues of the offence of rape, including the evidential presumptions as to consent in the **Sexual Offences Act 2003** and the reckless infliction of grievous bodily harm under **s 20** of the **Offences Against the Person Act 1861**.

With regard to Joe, the crime here is rape. Under **s 1(1)** of the **Sexual Offences Act 2003**, rape is committed when a person (A) intentionally penetrates the vagina, anus, or mouth of another person with his penis, B does not consent to the penetration, and A does not reasonably believe that B consents. The problem question here is clear that sexual intercourse has taken place, therefore the key fact in issue is that of consent.

Sexual intercourse has taken place here, so the *actus reus* element is satisfied. In terms of the *mens rea* for the offence of rape, the prosecution must show that the defendant intended to have sexual intercourse and that he did not reasonably believe that the victim was consenting.

In other words, where the defendant claims he believed that the victim was consenting, if such a belief is proved to be unreasonable, the jury should convict. This is the case even where the belief is held honestly.[1] In deciding whether the defendant's belief was unreasonable, the jury should have regard to all the circumstances, including any steps the defendant could reasonably have been expected to take to ascertain whether the victim consented (**s 1(2) of the Sexual Offences Act 2003**). This provision places an onus on the defendant to ascertain whether or not there is consent in situations where there might be doubt. In certain carefully defined circumstances, the Act provides for particular evidential presumptions to be raised against consent. These include a situation where the victim may be in fear and a situation in which the victim is not acting in full capacity due to ingesting a substance. If it is proved that the defendant did the relevant act and one of the circumstances existed at the time, it will be presumed that the complainant did not consent to the act, and the defendant did not reasonably believe that the complainant consented unless the defendant adduces sufficient evidence to raise an issue to the contrary.

Section 76 allows the court to presume, conclusively, that consent was not valid in circumstances of fraud.

The prosecution needs to prove the absence of consent beyond reasonable doubt as part of the *actus reus* of the offence. The Act contains the definition of consent in **s 74**: 'a person consents if he agrees by choice, and has the freedom and capacity to make that choice'. The section makes it clear that one will not be consenting unless there is agreement by choice, freely entered into, by a person with capacity. In *R v Bree*, the issue of capacity was raised in terms of a complainant's ability to give consent under the influence of alcohol. The key question here was whether the complainant had the capacity to decide whether to engage in sexual activity.

Helen's capacity may well be diminished by alcohol, but the facts do not elaborate on this. The better approach for the prosecution here would be to consider the evidential presumption in **s 75**.[2] **Section 75** states that if the *actus reus* of the act is proven and that one of the specified circumstances applies, then the complainant is to be taken not to have consented to the relevant act unless sufficient evidence is adduced to raise an issue as to whether she consented, and the defendant is to be taken not to have reasonably believed that the complainant consented unless sufficient evidence is adduced to raise an issue as to whether he reasonably believed it. Furthermore, **s 75(2) f)** states that one of these circumstances is as follows:

any person had administered to or caused to be taken by the complainant, without the complainant's consent, a substance which, having regard to when it was administered or taken, was capable of causing or enabling the complainant to be stupefied or overpowered at the time of the relevant act.

[1] The **Sexual Offences Act** reverses the previous common law position—see *DPP v Morgan* (Question 1) on this point—on the concept of reasonable belief.

[2] Note—**ss 75** and **76** work alongside **s 1** to enable the prosecution to show that in certain circumstances, the defendant could not have believed in consent.

Joe slips a sedative into Helen's drink and then proceeds to have sexual intercourse with her. It can safely be said therefore that if Helen drank the tea with the sedative in it, the court will presume that Helen was not able to give her consent in these circumstances. It will be difficult for Joe to adduce any evidence to the contrary, and he has, therefore, committed both the *actus reus* and *mens rea* of rape.

Mike's threat to Sue, followed by sexual intercourse which appears to be consensual, will be examined next. The *actus reus* is satisfied, and again the key issue here is whether the consent given by Sue can be said to be valid. If it is not, Mike will also be guilty of rape. In relation to consent, it can be said that Sue has not truly consented, but instead has submitted to sexual intercourse. The common law tenet that there is a clear distinction between consent and submission as reviewed in *R v Olugboja* (1982) is now an integral component of s 74.[3] Dunn LJ *obiter* stated that the jury should be directed to concentrate on the state of mind of the victim having regard to all the relevant circumstances.

[3] The old distinction between submission and consent, therefore, is no longer tenable.

Alternatively, the court will presume, again under s 75, that consent was not obtained, as the victim was in fear. **Section 75(2)(a)** states that a rebuttable presumption applies in circumstance in which the following circumstances apply:

any person was, at the time of the relevant act or immediately before it began, using violence against the complainant or causing the complainant to fear that immediate violence would be used against him.

The fact that Sue is very frightened by the threats made to her by Mike suggests that this presumption could be raised. Furthermore, as Mike places a knife on the sideboard, the threat of violence is clear. The court will therefore presume that no consent was obtained in these circumstances.

The men's claim that they thought they had obtained consent will fail due to the provisions above. Furthermore, the old defence of 'honest mistake' or the 'young man's defence' is eradicated in the new Act. Under the pre-**Sexual Offences Act 2003** law, *DPP v Morgan* **[1975] 2 All ER 347** would have required Joe and Mike to be judged on the facts as they honestly believed them to be.[4] Under the **2003 Act**, the onus instead is on the men to obtain the girls' consent.

[4] This was the case even if it was unreasonable to make this mistake. The decision was heavily criticized, and the idea of reasonable belief now effectively entrenches this reversal into statute.

They may want to argue that they were intoxicated and therefore unable to form the sufficient *mens rea* for rape and that they were so drunk that they mistakenly, but reasonably, had a belief in consent. This is highly unlikely to succeed, as Joe gave Helen a sedative and also went out for the night with the intention of having sexual intercourse: neither of these facts appear to support a case that he was even concerned with Helen's consent.

[5] Effectively, rape is a crime of negligence, so it cannot be said to be a crime of specific intent.

Although it is still uncertain, it is likely that rape will be classified as a crime of basic intent.[5] Following **DPP v Majewski**, the defendant was not able to argue that his attack on a police officer lacked sufficient *mens rea* because of intoxication. The House of Lords held that the defendant's recklessness in taking drugs rendered his behaviour uncontrolled and unpredictable and was in itself a sufficient substitute for the *mens rea* of the offence. Likewise, Joe's voluntary consumption of alcohol, even if excessive, is unlikely to succeed as a defence or negate a charge of rape.

Tim may also be guilty of rape under **s 1** of the **Sexual Offences Act 2003**. Sexual intercourse, again, has taken place so the question will be whether the consent given by Jane is valid consent. Tim has lied to Jane about his intentions. The presumption under **s 76** will be brought into play here, as the prosecution seeks to establish that Tim did not reasonably believe in Jane's consent. Under **s 76**, the jury will be entitled to presume (and Tim will not be able to rebut this) that Jane was not consenting if the prosecution can prove that, in order to have sexual intercourse with her, he intentionally deceived her as to the nature or purpose of what he was doing, or that he induced her to have sexual intercourse by impersonating a person known personally to her. As Jane does not know the footballer personally, the latter is unlikely. It is also unlikely that Jane is deceived as to the purpose or nature of the activity.

 LOOKING FOR EXTRA MARKS?

- This type of question requires advanced fact management skills and a clear structure—ensure you relate each fact to the particular part of the provision.

- Some facts may be left deliberately open—concentrate on how certain issues will be put to the jury.

 QUESTION | **6**

Bob and Will are in a pub with a group of friends. Bob invites Will and his friends to come back home with him to have sex with his wife, Jen. He tells them that if Jen objects, this is part of the game and they should ignore her protests and carry on. Bob returns home with Will and his friends and Bob and Will both have sexual intercourse with Jen, despite her protests. Bob slaps Jen hard on the cheek, and she stops protesting. One member of the group, Tony, does not want to participate, but asks if he can watch. Bob agrees. After a few minutes, Tony decides he is bored and whilst the men are in the bedroom with Jen, he goes downstairs and takes a valuable silver jug from one of

⊙

the cabinets in the living room. When he is caught, he says that he believed he had the right to take the jug, as Bob owed him £500 and was refusing to pay him back.

Will, who works in a bank, tells Bob that he can get him a mortgage at a very low interest rate if he lets him do the same thing with Jen again. Jen says later that she feels severely traumatized by the events of the evening and that she did not consent to sex with either man. Will cannot authorize decisions on mortgages as he is a cashier. Will goes out that evening and has a meal in an expensive restaurant, but leaves before the bill arrives, checking carefully before he does so that the waiter is looking the other way. When Bob finds out that he can't get the mortgage after all, he finds Will and punches him in the face.

On his way home, Tony decides to buy an expensive box of chocolates for his wife. He goes into a shop and changes the label on the box he wants for a much lower price—he hopes the shop will not notice and charge him the lower price. He also picks up a bottle of wine and puts it in his coat pocket. When he gets to the cash desk he pays for the chocolates, for which he is charged the lower price, but changes his mind about the wine and replaces it on the shelf.

Discuss the criminal liability of Bob, Will, and Tony.

CAUTION!

- This question requires an appraisal of both property offences and offences against the person, including sexual offences. An excellent structure is very important, to ensure clarity.

- In dealing with the fraud offence at the bank, be careful with the *mens rea*.

DIAGRAM ANSWER PLAN

Bob and Will may be charged with rape contrary to **s 1(1)** of the **Sexual Offences Act 2003**. The *actus reus* is defined as penile penetration of the vagina, anus, or mouth of another where the victim does not consent. The *mens rea* aspect is intentional penetration and a lack of reasonable belief in consent.[1]

[1] Start with a definition of the offence in question.

Bob may have committed rape because the *actus reus* has been committed intentionally. He did not have this reasonable belief in consent. **Section 74** of the Act states that a person consents if he agrees by choice, and has the freedom and capacity to make that choice.[2] The purpose of defining consent in these terms was to draw a line between consent and submission. Prior to the Act, the case of *R v Olugboja* **[1982] QB 320** had established that submission was not equivalent to consent, and this is now entrenched in the Act in the concept of reasonable belief.[3] As Bob has shown violence towards Jen, she may be too frightened to protest further and submits rather than consents.

[2] It is always important to start a discussion of consent with this section.

[3] Note that this is now entrenched in the Act in the concept of reasonable belief.

In addition, **s 75** applies to an offence under this section. This sets out, in **s 75(2)(a)–(f)**, six circumstances in which an evidential presumption regarding consent will arise.[4] If the facts of a case fall into these circumstances, it will be presumed that the complainant (Jen) did not consent. Violence is one of these circumstances. No facts are given in this scenario which would enable Bob to rebut this presumption, other than his assertion that violence is part of the act. Jen's evidence that she did not consent will probably prevent Bob from raising any such evidence.

[4] This can be rebutted by the defendant.

Bob will also be guilty of a non-fatal offence towards Jen, at least to the degree of common law battery, and this might be extended to an offence under **s 47 of the Offences Against the Person Act 1861**. The defence might try to argue that no actual bodily harm was sustained; however, if the definition in *R v Donovan* **[1934] 2 KB 498** is followed, it can certainly be argued that this action 'interferes with her health and comfort'. On the other hand, as no injury is caused, it may be difficult for the prosecution to sustain the argument. Overall, a common law battery is probably the best option.[5] Finally, Bob's assault on Will when he finds out that he cannot get the mortgage is a statutory assault under the **Offences Against the Person Act 1861**. If the punch does not result in grievous bodily harm, the appropriate charge will be under **s 47**—that of an assault occasioning actual bodily harm, which a punch will satisfy.

[5] Discuss alternatives for the different offences against the person.

Will has also committed the *actus reus* of rape, as he penetrated Jen without consent.

He will argue that he honestly believed that Jen was consenting due to the information he was given in the pub by Bob. The jury will need to assess this belief, which appears to be unreasonable. In order for the jury to do this, it will need to be convinced that the belief he held was both honest and reasonable—here, it is not. This reference to reasonable belief reverses the common law position in *DPP v Morgan*, which prior to the Act had held that a defendant could not be convicted of rape if he mistakenly believed that the woman consented even though he had no reasonable grounds for that belief.[6] Clearly, this is an unreasonable belief on his part—he lacked a reasonable belief in consent. The court will also be mindful of s 74. Jen does not make a free choice here.

When Will tells Bob that he may be able to get him a mortgage for a reduced rate, he may have committed a fraud offence under **s 1** of the **Fraud Act 2006**. Fraud may be committed where there is a false representation, where the defendant has failed to disclose information, or where there is an abuse of position. This last type of fraud would seem to be relevant here. **Section 4 of the Fraud Act 2006** is the relevant offence. A person will commit this offence if he occupies a position in which he is expected to safeguard, or not act against, the financial interests of another person (**s 4(1)**). He must dishonestly abuse that position and intend to make a gain or cause a loss or expose another to the risk of loss. Dishonesty must also be proven. The test in *Ivey v Genting Casinos* **[2017] UKSC 67** will apply to fraud as well as theft, although this has been disputed in some academic circles. 'Gain' or 'loss' are defined in financial terms, so the fact that Will hopes to sleep with Jen again will mean that he may not be guilty of this offence. With regard to the restaurant, Will may have committed fraud by misrepresentation according to **s 2(1)** of the **Fraud Act 2006**. A false representation is any representation made according to fact or law, and may be express or implied. By entering the restaurant, he implies that he intends to and has the ability to pay (**s 2(2)** of the **Fraud Act 2006**). The offence is complete as soon as the false representation is made, if the defendant has a view to gain or cause loss, and he does so dishonestly. Alternatively, he may have committed the offence of making off without payment under **s 3** of the **Theft Act 1978**.[7] This offence applies wherever goods or services are supplied for which payment on the spot is required or expected and the defendant dishonestly makes off without having paid as required or expected, with an intent to avoid payment. This may apply here.

[6] This case attracted a lot of criticism, and the position is now rectified by the emphasis of reasonable belief in the Act.

[7] Note that these offences may overlap and it is possible for both to be charged. This is a good example of the piecemeal development of the criminal law.

With regard to the jug, Tony may be convicted of burglary under s 9(1)(a) or (b) of the **Theft Act 1968**. The key question will be whether he has trespassed. If this is not successful, he may be found guilty of theft. Theft is defined as the dishonest appropriation of property belonging to another with the intention to permanently deprive the owner of the property (s 1 of the **Theft Act 1968**). He has appropriated the jug, which is property and belongs to Bob. With regard to *mens rea*, Tony might argue that he was not dishonest as he honestly believed that he had the right to take it, given that Bob owed him money. The **Theft Act 1968** sets out three situations in which a defendant is not to be regarded as dishonest. The defendant must hold one of the following beliefs: (i) a belief in the legal right to the property; (ii) a belief that the owner would consent; and (iii) a belief that the owner could not be traced by taking reasonable steps. The first of these is most appropriate for Tony. He will not be dishonest if he honestly believes he has the legal right to the property. This will be a matter for the jury to consider.[8]

[8] Note that it is a subjective belief, genuinely held by the defendant.

A further question will be whether, in addition to theft, Tony could be found guilty of burglary. This question turns on whether he is a trespasser. He will argue that Bob invited him into the house. In *R v Jones and Smith* [1976] 1 WLR 672, the two defendants were found guilty of burglary, despite a prior invitation to enter. The court held that a person was a trespasser if he entered the premises of another and acted in excess of any permission granted. If he is a trespasser, it is likely that he will be guilty under s 9(1)(b), as he did not have the intent to steal when he entered the property, but formed it later.[9]

[9] This matter is open to interpretation. The definition of trespass is not entirely certain, as it will depend on a number of other factors such as entry (see *R v Collins* [1973] QB 100).

In terms of the theft, appropriation is defined in the Act as an assumption of the rights of an owner (s 3(1) and *R v Morris* [1984] AC 320). When he switches the labels in the shop, he may have assumed one of the shop's rights and therefore have appropriated the chocolates.[10] He does the same with the wine by picking it up off the shelf. Both of these objects will count as property under s 4(1). They belong to the shop (s 5(1)). A more difficult question may be whether Tony is dishonest and whether he intended to permanently deprive the shop of the property. Although this argument is easily satisfied with regard to the chocolates, he will argue that he intended to replace the wine. The fact that he replaces it does not prevent him from being regarded as intending to permanently deprive the shop of the property if there are circumstances amounting to an outright taking or disposal. As the wine has remained in exactly the same state as it was when he appropriated it, the prosecution may not be successful on this issue.

[10] An assumption of a right applies to any right.

LOOKING FOR EXTRA MARKS?

- Make sure you carefully examine the legal definitions in the property offences. These may overlap, and the law does not always provide certainty. If you can identify the problematic areas, this will add depth to your answer.

- Try to provide alternatives to arguments throughout your answer. This shows good legal reasoning.

QUESTION | 7

Pete and Veronica, who had been going out together for a number of years, were going to get married. One evening, Veronica told Pete that she was having an affair with a work colleague and that her relationship with Pete was over. Pete was very shocked by this and felt hurt. In a state of confusion, he decided to go to Veronica's house to see if he could find something to take in memory of her.

To gain entry into her house, Pete used a spare key, which she had previously told him she kept under a stone by the front door. Pete made his way to her bedroom. On her dressing table he saw the engagement ring that he had given her and he took it. He thought to himself that she had no right to keep it now that she had broken off the engagement. He then sprayed her teddy bear with her favourite perfume and stuffed it inside his jacket. He was about to leave her bedroom when he saw a photograph of Veronica and her new boyfriend on her bedside table. Incensed, he grabbed her pyjamas from her bed and ripped them apart. As he was doing so, the teddy bear fell out of his jacket. He left it on the floor and ran out of the house.

Pete was arrested later that night but told the police that he barely remembered anything he had done after his conversation with Veronica because he was in shock.

Discuss any criminal liability arising from these facts.

CAUTION!

- There are a number of different property offences and defences in this question. Deal with them systematically before coming to an overall conclusion.

- Insanity and automatism are closely linked. Be sure to explain why one rather than the other might apply.

DIAGRAM ANSWER PLAN

Identify the issues	■ Consider burglary, automatism, criminal damage, and theft.
Relevant law	■ This includes **s 9(1)(b)** of the **Theft Act 1968** and **s 1** of the **Criminal Damage Act 1971**.
Apply the law	■ Has Pete 'entered' the property? Is he dishonest or does he have a claim of right? ■ Will automatism or insanity be the more successful defence?
Conclude	■ Automatism is unlikely on these facts and there is lack of an external factor. ■ Arguments on *mens rea* are unlikely to succeed, given the lack of a legal rather than a moral right to take the ring.

SUGGESTED ANSWER

[1] Set out the relevant offences at the outset.

Pete appears to have potentially committed three counts of burglary, and possibly criminal damage. In addition, he might have a defence of automatism.[1]

Burglary can be committed in two ways. Under **s 9(1)(a)** of the **Theft Act 1968**, a person is guilty of burglary if he enters any building or part as a trespasser with intent to steal, inflict grievous bodily harm on any person therein, or commit criminal damage. Under **s 9(1)(b)**[2],

[2] Note that you do not need to repeat the statute verbatim—simply summarize the effect of it. In an exam, no credit will be given for copying out.

a person is guilty of burglary if, having entered as a trespasser, he steals or inflicts grievous bodily harm on any person therein or attempts to commit either of these offences. Under **s 9(1)(b)**, it must be proved that D has committed any of the further offences.

The three common elements of the *actus reus* of either type of burglary do not appear to be in issue here. Pete has clearly entered a

[3] There are conflicting cases on this point; you do not need to go into great detail.

building (**R v Collins** [1973] QB 100). His entry was not only effective (**R v Brown** [1985] Crim LR 61), but also substantial.[3] He was presumably a trespasser because his entry was without consent. Pete might argue that he had permission to enter, but the court is likely to find that Veronica must have implicitly withdrawn permission upon termination of their relationship. Given Pete's intention upon entry as a trespasser, to find a memento of Veronica, he appears to have potentially committed **s 9(1)(a)** burglary, ie entry as a trespasser with intent to steal. The clandestine nature of his nocturnal visit to her house is strong evidence of an intent not only to trespass, but also to steal.[4] Pete would therefore appear to have committed **s 9(1)(a)** burglary at the point of entry. One might argue that a conditional intent to steal is insufficient for theft (*R v Easom* [1971] 2 All ER 945) and therefore insufficient for **s 9(1)(a)** burglary. Further, it could be argued that his intention was not to steal, but to find something of sentimental value to which he believed he was entitled. Arguably, this would not amount to an intent to steal at the point of entry. Either way, the *mens rea* requirement of intention or recklessness as to entry as a trespasser would seem to be satisfied.[5] Given the uncertainty about his intentions at that point, the ulterior offences will be considered next in the light of the principles of **s 9(1)(b)** burglary.

First, Pete may have stolen Veronica's engagement ring, which had been a gift from him to her. Theft is defined according to **s 1** of the **Theft Act 1968** as the dishonest appropriation of property belonging to another with an intention permanently to deprive. Appropriation is defined in **s 3** of the **Theft Act 1968** as an assumption of the rights of ownership. Therefore, Pete appropriated the ring by assuming possession of it.[6] A ring falls within the definition of property under **s 4** of the **Theft Act 1968**, defined as money and all other property, real or personal, including things in action and other intangible property. The property must belong to another defined in accordance with **s 5** as belonging to any person having possession or control of it, or having in it any proprietary right or interest, whether it be a right of ownership, possession, or equitable right. Since the ring had been a gift from Pete to her, Veronica was the owner of it. Pete may therefore have committed the *actus reus* of theft.[7]

There appears to be no doubt that he intended to deprive Veronica of the ring permanently as opposed to temporarily, in which case **s 6** need not be explored. However, it must also be proved that his appropriation was dishonest. Dishonesty is not defined under the **Theft Act 1968**, but **s 2(1)** sets out that one is not to be regarded as dishonest if the act was committed with any of three beliefs: (i) a belief in a legal right to the property; (ii) a belief that the owner would consent; and (iii) a belief that the owner cannot be found by taking reasonable steps. In any of these situations, D's belief need not be correct or objectively reasonable, provided it is subjectively genuine. Pete would find it impossible to assert either of the latter two beliefs, but the facts state that he does think Veronica has no right to it, having broken off the engagement. He will not be dishonest if he genuinely believes he has a legal right to the property. Unfortunately for Pete, it rather looks

[4] Apply the legal principle to the facts of the problem.

[5] Don't forget the *mens rea*.

[6] The statutory provision needs to be applied to the facts, just as a case would be.

[7] Here, we have worked systematically through the statutory requirements of *actus reus*, before moving on to *mens rea*.

as though his belief is based on moral rather than legal grounds, and is unlikely to provide him with a defence of lack of dishonesty. He may try to assert that although his conduct appeared dishonest according to the ordinary standards of reasonable and honest people, he did not consider what he had done to be dishonest according to those standards. In the past, he may have had the benefit of the subjective element of the test set out in *R v Ghosh* [1982] QB 1053, genuinely believing that he was not dishonest by ordinary standards given Veronica's reprehensible behaviour. The new test in *Ivey v Genting Casinos* [2017] UKSC 67 now means that the court will not have regard to this belief. In any event, a jury is unlikely to find that his retrieval of the ring was honest on the basis of these facts.[8] Consequently, we can argue that Pete may have committed s 9(1)(b) burglary on these grounds.

Second, there is no evidence that he damaged the bear by spraying it with perfume, and therefore criminal damage will not be considered. However, he appears to have stolen it, despite the fact that he leaves it behind when he runs from the house. He appropriated the bear when he assumed possession of it by picking it up. Appropriation is defined as any assumption by a person of the rights of an owner (s 3 of the **Theft Act 1968**). If, at that moment, the appropriation was dishonest with an intention permanently to deprive Veronica of the bear, theft is complete. The fact that it remains behind is irrelevant. It is unlikely he would succeed with this defence, given the circumstances. He has therefore committed both theft and s 9(1)(b) burglary.[9]

Third, in ripping apart Veronica's pyjamas, Pete has committed criminal damage contrary to s 1(1) of the **Criminal Damage Act 1971**: a person commits criminal damage if without lawful excuse he destroys or damages property belonging to another, intending or being reckless as to whether such property will be destroyed or damaged. Subjective recklessness is required according to *R v Cunningham* [1957] 2 QB 396 and *R v G and Another* [2004] 1 AC 1034. Pete has certainly destroyed the pyjamas; they do not belong to him. He has therefore committed criminal damage. This offence does not support a charge of s 9(1)(b) burglary.

However, Pete may use the defence of automatism. Automatism is a plea that the link between mind and body is missing, resulting in a lack of voluntary control over one's actions.[10] In *Bratty v Attorney-General for Northern Ireland* [1963] AC 386, Lord Denning defined the defence as 'an involuntary act … done by the muscles, without any control by the mind'. It provides a complete acquittal because lack of voluntariness negates the *actus reus* of the crime. Automatism is closely related to insanity. However, in automatism the cause of involuntariness must be external, whereas in insanity it must be a disease of the mind, caused internally. It is unlikely that a mere emotional

[8] Be sure that you have understood the changes made to the law by *Ivey*. In particular, Lord Hughes' judgment is useful.

[9] It is useful to draw a mini conclusion on the facts at each stage of your argument.

[10] Always provide a definition.

state will suffice as a disease of the mind. Otherwise, the defence must be based on insanity which, if successful, leads to a verdict of not guilty by reason of insanity, with disposal ranging from indefinite detention in a secure mental hospital to an absolute discharge (**Criminal Procedure (Insanity and Unfitness to Plead) Act 1991** and the **Domestic Violence, Crime and Victims Act 2004**). The defence is defined according to the *M'Naghten* Rules 1843 as a defect of reason due to a disease of the mind so as to deprive D of either knowledge as to the nature and quality of his actions or knowledge that the act was legally wrong. The concept of disease of the mind is wide enough to include physical as well as mental disorders (ie epilepsy (*Bratty v AG*) and diabetes (*R v Hennessy* **[1989] 1 WLR 287**)). A defect of reason excludes temporary confusion (*R v Clarke* **[1972] 1 All ER 219**) and this may be how one could describe Pete's mental state. However, the narrowness of the two cognitive tests (knowledge of nature or wrongness, meaning 'legally' wrong (*R v Windle* **[1952] 2 QB 82**)) excludes even seriously mentally ill people who know what they are doing. The *M'Naghten* Rules presume that every man is sane, therefore the contrary must be proved on a balance of probabilities if D wishes to rely on this defence. Automatism, on the other hand, does not need to be proved according to a legal standard, but D is cast with an evidential burden of proof to establish by means of medical evidence the necessary condition. It is possible but unlikely that Pete will be able to satisfy the court of automatism here.[11] Neither is it likely that he will be able to use insanity, given that his mental condition appears to be temporary and he appears to know what he is doing. As to whether he should be advised to plead insanity to his crimes, this is doubtful. If successful, the disposal will be uncertain and may result in detention in a secure mental institution for a period of time.

[11] This is because he can probably not show any evidence of an external factor.

LOOKING FOR EXTRA MARKS?

- You can do very well on this kind of question by showing that you have some broad knowledge of the syllabus and are able to compare and contrast. As there are a lot of issues, you are usually not expected to deal with them in too much depth.
- Remember to evaluate the three mental defences, and advise on which is preferable.

Online Resources

www.oup.com/uk/qanda/

For extra essay and problem questions on this topic, as well as advice on revision and exam technique, please visit the online resources.

10 Skills for Success in Coursework Assessments

In Chapter 1, we considered some of the challenges which you might face in studying criminal law. These related to the overlap between topics, and to the fact that although criminal law may be enjoyable to study due to its media presence, it is technical, yet sometimes philosophical, especially when considering the state of mind of the defendant. In addition, we have seen that criminal law contains some contradictions and uncertainties, for example in its application of the subjective and objective approaches to liability. This can be confusing for students. Criminal law assessments must therefore be approached logically, and be very well structured. Your task is to build a convincing argument using the 'evidence' of case law and statutes to apply to the facts of your problem, or to essay questions. You need to do this systematically, avoiding mere descriptions of the facts academic arguments,.

In this chapter, we look at answering coursework questions. It may be that coursework is the whole assessment for your criminal law module, or just part of it. In this type of assessment, examiners are generally looking for a balance of quality, accuracy, clarity, and relevance, as well as depth of analysis and argument. In terms of structure and content, answering coursework questions in criminal law is really no different to answering examination questions. The distinction is in the depth of the answer, and in the way in which you are able to prepare for and approach the task set. Remember that examiners are likely to be much *less* tolerant of mistakes or failure to explain issues in depth in coursework than they would be in an examination, as they know that the material you have researched is likely to be in front of you as you write. As such, there are no excuses for basic errors!

Some coursework questions may be in the form of one or two problem-style questions. Alternatively, the question may be in the form of a quotation from a judgment or an academic article, which you may be expected to critically evaluate. Make sure you know what the 'instruction' or process words mean in an essay—this is discussed below.

In coursework questions, unless you have been advised otherwise by your lecturer, it is crucial that you provide *full references and citations* for sources that you refer to. The recognized citation system for academic writing in law is the Oxford Standard for the Citation of Legal Authorities (OSCOLA) (https://www.law.ox.ac.uk/sites/files/oxlaw/oscola_4th_edn_hart_2012.pdf).

It is worth getting to grips with this system early on in your course, as you will certainly need to use it when you tackle longer essays or pieces of substantial legal research, such as a dissertation or an extended essay. It is a straightforward referencing system, involving the use of footnotes, and is better suited to legal writing than in-text referencing and citation such as Harvard. For the specific structure of essays and problem questions, please do refer further to the sections in Chapter 1 on examination success.

The 'blank page' syndrome

The most difficult thing about coursework is how to get started. Instead of starting to write straight away, start researching the general area. This will give you the confidence to tackle the question head on. You could make a mind map of different aspects of the topic, for instance. You also do not have to start at the beginning! You can tackle whichever part of the coursework you like first, as long as you organize it and present it in a logical order later. A common and useful technique is to write the introduction last. This helps you to explain what you are going to write about. Your introduction should not include the argument itself, but an indication of what that argument is and a link to the question. You could, if you wish, include an explanation of the general approach and structure you intend to take.

Researching, planning, and preparing to write

When you have an exam to sit, you will no doubt gather all your materials and start to consolidate them into a form from which you can start to revise and memorize them. You may not have thought about doing this for coursework, but it does have a big advantage—you know what the question is in advance. The first thing to do, therefore, is to gather all the material you have on the topic set, and ensure that you know the law. Now is the time to iron out any problems, or areas you have not fully understood. An important factor here is making sure you understand the question that has been set. Often, an essay question contains terms such as 'critically evaluate/assess', 'outline', 'discuss', or 'analyse'. Make sure you actually do what the question is asking you to do. The question may direct you to a particular area of the law, so keep within these parameters. One of the most common comments made by examiners on coursework is 'failure to answer the question set'. You should also think about breaking down the question in order to answer it thoroughly.

The next thing you should do is plan your answer. If the question set is a problem question, use the IRAC method to do this and to build up a coherent argument (*identify* the legal issues, explain the *rules* of law which are relevant, *apply* these to the facts, and *conclude* by offering legal advice to the person you are advising). In an essay-style question, remember to back up each point you make with evidence in the form of case law, statutory provisions, or academic authority and analyse these thoroughly.

Critical analysis and evaluation

This can be a tricky part of any essay or problem question. In problem questions, it means applying the law to the facts and reaching a conclusion in a reasoned way to give legal advice. It is not enough to simply state the law.

If you have stated a legal rule, make sure you apply every part of that rule to the facts of the question. What does the rule mean for this defendant, charged with this offence? Are there any cases which suggest that the opposite conclusion may be drawn? Are there any particular facts, unique to this problem, which you need to discuss?

In Chapter 1, we discussed the structure and order of problem questions. In doing this type of question for coursework, remember that you should have a brief introduction, setting out the issues, before following the IRAC method to answer the question in full.

In essays you are trying to formulate an argument, often for or against the particular statement or assertion the question makes. Again, you should avoid discussing everything you know about a given topic and instead ask whether each statement you make actually answers the question. This type of essay should have a more traditional introduction, a main body (containing your arguments and analysis), and a conclusion. Link each point you make back to the question set.

Be careful with the introduction. You should simply be setting out the problem here, and explaining what the essay will cover. Do not start explaining the law or the issues in detail. You could introduce some of the contentious issues raised in this particular area of law. For example, if you are asked whether the defence of loss of control contained in the **Coroners and Justice Act 2009** improves the situation for abused women who kill, you could start by explaining what the problems were in the previous law, and set out the approach you will take in the essay. Break down the question to determine what your overall structure will be.

In the body of the essay, the kinds of things to consider relate to whether there is a problem with this area of law. Are there any gaps in the scope of legislation, for example? Do the cases conflict? Is the law unclear or unfair to a particular group of people? In order to ascertain these points, you will need to refer to secondary sources of law, such as Command papers, other consultation papers, and academic journal articles. This is where you can show the examiner that you have thought about the topic, and use your skills of critical analysis. In an essay, critical analysis means evaluating the law as it is, and identifying the problems. You may have thought about problems yourself, but the best thing to do is to identify what other people think about it. Refer to academic journals and other academic commentary to help you to identify key areas for critique and reform. Above all, you need to avoid being too descriptive.

Your conclusion should summarize these issues, and possibly choose a proposal for reform which appeals to you.

Relevance and sticking to the word limit

Lack of relevance is another common comment made by examiners on student work. You need to select the correct legal rule for the scenario. For example, when discussing *novus actus interveniens* in legal causation, there are a number of factors which *may* allow the defendant to argue that the chain of causation is broken. These include third-party intervention, negligent medical treatment, and the victim's own contribution. You should not discuss all of these, only the ones which are relevant on these facts.

Similarly, in a non-fatal offences question, several offences may technically be appropriate. However, realistically, the prosecution will not charge the defendant with common law battery if there is sufficient evidence for a charge under **s 20 of the Offences Against the Persons Act 1861**.

Lecturers often hear complaints from students that the word limit for a given piece of coursework is not long enough. It is true that word limits can be tight, but it is an important legal skill to be able to stick to what is relevant and answer the question set. On further scrutiny, it becomes apparent that the student has included material which is in the general topic area but is not relevant to the question set (the 'shotgun' approach). In a problem question, this means adding facts, or giving several examples of, say, a break in the chain of causation, instead of just one. This is a problem which occurs in coursework rather than in examinations, as the scope is much larger. It is also related to knowing the law before you start, as it is difficult to issue-spot if you do not know which issues you are looking for! In terms of whether you are allowed to exceed the word limit at all, check with your tutor. Some law schools will allow, say, a 10 per cent leeway. If you do exceed it, you should try to stay as close to the limit as possible.

Referencing and citation of legal authorities

In coursework, you are usually expected to follow academic standards of citation, including providing a bibliography, footnotes, and proper citation of authorities. The reason for this is to encourage academic integrity and the avoidance of plagiarism. Any material which is not your own must be acknowledged in the body of your work in the form of a footnote, and you need to provide a separate bibliography listing cases, statutes, and secondary sources. Some institutions also require a separate table of cases and a table of statutes.

Writing up, proofreading, and checking before you submit

A key part of any writing process is the checking, editing, and proofreading at the end. You should ask yourself whether each point flows naturally to the next. Does it flow or does it appear disjointed? Put your work through a spellcheck. When you are ready to write up, use your plan to help you structure your answer. Be sure to write a draft first before you submit. As in all law assessments, you should adopt a formal written style and avoid personal opinions, journalistic language or use of 'I'.

Checklist for coursework in criminal law

- Have I produced a plan?
- Have I included sufficient cases and statutory material?
- Does my work include a bibliography? Footnotes? Properly cited cases?
- In problem questions, have I considered the effect of any defences, and concluded on guilt?
- In essay questions, have I considered academic opinion in the form of learned journals, and evaluated the strengths and weaknesses of those opinions with reference to the question set?
- Have I kept descriptions of the law to a minimum, but instead concentrated on application of the law to the facts (problems questions) or evaluated arguments for reform (essay questions)?
- Have I proofread my work and put it through a spellcheck?
- Have I followed the presentation and submission instructions?
- Have I stuck to the word limit?

EXAMPLE 1

The House of Lords in *R v G and Another* [2003] was correct in its decision[1] to overrule itself in *MPC v Caldwell* [1981].[2]

Discuss.

[1] Here a position is being taken—this is what you should focus on in your answer.
[2] Ensure that you explain both of these cases, along with their legal impact.

Answer guidance

A full discussion of the concept of recklessness is needed in this essay, and an appraisal of the House of Lords' decision in *R v G*. You should start with a brief definition of recklessness and how it can be distinguished from intention. Here, it is important to distinguish between subjective and objective recklessness. This should be followed with a brief discussion of subjective and objective recklessness. A brief definition of each of these terms would be useful here. This should include a description of the development of the law with reference to *R v Cunningham* [1957] **2 QB 396**, the change of the law in *R v Caldwell* [1982] **AC 341**, and finally the decision in *R v G* [2003] **UKHL 50**. At this point, it is worth highlighting some of the problems in this decision (eg the case of *Elliott v C* [1983] **1 WLR 939**, widely seen as being unfair) and the reasons for the return to the objective test. A brief description of *R v G* should then follow. Lord Bingham's speech in *R v G* could be contrasted with that of Lord Diplock in *MPC v Caldwell*. The majority's interpretation of 'recklessly' in **s 1** of the **Criminal Damage Act 1971** was a misinterpretation. He asked what Parliament had meant in using the word 'reckless' in **s 1(1)** and **(2)** of the **1971 Act**. The Law Commission clearly meant recklessness to mean the same as maliciousness and Parliament cannot have meant anything different from the Law Commission. In treating *Cunningham* as irrelevant, the majority in *Caldwell* fell into 'understandable but demonstrable error'. This last point, along with a summary of Lord Bingham's reasoning, should form the basis of your conclusion.

EXAMPLE 2

Diane is a railway enthusiast and volunteer[1] at the London Steam Railway Society. She operates the gates at one of the level crossings on the railway during public open days, opening the gates when safe and closing them as trains approach. She is very annoyed that no one has brought her any lunch one day and marches off to get a sandwich, leaving the gates open.[2] A young child, Vicky, runs across the track as a train approaches and falls under the wheels. Olly, who lives next door to Vicky, sees the danger, but fails to shout a warning.[3] Vicky is taken to hospital and put on a life support machine, which Ralph the doctor disconnects two weeks later because Vicky is in a coma and has no hope of recovery. She dies within days.

Discuss.

[1] This is an important fact and should be discussed carefully.
[2] This is the point at which the duty may arise.
[3] Don't forget to deal with all the defendants separately.

Answer guidance

This question concerns involuntary manslaughter and the structure of this question is essential, given the different protagonists. You should start by stating that a murder charge would not be appropriate due to the lack of intention, and then move to gross negligence manslaughter. At this point, give a definition of the offence as set out in *R v Adomako* [1995] **1 AC 171**. This is the best choice, as there is an omission on Diane's part. The first thing to establish is whether she owes a duty of care to Vicky. She has a responsibility to open and close the gates; however, she is not an employee, but a volunteer. The cases of *R v Pittwood* [1902] **TLR 37** and *R v Stone and Dobinson* [1977] **1 QB 354** should be discussed here. Most students will think that *R v Pittwood* is appropriate here—however, as Diane is a volunteer, it is unlikely that she has a contract. The duty therefore needs to be found elsewhere. Consideration should then be given to whether Olly or Ralph have broken the chain of causation. It is unlikely that Olly, as a neighbour, would have a legal duty, therefore the chain of causation remains intact. It is well established that medical treatment, even where it is negligent, does not affect the defendant's liability (*Malcherek and Steel* [1981] 2 All ER 422). Ralph's liability should then be considered separately. Any offence will depend on whether he is in breach of a duty of care and, possibly, whether he commits an act or omission (*Re A*, it should be noted, doubts this distinction). Consider *Airedale Trust v Bland* [1993] AC 789. Is it in Vicky's best interests to end her life support? A charge of gross negligence may be considered, but is unlikely.

TAKING THINGS FURTHER

- Finch E and Fafinski S, *Legal Skills* (7th edn, OUP 2019).
- McVea H and Crumper C, *Exam Skills for Law Students* (2nd edn, OUP 2006).
- Strong S I, *How to Write Law Essays and Exams* (5th edn, OUP 2018).

Online Resources   www.oup.com/uk/qanda/

Go online for extra essay and problem questions and a podcast with advice on revision and exam technique.

Index

D